Francesco Saverio Nitti

Population and the Social System

Francesco Saverio Nitti

Population and the Social System

ISBN/EAN: 9783337036256

Printed in Europe, USA, Canada, Australia, Japan

Cover: Foto ©Suzi / pixelio.de

More available books at **www.hansebooks.com**

POPULATION

AND

THE SOCIAL SYSTEM

BY

FRANCESCO S. NITTI

TRANSLATED UNDER THE AUTHOR'S SUPERVISION

LONDON

SWAN SONNENSCHEIN & CO.

NEW YORK: CHARLES SCRIBNER'S SONS

1894

TO ACHILLE LORIA.

NAPLES, *September, 1893.*

MY DEAR FRIEND,—Do you remember Hobbes' immortal aphorism? When reason is against a man, then man is an enemy of reason. To become convinced of the profound truth contained in this saying of Hobbes, it would be sufficient to examine the historical causes of economic theories, to make up, as you have once said, the economic theory of economic writers. If our science has made and still makes so little progress, it is because it is concerned with vital and real interests; to accept one of two directions is not for us, as for the followers of other sciences, merely a question of method, but it means, moreover, that different and opposite conclusions are reached, and that fixed forms of social organisation are justified or condemned. Had the propositions of Euclid affected economic interests, they would not now rank among the definite conquests of science, but would still appear doubtful hypothesis of arduous solution.

Metaphysics, driven out of all the other sciences, have taken refuge in ours, and I daily ask myself what can be the purpose of so many and such useless and vain researches, grounded upon pure hypotheses.

They are very few among the studious who follow a masterly road; just as there are but very few who do not sacrifice objective research to class interests. We have a philosophy of wealth and a philosophy of poverty; what we really lack is a broad and impartial philosophy. On the one side there are those who can see nothing but the miseries of the present hour, and there are those who would wish to change everything. Goethe had for a motto—*to see all the sides of things.* On the contrary, what is now wanted is just this exalted and serene vision, this calm, objective character in research and examination.

During the reign of Frederic II., Sömmering, the anatomist, in an inaugural dissertation at the University of

Mayence, foreseeing a great scientific truth, maintained that the anatomical conformation of negroes in their savage state approximated much more to monkeys than to white men. The canons of Mayence, who preserve the relics of the three Magi, one of whom, Melchior, would seem to have been a negro, were scandalised at this, and protested so vehemently that the honest Sömmering was severely blamed and punished. The teaching of the Darwinian hypotheses is now permitted in the Universities; but if an economist dares to sustain that some economic maxims held sacred hitherto are without any real foundation, or that, like the good Melchior, some economists belong much more to some inferior species of thinkers than to a superior one, he can be certain that he will be anathematised by the canons of our science.

Love, favour, and sympathy are bestowed only upon extreme theories, which gratify the interests of one class or another. On the one hand, quite a host of economists support no hypothesis that does not imply fatality, necessity, and immutability; on the other hand, a herd of authors flatter the passions of the populace, making themselves the apostles of views which necessitated immediate changes and profound convulsions. Both classes are outside of the right way, and have abandoned the great channel of objective research.

I am of the number of those who recognise the full moral and economic importance of modern socialism; to me it seems a great and beneficent reaction of optimism against blind and baneful pessimism, which had penetrated both the souls and minds of men. Hence I have studied socialistic literature with great affection for many years. And though greatly admiring the spirit which animates it, I am necessarily convinced that, after the book of Marx, so defective and yet so great, collectivism has been unable to produce a true and deep work. This is because both revolutionary and conservative collectivism are chiefly theories of an occasion, each destined to safeguard the interests of a different class; and if the former be inspired by broader and better intentions, it also proceeds through a stormy sea of error and illusion.

I do not know if the historic conception of Saint Simon

appears large-minded to you as it does to me. And although I accept it but in part, I am at least convinced that there are organic and critical periods in human history. During organic periods humanity accepts with profound conviction systems of positive belief more or less true or useful. Under the influence of these beliefs, men make all the progress of which the theories are capable, and then at last they come to find themselves in difficulty. Then succeeds a period of negation and criticism, during which mankind loses its former convictions, without acquiring other authoritative ones, except that of judging the former theories to be erroneous. And this is a view which has much truth in it, and which completes that materialistic conception of history which has gained so great a progress during recent years, and that, chiefly, thanks to your endeavours. And now we are truly in a critical period, and the society of our day is, as Dante would say, *entomata in difetto*, from which, if the *angelica farfalla* dreamed of by Utopian reformers does not issue, at least there should issue something better and healthier than our present state.

The economic forms around us are changing, and with them are changing the moral sentiments ; and if the critical period be not yet about to end, the more elect spirits are already in great part emancipated from the pessimist stage of thought, to which they have been subjected so fatally and so long.

The part of political economy which is still less studied every day is that which concerns the distribution of wealth. Walras maintains that "the fact of appropriation is an essentially moral fact, and the theory of property is an essentially moral science." And, in fact, where are the laws which regulate the distribution of wealth, and which can be accepted without essential modification or change ? Turgot's classical figure about the rate of interest is anything but exact ; Ricardo's theory on income has at least as many opponents as upholders ; Lassalle's iron law about wages is now repudiated even by socialists ; Malthus' hypothesis is belied by a century of research ; the deductions of the new Austrian school are in truth a building upon sand ; the other theories of Turgot, Smith, Ricardo, and Mill are either false or incomplete.

Among all these essential problems still a prey to prejudice and error, the most important of all is doubtless that of population, from which it would seem as though every other were derived. Intelligent demographists and economists have written with sufficient fulness on this subject in recent times; you yourself have studied it with that admirable method and great acumen which are recognised in you by friends and enemies.

Remembering what has been written on the subject hitherto, I believe that I have studied the question of population solely according to its objective aspect. In the first part of this book I have demonstrated how all the most important theories are directly derived from the surroundings which produced them; in the second I have striven, with the help of biology, statistics, and political economy, to formulate what I consider to be the true law of population.

Le savant doit avoir l'ésprit douteur is a saying of Claude Bernard. And although I have performed the present research with sincere desire, I do not dare to think that my conclusions are absolute truths. If you or others should wish to demonstrate the falsehood of my thesis, I may regret that I have laboured in vain, but I shall be the first to recognise the truth, by whomsoever or however it be made clear.

I have resolved to dedicate this book to you simply in order to testify to you my sincere admiration and friendship. Reading it you will see that we are not always in agreement, and that some of my conclusions differ from your own. But what does it matter that we are not in perfect agreement?

Comte had for motto—*Love as a beginning, order as a basis, progress as a purpose.* Morality, economy, and politics have not yet been able to invent anything better. And in your great and noble work, as in my small and humble one, the same sentiment is active which suggested to Comte his immortal motto, and one passion—the single passion for what is truthful and good—influences both your mind and mine.

I beg you, therefore, my dear friend, to accept the dedication of this my book, to the fortune of which, I am convinced, your name will contribute not a little.—Affectionately yours,

F. S. NITTI.

CONTENTS

—— ∞⁙∞ ——

BOOK I.

THE HISTORIC CAUSES OF ECONOMIC THEORIES ON POPULATION.

BOOK II.

POPULATION AND THE SOCIAL SYSTEM.

SUMMARY of the theories of population, 87—Gradual abandonment of the Malthusian hypothesis, 88—The experience of centuries, 89—Burdett's defence, 89—Absurd consequence of the Malthusian hypothesis, 90—Comparisons between population and the means of subsistence, 91—Increase of population in the nineteenth century, 91—Population and wealth in England, 92—Population and wealth in

POPULATION AND THE SOCIAL SYSTEM

BOOK I.

THE HISTORIC CAUSES OF THE ECONOMIC THEORIES WITH REGARD TO POPULATION.

A LEARNED German economist recently maintained that all the systems of economic ideas are embodied in two groups, one of which can be rightly characterised as the Philosophy of Wealth, the other as the Philosophy of Poverty.[1]   Destined as a defence or support of one or the other of these systems, no fundamental theory of social economy can be theoretically studied, except by taking into account the historical circumstances of its birth and development.   Still more account should be made of the historical circumstances of the terrible law of population, which once seemed to the demographists and the economists of the past to contain an insoluble and profound problem, but which later became the mainstay of economic individualism.

The Philosophy of Wealth and the Philosophy of Poverty.

For nearly a century, since the time when Malthus startled England by the desolate conclusion from his great economic law, no problem has been more deeply studied than this, which involves the great mystery of

The Mainstay of the Individualist Theory.

[1] "The two great systems of economic ideas can be summarised in two groups, one of which is rightly called *the philosophy of wealth,* the other *the philosophy of poverty.*"   A. von Miakowski : *Die Auflange der Nationalökonomie,* Leipzig, 1852, p. 7.

A

human history, and from which awful and complex source every other would seem to be directly or indirectly derived.

All the other questions of economic science, whether those regarding the distribution, or those concerning the production of wealth, are secondary compared to the problem of population, or, rather, are but aspects, as it were, of one vast prism. A brilliant Italian economist says that this is "the most momentous and difficult economic problem, always of present importance";[1] it is the problem which, as Rossi well said, "concerns everything, morals and politics, national and domestic economy."

The Problem of Population always a Problem of Present Importance.

It is vast and terrible as the Egyptian Sphinx, and whoever wishes to study the mystery underlying the history of mankind, or to push his active inquiries into the future, must, perforce, question it acutely.

But the question of population, not less than the other problems of the moral sciences, has not escaped the evil effect of the two opposite influences, which have hitherto impeded every study grounded upon its objective truth : namely, political influence and national influence; so that for a long time mere biological hypotheses have become, or, at least, appeared, unquestioned canons of economy, against which but a few independent spirits have dared to rebel.

The Two Fatal Influences in the Science of Political Economy.

Before Malthus, the economic theorists had not studied the question of population at all, or had thought that the duty of sovereigns and states consisted in procuring an increase of population by every means in their power.

The very word *population,* in the sense in which it is now used, had no precisely corresponding term in the sixteenth century in Italian, French, or German.

The Term and Idea of Population.

The word *population,* in its present sense, was used, perhaps, for the first time in English in one of Bacon's *Essays.*[2]

---

[1] Messedaglia : *L'Economia politica in relazione colla sociologia e quale scienza a sè,* Rome, 1891, p. 8.

[2] Bacon : *Essays,* London, 1597: *Of the True Greatness of Kingdoms and Estates.*

And the two French translators of Bacon's *Essays,* Badouin in 1621,[1] and the *Abbé* Goujet in 1734,[2] as though reluctant to use the new word, translated it by *peule, monde,* etc.

And as from the beginning the chief necessity was or seemed to be that of increasing the number of citizens, *population* was always understood in the sense of *the act of populating;* it was only later when the phenomenon of an abundant and disordered birth-rate appeared that the word assumed its actual meaning.[3]

The word, therefore, did not exist because the idea did not exist, and anxiety with regard to numbers, had not yet made itself felt.

Even in 1751, Voltaire had not yet made use of the word *population,* so often afterwards used in all his works, and if he made use of the word *peuplade,* he said that the aim and duty of a Government was, therefore, *la peuplade et le travail.*[4]

This principle of sociology was supported by several reasons, both political and geographical.

In fact, until the time of Malthus, the continent of America, although already a long time discovered, was but slightly cultivated. Asia was in great part unknown. Africa was a continent as yet wholly unexplored, and the vast regions of the interior, if no longer, as in the Vatican maps, designated by the terrible words, *hic sunt leones,* were not the less enveloped in mystery. Australia was but very slightly colonised, and the indigenous races still resisted the fatal influence of European civilisation. Such imperfect knowledge of geography led to the belief that the space reserved to humanity was immeasurably great. No one suspected that the means of subsistence would ever fail, or that they would prove insufficient for the progress of mankind.

Why the Study of the Question of Population was neglected before the time of Malthus.

---

[1] Badouin, editor : Francois Julliot, Paris, 1621, one vol. in 12.

[2] Goujet, Paris, 1734, one vol. in 12.

[3] *Cf.* for the whole question Schoene : *Histoire de la population Française,* Paris, 1893, pp. 1-7.

[4] Voltaire : *Dialogue entre un philosophe et un contrôleur général,* 1751. Later in the *Dictionnaire philosophique,* in the *Essais sur les moeurs,* and in other works, Voltaire always used the word *population.*

But there was another and a more important reason still. During the Middle Ages, and down to the end of the eighteenth century, the phenomenon of over-population never occurred, or it occurred but rarely and within narrow limits. Indeed, the old economic organisation necessarily led to a slow and regular increase. The phenomenon, which suggested to Malthus his terrible law, occurred only with the birth of modern industry.

The Phenomenon of Over-population a Modern Phenomenon.

Not less grave political reasons prevented economists from studying the problem of population. At a time when society was governed by real military rulers, and the power of the sovereign had no other basis than military strength, the chief care of every State was that of having a large number of citizens fit for bearing arms, and hence, of promoting the increase of population in every way.

In the second half of the past century almost everyone was still agreed upon this point, that is, they believed that the increase of the population was rather to be assisted than restrained.

Frederic the Great of Prussia held it as an axiom that "the number of the population constitutes the wealth of the State;"[1] even Rousseau expressed the same idea in axiomatic form, and added, with full conviction, "that the Government under which the citizens increase and multiply the most is infallibly the best."[2]

In Italy, Filangieri, taking his inspiration from Montesquieu, dictated precepts which he judged to be certain for the increase of births.[3]

The science of statistics was but in its infancy, communication was slow and difficult; hence not even the keenest rulers succeeded in establishing even an approximative proportion between the population and the means of subsistence.

[1] Frederic-le-Grand: *Oeuvres*, edited by the Academy of Berlin, vol. iv., pp. 4, 6.

[2] Rousseau: *Contrat social*, book iii., chap. ix.

[3] Filangieri: *Scienza della legislazione*, 1780, book ii.

The opinion that the world had supported a much larger number of men in ancient than in modern times pre- Former Theories about population. vailed among the writers of the last century. There was some uncertainty as to the precise number. Montesquieu, in one edition of his *Lettres persanes*, thought that it was fifty, in another ten times greater than that in his day, in the *Esprit des lois* he simply states that the countries of antiquity *regorgeaient d' habitants.*

Very many writers followed the opinion of Montesquieu, assigning, as did Wallace in England, an enormous population to the nations of antiquity."[1]

Other authors, chiefly in Italy, followed the old opinion of Botero,[2] that the number of men was almost always the same, and that such must always be the case in the future.

In France, Buffon[3] dubitatively, and the *Encyclopédie* explicitly, assented to the thesis of Botero, and the *Encyclopédie* openly asserted that " the sum of men taken together is to-day equal to that of an epoch of antiquity, and to that which it will be in future ages. If there have been periods when a greater or lesser scarcity of men was apparent, it was not because the total number was less, but that the population was migratory, and that thus local diminutions of population took place.[4]

If the learned were so uncertain in their way of judging, the governing powers were not less so.

They were, therefore, very much the more inclined to attribute famine to the scarcity than to the abundance of subjects, and they only busied themselves with enlarging their dominions or increasing the population in order to win prosperity and riches for their subjects by wars of conquest.

Cf. Schoene : *op. cit.*, p. 67.

[2] Botero : *Ragione e Governo di stato*, in the chap. *del Matrimonio.*

[3] Buffon : *Quadrupèdes*, chap. xvi.

[4] See the article *Population* by *Damilaville* in Diderot's *Encyclopédie*, 1765.

A taste for easy erudition (Italians, says Laveleye, begin the
The Problem of Popu- study of all questions at the flood [1]) would
lation before Malthus. induce me to make an exposition of the theories of population held by the philosophers and political
writers of antiquity and the Middle Ages. But the labour would
be vain, and has been already pursued by others.[2] Certainly the
question was studied by the ancients generally, and especially by
the Greek cities, whose economic constitution inclined towards a
limitation of numbers.

The morality and science of that day did not hesitate to
The number limited in recommend three equally immoral expedients:
Ancient Greece. unnatural love, abortion, and the exposure of
infants. A whole series of legislators frequently attempted to
order, regulate, and restrain birth; quite a host of philosophers
penetrated the subtle problem which was to agitate the souls and
minds of men so many centuries later.[3]

But before Malthus no one had treated the subject scientifically
Until Malthus no one and with ample method; and even half a century
had scientifically
studied the Problem of before his day, in so learned and prolific a country
Population. as Germany, John Peter Sussmilch maintained that
the chief care of sovereigns desirous of procuring the happiness of
their people was that of increasing the population.[4]

[1] Laveleye : *Nouvelles lettres d'Italie.*

[2] *Cf.* Robert von Mohl : *Geschichte und Literatur der Staatswissenschaften,*
3rd edit., Erlangen, 1858, p. 409 ; A. Senigaglia : *La Teoria economica della
popolazione in Italia,* from the "*Archivio giuridico,*" Bologna, 1881 ; etc.

[3] *Cf.* Aristotle : *Politic,* book iii., chap. iii., sec. 6 ; chap. vii., sec.
4 ; book xiv., chap. xiv., sec. 6. ; Montesquieu : *Esprit des Lois,* book
xxiii., chap. vi. ; Durny : *Histoire des Grecs,* vol. iii., p. 104 ; Plato :
Republic, book v. ; Van der Smissen : *La Population,* Brussels, 1893, chap.
i., ii. ; Fustel de Coulanges : *La Cité antique,* book ii., chap. iii.; Schoene :
op. col. pp. 27 and foll.

[4] Suessmilch : *Die göttliche Ordnung in den Veränderungen des menschlichen
Geschlechts,* 1742. Concerning the encouragement given to human multi-
plication in the old legislations, see F. Passy : *Malthus et sa doctrine,*
Paris, 1868, p. 19 ; Voltaire : *Siécle de Louis XIV.,* chap. xxix ;
Forbonnais : *Finance de la France,* vol. i., p. 187. The Salic Law, in
pursuance of the above-mentioned idea, orders thus xxiv., 6-7 : *Si quis*

But, when the demographic phenomenon which marked the transition from the feudal to the capitalistic economic state began to clearly appear, some writers had become alarmed, so that if we examine the economists of the seventeenth and eighteenth centuries it is easy to discover some observations or hypotheses which later appeared in a much greater degree in the work of Malthus.

Even Machiavelli had suspected that there was a *physical cause* (the productiveness of the soil) which set limits to the indefinite increase of the human species; [1] The Precursors Malthus. and a century later Giovanni Botero still more clearly perceived what later became the Malthusian hypothesis.

Botero, who, moved by political considerations, judged the abundance of population to be an element of public prosperity, and suggested, in his work, *Ragione di Stato*, the means of promoting it, studied in a truly masterly way the obstacles to the indefinite increase of the number of mankind, and decided that it was not so much famine, pestilence, and war, as the disproportion between the *generative power* of mankind and the *nutritive power of the State*, that is to say, between population and the means of subsistence. And under the influence of this thought, he suggested the development of colonies. [2]

But these were pessimistic forecasts, which did not in any way modify current opinions, nor exercise the least influence upon the tendencies of writers and of Governments. [3]

It was only towards the end of the last century, when the rise of a new capitalist phase made itself quite evident, and produced a systematic excess of population, that in Italy, France and

feminam ingenuam postquam coeperit habere infantes (that is after sixteen years of age) *occiderit, solidos 600 judicetur. Post quod infantes non potuit habere* (that is after forty or fifty years of age) *solidos 200 judicetur.* See Fustel de Coulanges : *La Monarquie franque*, p. 482.

[1] Machiavelli : *Discorsi*, book i., chap. i.

[2] See Jandelli : *Il precursore di Malthus*, in the *Filosofia delle scuole Italiane*, Rome, 1881, vol. xxiii., pp. 147-160.

[3] *Cf.* Cossa : *Introduzione allo studio dell' economia politica*, 3rd. edit. Milan, 1892, chap. iii., sec. 1.

England, a certain distrust began to be felt for former demographic theories.

In Italy, Cesare Beccaria had already declared the problem of population to be intimately connected with that of the means of subsistence; and he counselled in opposition to the old views, that attention should be given rather to the development of the latter than of the former.[1]

But above all, Gianmaria Ortes, a lowly Venetian friar, though living in the complete retirement of his monastery, foresaw that pessimistic demographic hypothesis which later immortalised Malthus. Some pages of Ortes seem quite similar to those of Malthus; he comprehended the entire question, the geometrical progression of the population, and the arithmetical progression of the means of subsistence, the preventative action of man, and the repressive action of nature. There is even a great affinity in the remedies proposed by the Catholic friar and the Anglican parson. But Ortes was uncertain, undecided, and had no statistical preparation; his work, therefore, could not meet with success.[2]

The causes productive of economic pessimism were, so to speak, in the air; theory always conforming itself to the phenomenon, and being directly derived from it, it was no wonder if even in Italy, France, and England, the most different authors expressed similar or identical theories with those of Malthus, on the eve of the publication of his work.

In France a state of anxiety succeeded to the old optimist theories;[3] in England, where the new phase of industrial capitalism was more advanced, the works of Townsend, Temple, and above all, Stewart, contain in germ the Malthusian hypothesis.[4]

Therefore, even before Malthus, many writers had some per-

---

[1] C. Beccaria : *Elementi di economia publica*, sec. 31 ; *Della Popolazione* in the *Collezione Custodi*, vol. iii.

[2] G. Ortes : *Riflessioni sulla popolazione delle nazioni per rapporto all' economia nazionale*, 1790. *Cf.* Lampertico : *G. Ortes e la scienza economica al suo tempo*, Venice, 1865.

[3] *Cf.* Schoene : *op. cit.*, pp. 304-309.

[4] *Cf.* Cunningham : *The Growth of English Industry and Commerce in Modern Times*, Cambridge, 1892, p. 557 and foll.

ception of the disparity between the increase of mankind and of the means of subsistence.[1] But no one had dared to profoundly study the difficult problem ; hence all the theories of population must substantially fall into two great categories as we have shown, that of the theories before and after Malthus.[2]

Nevertheless, if no one gave precise expression to the doubt which began to arise, it was, so to speak, in the air.

Society was in a state of transformation, and this transformation itself originating a new demographic phase, chiefly effected a change of ideas. But it was more than anything else a general and indefinite unrest, destined to find its interpreter at a later time.

Nevertheless, not even did the great mind of Adam Smith,[3] founder of the economic science, doubt whether the increase of men moved equally with that of *Nor did Smith modify the Old Opinions.* the means of subsistence, and he has even asserted in one part of his immortal work, like all the economists who preceded him, that the truest indication of a nation's prosperity must be sought in the numerical increase of its inhabitants.

God gives children, and he will feed them : *Gott macht kinder der wird sie auch wohl ernüren.* This was Luther's declaration, and, until a few years before Malthus, the science of economy had abandoned itself to this optimistic fatalism.

Malthus, therefore, with his *Essay on Population,* an essay, at least in its primitive form, purely political, and inspired by the needs and tendencies of the Con- *Economic and Philosophic Optimism.* servative party, effected a real revolution in the field of social economy.

[1] Malthus himself enumerates the authors whose works suggested his principle of population. *Cf.* Ingram : *History of Political Economy,* Edinburgh, 1888, p. 115. But Marx is in error when he judges the work of Malthus to be "a scholastic, superficial, and priestly plagiarism from Sir James Stewart, Townsend, Franklin, Wallace, etc."

[2] Jolles : *Die Ansichten der deutschen nationalökonomischen Schriftsteller des sechszenten und siebzehten Jahrdunderts über Bevölkerungswesen,* in *Jarbücher für Nationalökonomie und Statistik,* Jena, 1886.

[3] A. Smith : *The Wealth of Nations,* book i., chap. viii.

But how did he come to conceive of an inevitable inequality between population and the means of subsistence? How was it possible that a theory, which so profoundly shocked the religious convictions of a religious nation, should find so many votaries even among devout men? Why did the economists accept it at once, almost without discussion, and transmit it as one of the most evident and undoubted canons of the economic science?

It was, as we shall see in the course of the present inquiry, The Malthusian Theory as the Basis of the Philosophy of Wealth. because the theory of Malthus concerning population was, or appeared to be, an efficient basis for the philosophy of wealth, and because, placing the disproportion and poverty in the very nature of things, it relieved the dominant classes of responsibility for either.[1]

Only twenty-two years elapsed between the publication of Adam Smith's great work and that of the casual essay of Malthus; the first appeared in 1776, the second in 1798. But in these twenty-two years what a profound change had been effected in the society and mind of England! When Adam Smith wrote, a great political and a great industrial revolution were taking shape around him; when Malthus wrote, the evil effects of both had made themselves felt. Adam Smith necessarily inclined towards optimism; Robert Malthus was necessarily pessimistic.

In the great work of Smith, which is the highest document of The Optimism of Smith's Great Work. economic optimism, breathes the spirit which animated the immortal works of the French philosophers of the eighteenth century.

Towards the close of the last century, there spread over the whole of Europe, from the France of the Revolution, not only the theories which proclaimed a new social faith, but also, and not less extensively, the most absolute trust in the goodness of natural laws and in human perfectibility.

The conception of natural laws governing society, like the The Optimistic Conception of Progress. physical phenomena, doubtless belongs to antiquity, but not to Plato, whose social science

---

[1] Ingram: *op. cit.*, p. 112, truly remarks that Malthus wrote "in the interests of a Conservative policy."

is but the vision of a prophet or a poet, but to him whom Comte calls the *incomparable* Aristotle. To this conception of the natural laws the philosophers of the French Revolution added the idea of progress. Antiquity was enslaved by the belief that a long and irremediable decadence was the necessary sequence of the primitive golden age. But Turgot, and still more and more widely than he, Condorcet, taking from the physical sciences the idea of a law, and from the natural sciences that of progress, while fore-seeing sociology as the universal science of social progress, became the apostles of human solidarity, which seemed to them a fatal corollary of the evolution of ages.

The spirit of the French philosophy, penetrating into England, necessarily suggested the most abundant hopes *England in the Time* to a people already in the train of a great indus- *of Smith.* trial transformation.

Between 1760 and 1770, that is in the period when Smith chiefly observed the facts of English life, and *Causes Originating the* conceived the plan of the *Wealth of Nations,* *Optimism of Smith.* *The Great Scientific* the great industrial discoveries had succeeded *Discoveries.* each other with dazzling rapidity. And, in fact, during those ten years, within the limits of England, Roebuck began to separate iron from scoria by means of coal, Brindley con-nected the new manufacturing centres with the sea by means of canals, Wedgwood discovered a method of producing cheap china of a good quality, Hargreaves invented the sewing machine, Arkwright utilised the discoveries of Wyatt and High in spinning by means of cylinders and applied hydraulic pressure in setting them in action, Watt discovered a means for the condensa-tion of steam, Crompton the machine for cotton spinning, and Cartwright the mechanic loom. Such a wonderful and dazzling succession of discoveries and inventions gave a very large basis to the French philosophy; however, imbued with optim-ism, it seemed as though the revolutionary theories received the most absolute confirmation from these facts and these dis-coveries.

The public opinion of England had an optimistic tendency, and the theories which originated in France accentuated this optimistic tendency more and more.[1]

Hence it appears why Adam Smith, drawing his inspiration directly from the physiocrates, and most of all from Quesnay and Turgot, found a public disposed to accept his views.

Natural phenomena, said Turgot, being subject to constant laws, are bound within an impassable circle. Everything comes back to life in order to perish again, and what remains behind bears the impress of what has passed away. On the contrary, the succession of the races of men from epoch to epoch presents a spectacle of continual change. Reason, liberty, and civilisation always bring about new events; this treasure of knowledge is transmitted and increases, and humanity inevitably progresses. The link between the different epochs, the constant growth of the human patrimony, the progressive amelioration of social institutions by the advance of reason and civilisation, constituted progress in the view of Turgot.[2]

The Optimist Theory of Progress.

Inspired by the French philosophic theories, and originating in a society which was in a state of transformation, Smith's economics bore traces of their origin, and were necessarily optimistic, just as that was an optimistic philosophical conception which entirely founded the purpose of human actions upon sympathy.

Sympathy, that is the innate tendency by which we feel in ourselves the pleasure and pain of others, and, so to speak, vibrate in unison with our fellow-beings, necessarily became the basis both of the economy and philosophy of the optimistic school. For Smith, the universal moral law consisted in acting in such a manner as to excite the sympathy of our fellow-beings and to avoid whatever could provoke the contrary feeling.[3]

Smith's Philosophy and sympathy as the scope of Human Actions.

---

[1] *Cf.* Cunningham : *op. cit.*, p. 430 and foll.

[2] Turgot : *Fragment d'un traité sur le vide.*

[3] A. Smith : *The Theory of Moral Sentiments*, 6th edition, London, 1790, part i., sec. i.

Schopenhauer, wishing to refute every moral system with one example, which he calls *a crucial experience,* supposes the case of a youth, who, being in love with a young woman, wishes to get rid of his successful rival. He answers himself according to Kant, Fichte, Wollaston, Hutcheson, Smith and Wolff. Reasoning from the premises of Adam Smith's Theory, he says: I foresee that my act will not in any way bring me the *sympathy* of the spectator.[1] Unintentionally the irony of Schopenhauer is a definition of Smith's theory.

Smith's work was in favour among the philosophers of the French Revolution, and no less a person than the Marquis de Condorcet translated it and gave it publicity.

At the time of Smith's death, in 1790, the French Revolution had just burst forth, and the choice spirits of the whole of Europe followed it with enthusiasm and trust. Very fortunately for himself, Smith did not see the days of terror and the ruin of the French Revolution, nor did he behold the frightful economic crisis which later resulted from the industrial revolution in his own country.[2]

In what different surroundings and under what different conditions Malthus conceived and published his work !

The French Revolution was stifled in blood, and upon the political horizon of Europe there already appeared the showers which announced the Napoleonic storms. The tyrant had been killed, the old privileges abolished, but the illusion had also proved false in a great and far-reaching way, for, in spite of reforms, society had remained essentially the same.

[1] Schopenhauer : *Le fondement de la morale,* translated by Burdeau, p. 146.

[2].On the causes of Smith's optimism, see Ingram : *op. cit.,* pp. 87-110; Price : *A Short History of Political Economy in England,* etc., chap. i.; R. B. Haldane : *Life of Adam Smith,* London, 1887, and W. Skarzynski : *Adam Smith als moral philosopher und Schöpfer der nationalökonomie,* Berlin, 1878, and Hassbach : *Les fondements philosophiques de l'économie politique de Quesnay et de Smith* in the *Revue d'économie politique,* Sept., Oct , 1893.

The life of England beheld by Malthus in his youth was not
less saddening.[1] Various successive seasons of
scarcity had impoverished the British agricultural districts, while, influenced by the rapid
development of industries, the population increased and the
phenomenon of over-population systematically occurred. Imports
and custom duties, not yet attacked by the reforming genius
of Peel, hindered the rapid progress of the means of subsistence and of exchange. The evils of war and famine
found a sad counterpart in the occurrence of a terrible industrial crisis, than which not even England has seen a sadder
or a vaster. The great number of discoveries had, in fact,
originated the formation of the great industrial system; and
crushed by this last, the smaller industries were violently injured
and unable to resist through lack of strength. Thus the old
industries died away on all sides, bringing down in their ruin
thousands of workmen, and causing a strong feeling of misfortune
to be felt by the whole of England.

The marginal note reads: *The Economic and Social Crisis of England at the time of Malthus.*

This evil state of things was the more deeply felt because
the new ideas, spread among the educated classes,
augmented the subjective causes of misery.

The marginal note reads: *The Evils of English Society in the time of Malthus.*

The poor laws, become a source of evil, far from remedying
pauperism, increased it. Government provisions in favour of the
poorer classes were inopportune and sometimes evil also, such as
the right permitted to parishes to give an increase of wages
(*allowances*).[2]

In short, the whole administration of public relief was so
defective, that it is impossible to conceive the
disastrous effect which it then produced in
England. Multiplying the relief given, enlarging the practice
of *allowances*, it ended by causing a progressive decline in wages.
Indeed, at one time, the tithe which the poor-rate levied upon
the tax-payers in general, became nothing else than a species of
subsidy given to manufacturers. In reality, the ratepayers were

The marginal note reads: *Public Relief in its hurtful consequences.*

---

[1] *Cf.* Cunningham : *op. cit.*, p. 491.
[2] *Cf.* Van der Smissen : *op. cit.*, pp. 156, 157.

not burdened for the benefit of the poor, but of the manufacturing classes, and the tax increased so much that the rate of the wages decreased while that of the reliefs increased.

Such were the causes which prepared and produced the pessimistic philosophy and economics of which Malthus was probably then the greatest interpreter. *The Causes of the Pessimism of Malthus.*

In the great disproportion originated by the large growing industry and in the rapid technical revolution, Socialism was already taking its rise.[1]

Further, true to its own nature, and a law which is inevitable in a state of society where the causes of discord were very grave, Socialism had a violent character in its origin. And, being as yet without scientific consistency, it oscillated between the need of practical and positive reforms, and the most Utopian anarchism.

The chief spokesman of the new theories, William Godwin, a very successful agitator and a genial if not *W. Godwin.* always a profound writer, but always most acute and daring, was placed more than any other in this grave contradiction.

It is in truth very difficult to gather a broad and complete system from Godwin's disordered work; what *Examination of Godwin's Optimistic Theory.* is chiefly wanting to it is stability of views. While in his celebrated book : *An Inquiry Concerning Political Justice* (1793), studying the forms of property, he distinguishes between the contrary systems of private property, of supply and demand, and declares himself favourable to this last system, and hence to that of common property ; nevertheless, he would have the great transformation to occur spontaneously, without revolution or the intervention of the legislature. The evils which oppress society belong in no way to the nature of things ; on the contrary, it is from human institutions that misery and injustice arise. Social wealth not only exists in sufficient quantity, but if properly distributed, could afford an easy existence in exchange of moderate labour.

---

[1] Ingram : *loc. cit.*

Let wealth be properly distributed, and give mankind sufficient time for education and culture, and un-
aided reason will become the guide of human
action, and there will be no further need of coercion and
violence. In short, Godwin's ideal was really an anarchical one,
but mild and pacific; in every work of his he attacks popular
revolutions, which he considers to be great catastrophes,
which only replace a decrepid tyranny by a new and powerful
one.

The Optimistic Ideal of the Pacific Anarchist.

Godwin was a changeable and unmethodical writer, but at the
same time very forcible and keen, and, of course, he had a large
following.

Condorcet, in his magnificent *Esquisse historique des progrès
de l'esprit humain,* written almost under the
knife of the guillotine—the noblest of books, and
written by the noblest of men, as John Stuart Mill has said—a
luminous essay, replete with illusions, but also vast and ingenious,
had summarised in three principal propositions the progresses
which he believed would be speedily realised. They were : (1) the
destruction of national inequalities; (2) the progress of equality in
each nation ; (3) the actual progress of the individual towards
perfection.

Condorcet and Progress.

Godwin was less optimistic than Condorcet, and, although his
ideas formed a contrast with the social difficulties
with which England was at that time struggling,
nevertheless they had won for him a large number of followers,
and were widely diffused, so that the interest of the British public
about the brilliant English author and his journal, *The Inquirer,*
was very intense.

Godwin and Condorcet.

The principle of human perfectibility was not, or did not seem
to be, a Utopia at that time ; the very assertions of Condorcet,
which raise a laugh now, formed part of the general conviction,
and seemed to be indisputable canons.

Everyone remembers Diderot's beautiful dream in the Rêve de
d'Alembert ?

Everything, therefore, seemed perfectible both in English

and in French society, and as though it could be modified and transformed under the influence of the new ideas. Faith in Human Perfectibility at the end of the Eighteenth Century.

At that time such dreams, Utopias, and hopes were possible, and even natural to a society not yet convinced by disillusions.

On the other hand, English society was, as we have last seen, in a very trying period of its existence. Industry, the child of man, was begotten, as is the offspring of woman, in pain ; the financial crisis grew worse, and the revolt of the colonies intensified it.

The condition of agriculture was miserable ; that of industry very difficult, since the great revolution effected by the new machinery had decreased the wages Causes of the Pessimist Reaction. of adults, increased child-labour and pauperism, and rendered desperate the economic view of the birth-rate.

Add to all this that the great revolution with regard to means of transport which occurred a few years after, and which made England pass from the industrial to the commercial phase, was yet to come. In fact, the first steamboat was only built in 1807 ; steam navigation was only introduced into England in 1812 ; the service of steam navigation across the ocean was only established very much later, in 1838, when Malthus had been four years dead.

In such a grave crisis, the optimistic views imported from France, and so widely diffused in England, coming into collision with their surroundings, naturally The Pessimist Reaction. generated a pessimistic reaction. And in fact the reaction did not delay in coming.

Amongst the greatest admirers of Condorcet and Godwin was the father of Robert Malthus. Not so the son. The study of history had shown him that progress, won by dint of sacrifices, was always very limited and always gained by main force amid resolute, insurmountable, unceasing obstacles. Therefore, he did not trust the views of his father or the philosophy of Godwin ; and it was while studying them that he conceived the plan of collecting the chief ideas, and in 1798, he published the work:

B

An Essay on the Principle of Population as it Affects the Future Improvement of Society, with Remarks on the Speculations of M. Godwin, Condorcet, and other Writers. Being an Anglican pastor, and belonging to the Conservative middle class, Malthus became the natural, and, perhaps, unconscious representative of the Conservative party, which felt itself fundamentally menaced by Godwin's subversive views.

"Malthus," says Wolowski, "wrote his work under the influence of a reaction which we can easily understand.

Publication of Malthus' Work.

For a generation the whole of Europe had heard it unceasingly maintained that trees could touch the sky, if only they were manured, watered and cultivated, according to the newest formula of a marvellous perfection."[1]

Malthus, therefore, represented the pessimistic reaction not only in the economic science but also in the whole social philosophy of his time.

Malthus the Precursor of Pessimism.

The mutual dependence of the economic sciences and philosophy, already foreseen by some brilliant writers,[2] has been too much neglected in our day.

Moreover, whoever wishes to penetrate into the study of these relations of dependence sees at once how close and continual they are. The economic discussions

Mutual Dependence of Economy and the Moral Science.

appeared for the first time in the *Ethics* of Aristotle: the economic principles of the Middle Ages are found in methodical form in that part of his *Summa* which Thomas Aquinas

[1] Wolowski: *loc. cit. Cf.* also Kerkup in the *Encyclopædia Britannica,* 1883, vol. xv., p. 343.

[2] *Cf.* on this subject Dargun: *Egoismus und Altruismus in der Nationalökonomie,* Leipzig, 1885; Sidgwick; *Principles of Political Economy,* 2nd edition, London, 1887, last chapter; Minghetti: *Dell' economia publica e delle sue attineuze colla morale e col diritto,* Florence, 1859; H. Bandrillart: *Philosophie de l'economie politique,* Paris, 1883; V. Cathrein: *Moral Philosophie,* Freiburg, 1891; Jodl: *Volkswirtchaftslehre und Ethik* in *Holtzendorffs deutschen Zeit—und Streitfragen;* Jahrg, xiv. (1886); Heft 224; Gustav Schmoller: *Sozial—und Gewerbepolitik der Gegenwart* in *Reden und Aufsaze,* 1890, pp. 204-246; Ziegler: *Die soziale Frage eine sittliche Frage,* Introduction; and James Bonar: *Philosophy and Political Economy in some of their Historical Relations,* London, 1893.

dedicates to ethical questions.[1] Smith, before inquiring into the nature and causes of wealth, wrote a theory of moral sentiments, and almost all the great English economists who succeeded him have been philosophers and moralists. Commercialism, and later, Parliamentarism, were in Germany the consequence of a system of national philosophy. Smith and the *physiocrat* were the outcome of economic optimism, prevalent in France and England : just as Malthus was the greatest and most sympathetic of the precursors of modern pessimism. This relation of mutual dependence between the economic sciences and philosophy will cause no surprise to anyone who reflects that both have in general rather succeeded and conformed to phenomena than preceded them.

The whole Malthusian theory is impregnated with so thorough a pessimism that it is difficult to say who, before the time of Malthus, had unfolded with great skill the theses which were afterwards largely developed in the works of Schopenhauer, Rolph and Hartmann.

Malthus and Pessimistic Fatalism.

All philosophers and economists have optimistic or pessimistic theses as the basis of their work ; hence it is that even those who appear to have the most different and opposite ideas have fundamentally the same conceptions. The most different and opposite men, such as Turgot and Spenser, Smith and Mill, Bentham and Hegel, Rousseau and Comte, calmly studied, do not appear other than men imbued with the same spirit of optimism.[2]

Optimism and Pessimism as the bases of all the Economic and Moral Systems.

Leibnitz, the greatest interpreter of optimism, against whose teaching Voltaire conceived and wrote *Candide*, asserts in the preface to *Teodicea*, that there are three kinds of fatalism: the Musulman, the Stoical and the Christian fatalism ; and he judges them equally dangerous to the future of mankind. The Musulman imprisons his stolid reason in the formula ; *it is written*, which is in itself nothing

The Three Forms of Fatalism according to Leibnitz.

---

[1] *Cf.* Ziegler : *loc. cit.*

[2] *Cf.* Renouvier : *Schopenhauer et la metaphysique du pessimisme*, in the *Année philosophique* for 1892, Paris, 1893, p. 5.

else but the very negation of reason. The Stoic considers nature to be quite as inexorable, and obeys her laws in a passive way, under the pretext that she directs whoever will accept her guidance, and compels whoever makes resistance. It is a forced resignation, which may have an aspect of utility, but which leads to nothing but discouragement. The Christian fatalism, grounded upon the doctrine of predestination, is not less absurd and dangerous, since, considering man as already destined to salvation or damnation, it weakens all his energy and unmans all his daring.[1]

But the fatalistic pessimism of Schopenhauer and his followers has nothing in common with these three systems : although it is also based upon a foregone conclusion, nevertheless, it attempts to find its *raison d'être* in the very nature of things, and in substantially it does not go further back than Malthus : it is a much more complex and profound conception.

The difference between Ancient and Modern Pessimism.

According to the optimistic theory of theology, evil is something which simply consisting in privation, is a partial negation of being and of good. On the other hand, according to the pessimistic conception, pain precedes pleasure : it alone is positive, and pleasure is but the satisfaction of a pre-existing pain. It is a foregone conclusion, which Hartmann has tried to correct in some way, but of which he never succeeded in furnishing an exhaustive demonstration.[2]

The Fundamental Theory of Pessimism.

The teaching of a German biologist, Rolph, has endeavoured to give a scientific foundation to this ungrounded conception. In fact, according to Rolph, all organic matter increases by diffusion, that is by absorbing and assimilating, by means of its extension, all the materials necessary for its life. The diffusion is a series of movements

Rolph and the Scientific Foundations of Modern Pessimism.

---

[1] It should be remembered that this is not the teaching of the Christian creeds indiscriminately, nor indeed of the more important among them (*Translator's note*).

[2] *Cf.* Renouvier : *loc. cit.*, and above all Fouillée : *La Psychologie des idées forcées*, Paris, 1893, vol. i., p. 77, 95

or *endosmosi*, which absorb favourable elements, exercising an influence on the *exosmosi*, and this diffusion is a mechanical effect. The various ways of exercising these mechanical functions in the organic substance explain in the first place all the phenomena of nutrition ; to be nourished is to absorb and assimilate. In the second place they explain the phenomena of the division and number of the cells, as a consequence of the extension of being outside the limits of the single and original cell. Finally, they explain the phenomena of reproduction, since in such a case reproduction is nothing else than a division of cells or of nutrition.

Rolph fixed no limit to the action of assimilation by *endosmosi ;* every cell, and consequently every organism, suffers from *insatiability*, and a *mechanical hunger* exists, and this is the consequence of all the actions of living organisms. At a certain point in the evolution, in correspondence with the mechanical hunger, there is developed a *psychical* hunger, which manifests itself essentially as a pain, and pleasure is but a secondary and derived phenomenon. Therefore, pain remains as the fatal mainspring of the universe.

Insatiability and Mechanical Hunger.

This striking theory, in which we see the boldest attempt ever made to give a scientific basis to pessimist assumptions, is contradicted by the very data of biological science. Indeed, it is unquestionable that there are pleasures which make themselves directly felt, without the sad medium of an intermediate pain, and that these pleasures can be the moving powers of our vital activity without the assistance of pain.[1]

The thought that pleasure and gratification are negative things, and that they are but the satisfying of a desire, and hence of a pain, was to be found in some old economists and philosophers. Verri, an Italian economist of the eighteenth century, had said, a few years before Malthus, that *pain precedes every pleasure*, and he had added that *pain is the only moving power in man.*[2]

P. Verri and the Pessimist Economy.

---

[1] Fouillée : *loc. cit.*

[2] Verri : *Sull' indole del piacere e del dolore*, 1781.

But these were but isolated opinions; Malthus was really the great precursor of modern pessimism.

In the Malthusian theory the irrestrainable generative instinct, *Relations between the Malthusian Theory and Modern Pessimism.* causing a disproportion between men and the means of subsistence, condemns them to pay a penalty, which is a part of nature itself; hence pleasure appears as a negative fact, and simply originates pain. So far, and not as in Schopenhauer and Hartmann, pain appeared to Malthus, not the eternal irremediable condition of beings, the penalty only to be escaped from by self-annihilation, but it was the fatal counterpart of every being, condemned to a perpetual conflict between two equally profound needs, love and hunger.[1]

The conception of Malthus not only preceded those of the *Evil Influence of Malthus upon Darwin.* later pessimists, but directly influenced them, having acted even upon Darwin, who had contrary tendencies.[2] Indeed, under the influence of the Malthusian ideas, in the conflict of beings he saw nothing but the need of *self-maintenance* and of *living normally*, and he did not perceive that, beyond the limits of both, there is an incessant and continual struggle for the bettering of the conditions of life in intensity and quality. Nor did he feel that it was only at the beginning of the evolution that hunger and sorrow are the sole stimulus which nature adopts, but that at a more advanced point in the life of beings pleasure becomes the certain spur of every activity by means of the idea which *anticipates* it.

When pessimism has become but a phase of spent philosophic thought, then and then only, judging it objectively, it will be seen to what extent the whole pessimistic theory was but the natural consequence of the Malthusian hypothesis.

Perhaps no English economist of the last or present *Malthus the sole Interpreter of Absolute Individualism.* century has ever had the rapid and immense success which befell Malthus, notwithstanding

[1] The great and direct influence exercised by Malthus upon modern pessimism has been very well observed by Renouvier : *op. cit.*, pp. 6, 7, and by Fouillée : *loc. cit.*

[2] "The Darwinian theories have been too much influenced by Malthus' law about population." Fouillée : *op. cit.*, p. 77.

that there have been others much more sympathetic and profound.

Upon what did his success depend ? to what unknown cause must it be attributed ?

A deep study of the history of economic theories has made me quite certain on this point. None of the English economists before Malthus, nor any of his contemporaries, or of those who lived for a short time after him, was more strictly individualist than he ; no one lent himself more to the justification of the abuses, the indifference, the privileges of the dominant classes. If the orthodox English school assumed so severely individualist and anti-democratic a character, it was simply by reason of Malthus.

It is true that Adam Smith declared the communist[1] ideal absurd, and that he utterly discredited the Adam Smith not opposed to the Radical View. beneficent influence of legislative intervention. But we must remember that he wrote at a time when the function of the State was disturbing and evil, and the cause of much more injustice than of good. Lastly, it is necessary to remember that Smith's whole work is redolent with a plentiful innovating spirit ; the Scotch philosopher, wishing to base the relations between men upon sympathy, is often involuntarily, and perhaps also unconsciously, a radical ; such in fact he is in the labour question,[2] still more so in the matter of imposts[3] and popular education.[4]

Ricardo, absorbed in his subtle economic theories, spoke in the House of Commons upon the labour question Ricardo's Individualism. only to say that he is *completely at war with the system of Mr. Owen.*[5] But the fact of his being in utter disagreement with Owen does not blind his clear-sightedness ; he is not, nor can he be, considered as an extreme individualist.

[1] Smith : *Wealth of Nations*, book iv., chap. ii.
[2] Smith : *op. cit.*, book i., chap. viii.
[3] Smith : *op. cit.*, book v., chap. ii.
[4] Smith : *op. cit.*, book v., chap. i.
[5] See Cannan : *The Malthusian Anti-Socialist Argument* in the *Economic Review* for January, 1892, p. 73,

Malthus' chief follower with regard to population, Stuart
S. Mill partly repudi-
ates the Pessimistic
Basis of Malthusianism
Mill, differs more than anyone else from the
terrible premises of Malthusian individualism·
If in the first edition of his work, written, moreover, too
hastily and in too short a time, he speaks of Socialism
as a Utopia, in the succeeding editions, and in his post-
humous fragments, on the contrary, he speaks of it with great
respect, as of a theory containing a great deal of truth. Mill
looks forward to a time when society will no longer consist of two
classes, one of idle and the other of working men, when the law
that only those who work shall have food will be applied to all
indiscriminately, when the division of the fruits of labour will
depend, not upon chance or birth, but upon some principle of
recognised justice, when, in short, men will be free to work
energetically and acquire profits which will not be exclusively
theirs, but which they shall be compelled to share with the
society in the midst of which they live.[1]

Even N. W. Senior, the most vehement adversary of factory
N. W. Senior.
legislation, the economist who, in the interests of
capital, invented the terrible expression, *starvation wage,* has frequently noble ideas, as when he maintains against the then prevalent opinion, that high wages do not in any way diminish the
production.[2]

England has had but one truly, absolutely and strictly indi-
Malthus the only
strictly Individualist
Economist.
vidualist economist, and this was Malthus, who
was led by an inflexible logic to the most extreme
and odious consequences of his social system.

The success of Malthus' short treatise was therefore and neces-
Malthus the great
Defender of the Philo-
sophy of Wealth.
sarily enormous. Naturally such, both on account
of the cause he defended, as well as on account of
the novelty and attractiveness of the theories which it exposed.

[1] Mill : *Autobiography,* chap. vii.

[2] Senior : *Political Economy,* 5th edition, London, 1863, p. 187, etc.
"But Malthus," says Cannan, *art. cit.,* p. 75, " was really an anti-Socialist,
and it is almost entirely from him that the anti-Socialist reputation of the
English classical school of economists is derived."

The pessimist reaction was, so to say, in the air. Owing to the wars which devastated the continental countries, the price of grain was very high, and the industrial crisis very grave. Meantime the English tax-payer was obliged to pay to the poor tax from five to twenty-five francs a year, according to the county.[1]

There was, therefore, every reason why a theory, which seemed to be simply a biological-economic one, should become a political theory chiefly.

When Malthus perceived the state of his theory, he saw that he must rewrite his work, enlarge it, and furnish it with new proofs. Therefore he travelled a great deal in Europe, collected a great deal of statistics, and gave to his book, which was of a purely ephemeral and political nature, a scientific foundation and gravity of treatment.

The privileged classes of English society, writes Ferrara, took notice of the new theory; and, although made public by a Whig, the staunchest Tories were seen to wildly applaud, enrolling themselves under the banner of Malthus, and entertaining the bold writer who had raised it. Those who possessed almost the whole of the land, and lived luxuriously in aristocratic affectation, felt their consciences relieved of a great weight. The sight of the miserable peasant, compelled to dig the earth during his entire life, caused them no fear; they could now answer his laments by reproaching him with his own imprudence, and imputing the inevitable effects of an imprudent marriage to his own fault. They could reply to every declaration of the insufficiency of the poor-rate that, instead of increasing it, it was necessary to diminish it at present in order afterwards to suppress it altogether. It seemed as though all the abuses, about which the progressists had made such a cry, were to find a justification and excuse in the theory of Malthus.[2]

Sympathy of the Privileged Classes with the Views of Malthus.

[1] In the financial year, 1817-1818, the poor tax for the whole of England, including expenses, reached the sum of nine millions sterling. See *Parliamentary Abstracts for the Session of 1820*, p. 744.

[2] Ferrara : *Malthus* in the *Annali di statistica*, Rome, 1890, pp. 223-24.

The defender of the philosophy of wealth received titles,
honours, and glory; the defender of the philosophy of poverty was at once forgotten. The
theory of human perfectibility, exaggerated and ridiculed,
still found supporters, but they did not appear till a late and
remote period. Notwithstanding his Utopias of a pacific anarchy,
after the successes of his youth, Godwin was compelled to lead a
poor life ; and the misunderstood prophet of the greatest reforms
died in poverty and neglect in 1836. His refutation of Malthus [1]
was read by only a few ; disordered, confused, and uncertain, it
was principally nothing else than a defence of social help. In his
old age he was obliged to find a livelihood in writing little books
for the use of schools, which he sold at a shop in London, and
which passed under the *nom de plume* of Baldwin. [2]

Success of Malthus and Failure of Godwin. Godwin's End.

Good fortune, therefore, befell the views of Malthus, as happens
to all those which imply fatality, necessity, and
unchangeableness. An entire class of society
found in them the defence of its interests, prejudices, and abuses,
which were on the point of being overthrown by Godwin's subversive theories. [3]

Success of the Fatalistic Views, and of those conducing to Inaction.

[1] W. Godwin : *An Inquiry on Population*, London, 1820.

[2] About the life, works, and teaching of Godwin, *cf.* L. Bouchez :
W. Godwin in the *Revue des deux mondes* for 1877, fasc. 21, and the article
W. Godwin, his Friends and Contemporaries, in the *Westminster Review* for
October, 1876.

[3] Malthus' teaching, besides flattering the passions of the powerful classes,
seemed and was a new and bold theory, destined to be seductive. It is
true that even Adam Smith had spoken of an utmost limit fixed by the
means of subsistence against the increase of the whole animal species (*An
Inquiry into the Nature and Causes of the Wealth of Nations*, i., 8); that Ortes
(*Riflessioni sulla popolazione delle nazioni per rapporto all'economia nazionale*, chaps. i., ii.) ; and Franklin (*Observations Concerning the Increase of
Mankind and the Peopling of Countries*, sec. 21) had shown that nature itself
provides with beneficent destruction against the evils resulting from the
generative power of all the animal species ; that Brueckner, Stewart, and
Townsend, had gone so far in their works (*cf.* Loria : *Carlo Darwin e l'economia politica* in the work entitled : *Carlo Darwin e il darwinismo*, published by Morselli, Milan, 1892, pp. 167, 168) as to show the results of ex-

Many years later, when the success of Malthus was at its greatest, Lord Brougham, speaking in the House of Commons, attributed the distress in England to the excess of population.[1]

Even Ricardo did not disdain to give the support of his uncontested authority to this movement.[2] Nay, even a great inquiry, instituted by the House of Parliament, declared the population to be over-abundant in many parts of England, Scotland, and Ireland, and attributed to this excess both the pestilence and the renewal of poverty.[3]

Naturally, all these facts afforded a solid basis to the invectives against the poor laws, and served to tranquillise the minds which the Godwin's philosophy of equality had profoundly disturbed.

And hence it was that not only in England but throughout Europe, even those men who, by their temperament, their religious tendencies, and their surroundings, were inclined to conclusions greatly differing from those of Malthus, accepted his teaching with ardour.

It was accepted even by Joseph de Maistre, the representative of the most aristocratic and conservative Catholicism, the bold and loyal defender of Legitimism and the Papacy.[4]

The Beneficence of Nature according to Turgot and Condorcet, and its contrary Disposition according to Malthus.

In the Malthusian theory lies the chief source of modern sociology ; the principle found in germ in Turgot and Condorcet, namely, that the human society, like other organisms, is guided by natural laws. But nature to them, as to Smith, appeared something beneficent, great and provident ; the principle is also found

cessive generation and of the destructive strife upon the perfectioning of the species. But the merit of having originally formulated an economic and biological theory concerning population exclusively belongs to Malthus.

[1] Speech pronounced in the House of Commons, and reported in the appendix to Godwin : *op. cit.*

[2] Ricardo : *Principles of Political Economy and Taxation*, chap. v.

[3] *Parliamentary Abstracts for the Session of 1826*, p. 185.

[4] De Maistre : *Du Pape*, book iii., chap. iii., sec. 3. It is only fair to De Maistre to allow that the moderate statement of his acceptance of Malthusianism on page 106 of the edition of 1821 would seem to show that he had not completely accepted the theory. (*Translator's note.*)

in Malthus, but *quantum mutatus ab illo !*   Nature is no longer
the provident Cybele of Condorcet and Smith, but a hurtful and
cruel influence, an avenging Nemesis who pitilessly kills anyone
who attacks her unchangeable laws.

The social causes which brought about the reaction of Malthus
were fundamentally the same as those which led
Thiers to write his famous book, *De la propriété.*

Causes of
Malthusianism.

Thiers rose up in defence of private property against the communism of Proudhon.   Malthus wrote his work on population
against the tendencies of Godwin, which wavered between Radicalism and Communism.   But in reality he neither wished or intended to defend anything else than private property against the
subversive Godwinian theories.   As an acute Belgian author says:
" What Malthus also wished to defend was property, the corner-
stone of the social edifice. [1]

What Malthus therefore wished to defend was what
Thiers afterwards defended, in his famous but
mediocre pamphlet, and the whole theory of Malthus is nothing
else but an endeavour to place the corner-stone of property
in the individualist edifice.

Malthus and Thiers.

According to Malthus men have a natural tendency to
multiply with rapidity ; unless this incessant process of multiplication found an obstacle either in the wise foresight of men, or the inflexible repression of nature, humanity
would double its numbers every twenty-five years.

The Views of Malthus.

On the other hand, the means of subsistence do not follow
any such progression, and while the population
increases in geometrical proportion, the means of subsistence
increase in arithmetical proportion.   In other words, while the
progression of the means of subsistence is 1, 2, 3, 4, 5, 6, 7, 8, 9,
on the contrary, that of the population is 1, 2, 4, 8, 16, 32, 64,
128, 256.   Population has, therefore, a tendency to surpass the
means of subsistence.

The Two Progressions.

In proof of the rapid increase of population according to geome-

---

[1] E. van der Smissen : *La Population,* Bruxelles, 1893, p. 157.

trical progression, Malthus had recourse to the   Grounds for the
example of the United States of America, where, in   Theory.
the twenty-five years preceding the publication of his work, the
population had more than doubled. And, on the other hand, in
proof of the arithmetical increase of the means of subsistence, he
turned to the example of the older country England, fallen a
victim to poverty and crisis in his day.

Products also can grow indefinitely, but the generative power
of men will so exceed them that in order that there may be a
sufficiency, it is necessary that a superior law should exist in
opposition to the progress of men, so that it may fix their limits
within proportion with the means of subsistence.

The checks put upon the increase of population may come
from either man or from nature ; they are hence   Preventative and R-.
preventative or repressive, and can be classed in   pressive Restraints.
three categories ; moral restraint, vice, and poverty. The repressive factors depend upon mankind, such, for instance, as war, and
are, in general, immoral ; or else they depend upon nature such
as epidemics and scarcity, and are then providential. But a far
more efficient one is moral restraint ; that is, to abstain from
matrimony by the preservation of chastity.[1]

By *moral restraint* Malthus simply meant that in order to
avoid the cruel restraints of nature, men should   Malthus and Moral
only marry when they were in a position to maintain   Restraint.
their children ; or, at least, that they should limit their number
according to their resources.

Not daring to recur to the immoral counsels and practices
propagated later among the elevated class of his followers after
his death, Malthus was too keen and truthful an observer to be
blinded to the fact that celibacy, chastity during a long period,

---

[1] Malthus : *An Essay on the Principle of Population*, book i., chap. ii.
Malthus being a Christian and minister of the Gospel, did not go so far as
to recommend those immoral practices to which the great body of his
followers had recourse later. The theory of *moral restraint* became, quite
contrary to what Malthus might himself have supposed, a real school of
moral degradation. Concerning these degradations of the moral sense, see
Ott's article in the *Journal des économistes* of August, 1888.

and abstaining from marriage were things of difficult, if not impossible attainment, and that they found powerful obstacles in the physiological order.

He asserted his belief that not many of his readers expected **Malthus' Doubts.** any general change of conduct in men in this respect.[1]

In the first edition of his book, which was more than anything else a political conservative *brochure* in opposition to Godwin's radical system, Malthus had roughly asserted that a man born into a world which is already full, has no right to demand maintenance.

There was no place for him at nature's banquet; nature **The Banquet of** itself bade him abandon it, and did not hesitate **Nature.** to carry her severe order into effect.

In succeeding editions of the work, the really moderate pastor of the county of Surrey, modified the rough assertion ; but the conception of the doctrine remained in its saddening simplicity.[2]

It was a sad and desperate theory, and set an irresistible and **Malthus' Distressing** fatal law against all the daring of human thought. **Conclusions.** You have thought, said Malthus, to increase your power by increasing the population, and you have only increased your poverty. And when you thought to remedy this last by help, the number of the poor has augmented instead of diminished !

Like Godwin's optimism, the fatalism of Malthus knew no **Extreme Consequences** limits. To Malthus it appeared a miserable ambi- **of the Fatalism of** **Malthus.** tion to wish to snatch the rod from the hand of nature, and the man who has begotten children without being able to maintain them, must submit to the terrible action of the laws of nature, which are the laws of God, and have con-

---

[1] Malthus : *An Essay,* book iv., chap. 3.

[2] The first edition of the work was published in 1798 : Malthus himself published the others in 1803, 1806, 1807, 1817 and in 1826, making essential modifications in all of them. At a later date he frankly said that it was possible he had exaggerated in one direction in order to avoid the opposite error ; and that he was always ready to modify his work according to the confirmed objections of competent critics.

demned himself and his family to suffering. Whoever generates beyond the limits of his economic capacity acts against the will of God.[1]

The teaching of Malthus was therefore not simply a biological and economic theory, but it was a political one also, and this assured its success. According to Malthus, society should abhor every kind of legal assistance ; those who have violated the law of nature must live a painful life, paying the penalty of its violation. Malthus even goes so far as to call for a law which would deny parish help to the children born in wedlock contracted within a year afterwards, and to illegitimate children born two years after the promulgation of the law itself. Without, in any way, excluding casual private charity, Malthus affirms that should even a provident man fall into distress he has no right to any social assistance, and that he should be considered as a man compelled to bear the pain of an unavoidable evil.

Malthusianism as a Political Theory.

The teaching of Malthus was therefore received with equal ardour by Tories and Whigs, both equally averse to Godwin's political system, as that which exonerated the powerful classes from all responsibility for the evil, and attributed all the causes of poverty to the improvidence and incontinence of the poor.

General Enthusiasm of the Richer Classes for the Teaching of Malthus.

The general enthusiasm for Malthus was so intense that no one dared to entirely controvert the new theory of population. Ingram says that the favour which the richer classes displayed towards the Malthusian theory is to be ascribed to the pleasure which they felt in being thus exonerated from blame, because Malthus asserted that the poor and not the rich were to be blamed for the evil state of the poor.[2]

Causes of the Enthusiasm.

[1] Malthus : *op. cit.*, book v., chap. ii.

[2] Ingram : *History of Political Economy*, p. 116. In the time of Malthus the science of statistics was only in its beginning ; but the Rector of Haileybury, in formulating his propositions, was not ashamed to ground his entire system upon a very weak and uncertain foundation of statistical proofs.

The mind was therefore no longer tormented by the doubt as to the rightfulness of wealth ; no one need reproach himself any more for egotism or indifference to the ills of society.

If there were poor the fault was certainly neither of the rich nor of the social order : the fault was, on the other hand, the blind improvidence and the unconscious egotism of the poor themselves.

A writer of weight in the *Quarterly Review,* combating the English laws on public assistance, said that they were not adapted to decrease the population : and he added that the problem of population had now become the personal interest of every individual.[1]

The pessimist conservative reaction therefore appeared not only rightful but useful.

As Godwin demonstrated, in affirming that population increases in geometrical proportion, Malthus was only mindful of the assertions of Petty, Styles, Franklin, Euler, and the example of the United States of America. Now, Styles was a mere rhetorician, Franklin asserted without proving, Price and Euler only calculated the numbers of an hypothetical progression.[2] The example of the United States neither had nor could have had any importance, since it was a new country, only a short time open to colonisation.

The Foundation of the Malthusian Hypothesis.

Even for the Malthusians, the two famous professions, as even his most fervent admirer, John Stuart Mill, has noted, are but a passing observation, indicating a real truth in a false way.

Errors about the Two Professions.

But granted even its erroneous formality, is the fundamental principle of the Malthusian theory true in substance notwithstanding ? Almost a century of observation and research has so profoundly modified the two principal propositions of the Malthusian theory as to render it irrecognisable, and to utterly destroy the fragile political

Inconsistency of the Malthusian Hypothesis.

---

[1] See the article in *l'Etat actuel et avenir de la Grande Bretagne,* given in the *Revue Britannique,* first series, 1829, vol. xxiii.

Godwin : *An Inquiry on Population,* London, 1820, book ii., chap. v.

edifice which the bold Rector of Haileybury had built up with so much care.

As we shall afterwards see, the fundamental error of the system of Malthus lies in his having confused *real* increase with *potential* increase.

Maupas has demonstrated that a single infusory becomes, within the space of one week, the progenitor of a family calculable only by millions. And Huxley has calculated that the progeny of a single parthenogenetic emittery, if it were not interfered with, would in a few months exceed the entire population of China.[1] Now, if we were to use the Malthusian argument, and to neglect the capital difference which lies between *real* and *potential* increase, we should have to conclude, that, in a few years, the whole world would be covered with emitteries.

But before applying any critical laws, having examined the atmosphere where the Malthusian theory originated and the reasons of a political and of a social kind which assured its success, it will be well to study the successive transformations which it underwent, and how it has continually modified itself in various ways under the influence of different causes, such as the birth-rate and productiveness of each country, and the dominant political views.

Historical and Ethnographical Causes of the various Theories of Population.

While in prolific Germany, Malthusianism still finds believers and apostles, in sterile France, where it was at first received and practised with enthusiasm, it is gradually losing ground. And whereas in England fifty years ago, it was the mainstay of social science, it has now lost the greater part of its supporters, owing to the check imposed upon the increasing birth-rate during recent years.

The Theories of Population and their Phases.

We shall also see later that the writers who follow the philosophy of poverty, have considered and still consider the problem of population in a very different way from those who follow the philosophy of wealth.

[1] Geddes et Thomson : *L'évolution du sexe*, vol. iii., of the *Bibliothèque évolutioniste*, Paris, 1892, chap. xx., sec. 1.

Indeed, I judge few other studies to be of greater utility than those which tend to show the close union between the theory and the phenomenon. It has been shown at length by clear-sighted authors, and most of all by Loria, that moral systems, political systems, and systems of law are scarcely ever anything else than the expression of the needs and tendencies of the dominant class.[1] For the demonstration of this fundamental truth it is sufficient to study the successive transformations of the Christian idea through the ages. Not simply does morality change with the change of needs, but after a wide study of economic theories logic itself appears to us excessively pliable and subject to change. And the impartial critic is surprised to find the same arguments employed at different epochs in the support of different theses; he is struck with astonishment at the spectacle of theories which were apparently fixed and unassailable, yet which none the less lend themselves to the upholding of causes repugnant to their primitive nature.

Relations between the Theory and the Phenomenon.

A very great number of economic theories, to anyone who wishes to penetrate them deeply, appear to be nothing else but a continual effort to legitimate interests or to defend abuses.

The Hidden Cause of the Economic Theories.

And it is still more wonderful that theories have always changed with the change of phenomena; far from overcoming them, they have been overcome by them; far from anticipating them, they have done nothing else but follow them.

From this point of view the history of the theories of population in Germany, England, and France is highly instructive.

More than any other European country, Germany was compelled, by economic and demographic reasons, to accept the theory of Malthus. Having still preserved, throughout the centuries, that traditional

History of the Theories of Population in Germany.

---

[1] *Cf.* Loria : *Teoria economica della costituzione politica*, Turin, 1886, and the *Annalisi della proprietà capitalista*, Turin, 1889, vol. i., and *Les bases économiques de la constitution sociale*, Paris—Turin, 1893.

fecundity which had profoundly impressed Tacitus,[1] it was menaced until the beginning of this century by a real excess of population (*Übervölkerung*), a menace which in recent times the result of a successful war, the modifications of the matrimonial laws, and, above all, the profound change effected in the economic legislation of the country have greatly strengthened.

Exhorting to fertility, Martin Luther had said to Germany, hindered in her expansion by long civil wars, religious discords, and the strife of classes : "God creates children, and He will Himself support them." But when a long period of peace, the end of the religious wars, and the legislative reforms had brought about a rapid and continual increase of births, economists and sociologists began to ask themselves with fear : Who will ever feed all these children of God? Then it was that a whole host of economists held the Malthusian hypotheses as indisputable truths, and that they became the undisputed foundation of the most varied and opposed economic systems.

Optimism of the old German demographers: pessimism of the new.

Roscher, accepting the teaching of Malthus almost in its integrity, has treated at length of all those who accepted it in Germany before his time.[2] Robert von Mohl, on his part, declaring himself to be also a believer in the Malthusian theory, has made a deep study of all those in Germany who, before or after Malthus, down to 1858, occupied themselves with the study of population, both from the demographic and economic point of view.[3] Whoever, therefore, is desirous of thoroughly understanding the causes of the success of Malthus among the German writers, may read what both these authors have written.

Roscher and R. von Mohl.

Nevertheless, it is only during the last twenty years that the question of population has strongly attracted the attention of the economists and writers of Ger-

Importance of the new studies.

[1] Machiavelli also attributes the invasions to the extreme fecundity of the Germanic races.

[2] W. Roscher : *Grundlagen*, etc., 18th edition, p. 644, etc.

[3] Robert von Mohl: *Die Geschichte und Literatur der Staatswissenschaften,* Erlangen, 1858, vol. iii., p. 465, etc.

many. Rümelin, Wagner, Oettingen, and Cohn, have, above all recent writers, the merit of having examined it with a depth and acumen than which it is difficult to expect greater.

Recently there were formed two schools among those who The optimist school and the pessimist school. studied the question of population; the one pessimist with Zacharias, Stille, Stein, Geffcken, Ferde, etc.;[1] the other optimist with Bötiker, Fabri, Mettenheimer, V. Otto, Grad, Mehring, etc.[2] Thus the optimistic and pessimistic views which, as we have seen, are found at the bottom of every economic system, naturally appear also in Germany with regard to the question of population.[3]

To Rümelin[4] the Malthusian system appears to contain such undeniable truths that, although not generally accepted, it may be considered as a definitive conquest of science (*ein festes Eigenthum*

[1] See Zacharias : *Die Bevölkerungsfragre in ihrer Beziehung zu den socialen Northständen der Gegenwart*, Jena, 1883. G. Stille : *Die Bevölkerungsfrage in ihrer Beziehung zu den socialen Verhältnissen vom medizinischen Standpunkt aus betrachet*, Berlin, 1879, and *Der Neomalthusianismus das Heilmittel des Pauperismus*, Berlin, 1880. H. Geffcken : *L'Allemagne et la question coloniale* in the *Revue de droit international et de législation comparée*, 1885, xvii., pp. 105-131. J. Stein : *Unbeschränkte Volksvermehrung oder sind viele kinder ein Segen?* Stuttgart, 1883. Ferde : *Der Malthusianismus in sittlicher Beziehung*, Berlin, 1885.

[2] See Bötiker : *Die Preussiche Aus-und Einwanderung seit*, 1844 ; Dusseldorf, 1879. F. Fabri : *Eindunkler Punkt*, Gotha, 1880. C. Mettenheimer : *Uber den sogennanten Neomalthusianismus in Betz's Memorabilien*, Heilbronn, 1883. Otto : *Künstliche Unfruchtbarkeit, eine volkswirthschafliche Studie*, Berlin, 1885. Ch. Grad : *La population de l'empire allemand*, in the *Revue des deux mondes*, for January 1st and 15th, 1885. F. Mehring : *Die socialreform und die Uebervolkerung* in the *Politische Wochenschrift*, 1882, No. 13.

[3] Vanni has minutely and learnedly examined whatever has been written about population during recent years. See his study entitled, *Questioni malthusiane in Germania ed il momento etico della teoria della Popolazione* in the *Saggi critici sulla teoria sociologica della popolazione*, Città di Castello, 1887, pp. 75-135.

[4] Cf. Rümelin : *Die Bevölkerungslehre* in Schoenberg's *Handbuch*, and the very important treatise, *Zur Uebervölkerungsfrage*, in the volume called *Reden und Aufsätze*, Tübingen, 1881, pp. 568-624 ; and a good book by Knapp : *Theorie des Bevölkerungswechsels*, Braunschweig, 1874.

der Wissenschaft). It is true that the famous progressions are un-founded, but it is equally true that the earth and its products cannot grow in parallel progression.

There are psychological motors which Malthus has neglected to consider, but which influence the birth-rate in a powerful way, and they are : the desire of a comfortable life, the fear of a numerous offspring, the need of maintaining oneself in the same condition, etc. Nevertheless, the disproportion between the increase of the means of subsistence and the increase of population always remains an unquestionable truth. Statistical inquiry makes it clear that the population of Europe has not in any way experienced the rapid increase which Malthus feared, and the increase which has occurred in this century cannot be considered except as a passing fact, and it is, moreover, true that civilisation causes men to increase much more in wealth than in number.

Summary of Rümelin's Teaching.

But in face of the fact that Germany is menaced by a real ex-cess of population, Rümelin does not hesitate to allow that obligatory assistance has contributed to intensify the evil. An inconsiderate legislation has abolished all the obstacles to matrimony without weighing the evils which will result from it in future. If everything were as simple as the empirics believe, if everything consisted in *laisser-faire*, we could never understand why for thousands of years, from the time of Plato and Aristotle down to our own day, so many thinkers have been perplexed in attempting to hinder the impoverishment of the people, which results from an excessive multiplication. We have allowed that every one is born into the world with a number of rights; society takes it upon itself to secure him the right of living, of bringing up, of education, work and food. Is it logical that this same society should not even know if it have the strength to take upon itself a new burden, and to guard against its becoming the plaything of caprice and chance? The higher classes impose upon themselves more or less grave restrictions, but the popular classes generate without any restriction. Hence, what occurs is most unsatisfactory, since the classes which

Rümelin's Practical Conclusions.

are superior by education and culture are those which multiply the least. In the face of all these facts *laisser-faire* would be a mistake; it is incredible that every man has the right to place as many children as he wishes at the charge of society.

But, being obliged to have recourse to preventive measures, Rümelin is only able to counsel the barren and useless remedy of suppressing obligatory assistance as being the chief encouragement to rapid generation.

Although writing in 1875, shortly after a fortunate war, and
Rümelin is, however, opposed to the Pessi- when Germany was still enjoying the illusions which
mist thesis. follow great victories, Rümelin could not but arrive at pessimistic conclusions. Therefore, although he speaks of the teaching of Malthus as of a fixed property and a definitive conquest of science, he endeavours to avoid the fatalist character in every way. "We may say," he even writes, " that there is no reason to be disquieted. Where a small brain cannot see any issue, the solution presents itself. It can be demonstrated that two hundred years ago the actual number of the population would have seemed impossible. We may reckon upon possibilities not to be now determined, on chemical discoveries, on industrial inventions, upon the consequences, not now possibly to be foreseen, of a gradual transformation of the universe. We can imagine that the air may become an aliment, that hydrogen will suffice for light and heat, that the forests will be planted with fruit-bearing trees, and that they will produce eatable fungi, that horticulture will replace agriculture, and that there will be two yearly harvests instead of one, etc."[1]

Adolphus Wagner, who also admits that the cardinal principle
A. Wagner. of Malthusianism is irrefutable, thinks, nevertheless, that although the present excess of population be not such as to render State-intervention and the violation of many individual liberties necessary, that the State has the right of intervention. The principle of population being the basis of every social constitution, no Socialist system can exist unless it limit the number of births.[2]

: Rümelin : *op. cit.*, vol. i., p. 323.
Wagner : *Grundlegung der politischen Oekonomie*, Dritte Auflage,

In every case, the ardent apostle of State-socialism immediately adds, it is necessary to accept with reserve all that part of Malthusianism which refers to practical applications.[1] A. Wagner and the application of Malthusian practices.

Nor does Cohn differ greatly from Wagner and Rümelin,[2] except by a greater and more marked tendency to pessimism. Cohn. He also believes that whatever may have been the political scope which led Malthus into exaggerations, the assertions of the English philanthropist are fundamentally correct. But the morality of men should tend to overcome physical impulses, and every state of civilised society must have recourse to moral restraint.

If the influence exerted by population upon the means of subsistence has occasionally been a cause of progress, nature most often acts recklessly, and Cohn and the Pessimistic Tendency. not only does no progress result from it, but even evil. In our present state of society, the majority of children do far otherwise than increase the productive power and the success of the labour of the parent, and, on the contrary, it generally happens that the lowest ranks of society are those where there are most characteristic anti-social qualities and apathy. Cohn's conclusions are, therefore, in reality, pessimistic; nor does he seem, at least, to believe with Rümelin and Wagner that State intervention and the suppression of obligatory assistance form a strong and certain remedy.

Even Brentano, who was so acute and so satisfactory, although

Leipzig, 1893. And, in fact, every communist system has always striven to limit the number of births. Even Plato, in his *Republic*, restricting the number of families to 5000, foresees the case where this number might be disturbed by the excess of births, and he establishes that the birth-rate should be promoted or lessened according to such cases. *Cf.* Duruy : *Histoire des Grecs*, tom. iii., p. 90. For the rest the Greeks had few scruples on this point. Aristotle openly advises abortion and the exposure of children who are born weak, and prefers this second means as more adapted to selection ; Duruy : *op. cit.*, vol. iii., p. 104.

[1] Wagner : *Allgemeine oder Theoretische Volkswirtschaftslehre*, I., Teil, 1876, S., 1321.

G. Cohn : *System der Nationalökonomie*, p. 231, etc.

he has shown with singular force that Malthusianism was in no way a fit remedy for the social question,[1] has not attacked the foundations of the Malthusian system.

After the studies of these vigorous theorists, a whole host of German economists and writers devoted themselves to the study of the problem of population, considering it chiefly from the German point of view. The followers of the optimistic **The followers of the optimistic tendency; their feeble successes.** tendency, whom we have above mentioned, have either endeavoured to deny the peril of over-population, or have found that it is unnecessary to study the relation between the number of the inhabitants and the district occupied, but that two decisive elements only must be taken into account : wages and the demand for labour. Others have asserted that population and subsistence are correlative terms ; the augmentation of the first necessarily implies augmentation of the second. Others still using the argument, which we shall afterwards examine, and which Rümelin has already thoroughly criticised, have maintained that when the surface of the nation shall have been totally cultivated and become insufficient for the needs of the people, there must necessarily result from the popular need a development of industrial products, which can be exchanged without any loss for the country products of nations upon an agricultural footing.

But the theories of pessimist demography have taken quite a **Prevalence of the pessimistic view.** different hold of men's minds, owing to the state of thought, the fatalist tendencies, and the profound demographic disproportion.

The increase of the German birth-rate has assumed the form and dimensions of real over-population (*Übervölkerung*) during the last half century, but still more so during the last twenty years. The population has grown rapidly, and not only has it grown, but **Reasons for the pessimism of the new German demographists.** owing to higher instruction and increased civilisation, it has acquired new needs, so that the standard of living has been greatly raised. Property being

---

[1] See Brentano : *Die gewerbliche Arbeiterfrage* in Schoenberg's *Dictionary*, 1st. edition, p. 905 and following, and the article on *la Question des huit heures en Angleterre* in the *Revue d'économie politique* for November, 1891.

much more concentrated than in France, and the number of hired labourers greater, the masses of the people have become improvident, and have abandoned themselves by reason of an inevitable and fatal necessity to an abundant and disordered multiplication. With the exception of Hanover, Schleswig-Holstein and Westphalia, all the rest of the Empire, especially Pomerania, Silesia, Western Prussia and Posnania are under the rule of the great landed proprietor. Hence the cultivation of the soil experiences very slightly indeed, the progress required by the heightened civilisation and the development of technical knowledge, and the extraordinary and dangerous exodus from the country to the city is continually on the increase.[1] Moreover, the primary schools, not being altogether an end in themselves, during late years there has been a large class of persons who are desirous of civil occupations.

Very many persons gifted with a certain culture hourly strive for the least remunerative positions; school-masters and evangelical ministers, at one time too few, now abound. Wherever a civil occupation is sought the answer is: everything is taken up, everything is overcrowded (*überfüllt*).[2] The extraordinary exodus from the country, the irresistible force of home and foreign competition, create difficulties for the state of commerce; while, on the other hand, an excessive body of middlemen, chiefly due to the competitive system, exists like a fatal parasite to the loss of consumers and producers. The strong current of emigration has not at all succeeded in removing or alleviating the causes of evil. On these accounts the struggle is always growing more severely intense, and forcing the minds of men to a continual tension, and originating on the one hand the historic phenomenon of a social democracy and the strife of classes, and on the other the

The disproportion in the social life of Germany.

The two pathological phenomena of German life.

---

[1] Concerning the bad distribution of wealth in Germany, see chiefly Stoeber: *Umfang und Vertheilung des Volks—Einkommen in Preussischen Staat*, 1872-1878; Leroy-Beaulieu: *Essai sur la répartition des richesses*, Paris, 1881, chap. xix.

[2] See Vanni; *op. cit.*, p. 84.

pathological phenomenon of the perpetual diffusion of nervous diseases.[1]

Historical and economic inquiry has already shown us that economic theories have been and are still the result of the conditions and actual needs of the epochs when they have arisen. The history of human thought has shown us no trace of any thinker,

Economic theories as resulting from the surroundings in which they are developed. economist or philosopher, who has entirely lifted himself above the conditions and needs of his surroundings. The most abstract theories are, therefore, almost always the result of determining historical circumstances.

So it has happened in Germany with regard to the theory **The übervölkerung.** of population. The *übervölkerung* or excess of population, caused by the economic circumstances and the industrial struggle, has greatly impressed the students of demography, and has caused a vast prevalence of the pessimistic over the optimistic influence.

The proposals of the English Neomalthusians, tending to check the birth-rate, have hence necessarily found a large acceptance notwithstanding their distasteful character, which would have caused their repudiation by a nation imbued with ideality and the Christian spirit.

Already in 1866, a German magistrate, Kirchmann, took up its defence,[2] and he found many disposed to approve and follow his advice.

Although the more illustrious economists, and the more distinguished statisticians, such as Wagner[3] and **The German economists and demographists and the practical application of the Malthusian theory.** *Oettingen*,[4] have demonstrated the fallacy and inefficiency of the efforts of the Neomalthusians, nevertheless, some economists of weight, such as Rümelin, have spoken of them with sympathy,[5] and scientists of great name, such

On the diffusion of nervous diseases in Germany as a more or less direct consequence of the economic struggle, see W. Erb : *Ueber die nevere Entwickelung der Nervenpathologie*, Leipzig, 1880, p. 16, etc.

[2] Kirchmann : *Ueber den Communismus in der Natur*, Berlin, 1866.

Wagner : *Volksvermehrung und Auswanderung*, I.

[4] Oettingen : *Die Moralstatistik*, sec. 24-26.

[5] Rümelin : *Zur Uebervolkerungsfrager* in *Reden und Aufsätze*, pp. 613-617.

as Mensinga, have even pretended that doctors should regulate the generative functions, and supply a timely remedy to the evils of excessive child-bearing.[1] But against all the efforts of the Neomalthusian school, notwithstanding the dangerous excess of births, there has been formed and is still forming a strong current of opposition ; doctors and demographists daily protest against a school, the principles of which if carried into effect would change matrimony into a monogamic prostilation, and would gradually lead to the weakening of social relations and to the degradation of the moral sentiments.[2]

It is easily conceived that in a country like Germany, menaced with a real crisis of over-population, the socialist writers should have felt, and should still feel, the influence of the Malthusian theory.[3] German socialism and the theory of popula-tion.

In any case, only the theories which fundamentally differ from Malthusianism have ever been exposed and defended by socialist writers.

Rodbertus, without denying the disproportion between the increase of the population and of the means of subsistence, judges, however, that when the working-man shall have the entire fruit of his work, he will acquire foresight, which is at present a virtue attainable only by the upper classes.[4] Rodbertus.

Marlo, who also acknowledges that Malthus insisted excessively upon the disproportion between the population and Marlo.

[1] C. Hasse (Mensinga's *nom de plume*) : *Ueber facultative Sterilitat beleuchtet vom prophylachtschen und hygienischen Standpunkte*, 4th edition, Berlin, 1885.

[2] About all those who have attacked the errors of Neomalthusianism in Germany, see Vanni : *op. cit.*, pp. 114-116. Nevertheless, it is well to observe that even in 1859, an acute statistician had declared that "the number of births is in an inverse ratio, not to the density of population, but to the difficulty of procuring the food necessary for a family." Wappaues : *Allgemeine Bevölkerughstatislik*, Leipzig, 1859-1861, I., 173.

[3] Soetber has published an accurate study upon the theories of German Socialists in the question of population. *Die Stellung der Sozialisten zur Malthus' schen Bevolkerungslehre*, Göttingen, 1886.

[4] K. Rodbertus Jagetzow : *Zur Beleuchtungder socialen Frage*, 1875. About the views of Rodbertus consult H. Soetber, *op. cit.*, pp. 65-75.

the means of subsistence, does not at all deny that such a disposition exists. But, instead of speaking of moral restraints, his opinion is that it would be much better to hinder marriages by a wise legislation, except under given conditions. Every death which is the result of the repressive obstacles presented by overpopulation is a real assassination, committed by those liberal legislators, who have been unable to hinder imprudent marriages.[1]

K. Marx has exposed far more profound and original views ; and The teaching of Marx. although they can only be accepted in part, and although they often conflict with the results of statistical research, nevertheless, for their original and truthful character, they stand apart from what his predecessors in and out of Germany have maintained. According to Marx, "an abstract and unchangeable Summary of his teaching. law of population exists only for plants and animals, and for these only in so much as they are independent of human influences."[2]   On the other hand, every period of human history has a special law of population, which is applicable to it only and not to any other. On this account our capitalistic society has a special law for its relative excess of population. Although there is not a greater working population than that required by the wealth which is being accumulated, there is, however, a very bad distribution of work, which weighs heavily upon the one class while keeping the other unoccupied. In this way one part of the population performs the work which all should do, and Capitalism avails itself of the industrial reserve, that is of the great body of unemployed, to compel those who work to accept a slender salary. The variations in the rate of wages are determined by the proportions between the men who labour and those who form the so-called industrial reserve, and

[1] K. Marlo : *Untersuchungen über die Organisation der Arbeit, oder system der Weltökonomie*, Tübingen, 1885, 2nd edition.

[2] Marx : *Das Kapital*, Hamburg, 1873, 2nd edit., chap. xxv., sec. 3. Even Soether, notwithstanding his small sympathy for Socialism, confesses that Marx has brought a new and original contribution to the theory of population; *op. cit.*, p. 46,

not by the total number of the population. The The capitalist regime and the excess of population. relative excess of the population, which divides capitalist society, assumes three forms ; the fluctuating, the latent, and the stagnant.

The fluctuating form is determined by the attraction and repulsion of working men exercised by modern The three forms of relative excess of population. industry. The latent form, on the contrary, is caused by the fact that capital, after having made use of the working men up to a certain age, discharges them, and has recourse to younger strength ; hence it increases the female population to the detriment of the male population, and marriages are necessarily premature. The last form, that of a stagnant population, is also to be found in the active industrial army, but only in those working men who are always engaged in such irregular occupations, that they may rightly be considered as disposable forces. Accustomed to poverty, these come to be recruited among the supernumeraries of the larger industry and of agriculture.

Now, it is quite easy to perceive at a glance all the weak points of the teaching of Marx,[1] which, while Deficiencies in the teaching of Marx. containing a great deal of truth, is founded upon the error that there is no tendency in the human species to multiply itself beyond the intrinsic and natural limitation of the means necessary to it. If, therefore, K. Marx have the great merit of having been, perhaps, the first to recognise the existence of a systematically excessive population, he is wrong, however, in denying altogether, and at all costs, the existence of an automatic excess. Yet, it is not presumable that the capitalist class should *always* induce the development of a systematic over-population in order to obtain a more rapid expansion of production upon every demand for products ; the loss which capital experiences when one part of the population becomes excessive, is much graver than the advantage which Marx presumes to be derived from it. None the less, Marx, despite the deficiencies in his teaching, has

---

[1] Lange has criticised it very cleverly : *Die árbeiterfrage, ihre Bedeutung für Gegenwart und Zukunft*, p. 212, etc. ; and Loria : *Analisi della proprietà capitalista*, vol. i., pp. 638-640.

the great merit of having demonstrated with abundance of facts and proofs, that the principle of population must be considered, not only under the biological and demographical aspect, but also, and chiefly, with relation to the prevailing economic system.

E. F. Schäffle, although differing greatly from the precipitate **Schäffle and his views on population.** conclusions of democratic Socialism, has exposed a theory of population, which, especially in its practical and positive part, savours not a little of the influence of Marlo and Rodbertus. For Schäffle the law of population is a special part of the law of selection, which rules the entire organic world; the excess of population, in originating the social strife, was the first and palmary cause of progress. Bearing in mind the features which differentiate human from natural selection, the law of population forms part of the current of evolution, and has an absolute, not a relative value. It is an historical law, which **The law of population as an historic law.** has undergone, and will still undergo, other essential modifications.[1] Recognising withal the present disproportion between the population and the means of subsistence, Schäffle in his practical deductions, adheres almost entirely to Marlo, that is, he desires the restriction of the matrimonial right, stipulating, however, in the first place, a vast **Practical conclusions of Schäffle.** network of social reforms. Since the right to existence excludes that of unlimited generation, the law must intervene, limiting marriages and placing an obligation upon all husbands, whether proprietors or otherwise, to assure a dowry to the wives in case of widowhood, and securing on the part of both parents a patrimonial fund for the children, which last fund must be determined according to statistical returns about the average of births.[2]

This theory of Schäffle, apparently socialistic, but substantially **Consequences of Schäffle's theory.** derived from the old Germanic legislation, were it possible of application, would make matrimony the

---

[1] Schäffle : *Bau und Leben des socialen Körpers,* vii., 5.

[2] Schäffle : *Bau und Leben,* etc., ii., 2 ; viii., xii., 7 ; *Das gesellschaftliche System der menschlichen Wirthschaft,* sec. 332, 354 ; *Kapitalismus und Socialismus,* p. 680, etc.

privilege of a few fortunate people, and would give an irresistible impulse to improvidence and illegitimate births, and would be a direct cause of a fresh degeneration of the moral sentiments.

Nevertheless, Schäffle, agreeing in this with economic radicalism, firmly believes that nothing can be done to limit the birth-rate unless " a good legal organisation of the production of goods and of the division of social revenues be found and carried out." When the births among the lower classes shall have been limited, the diminution of offers of labours " will create so favourable a condition for the working men that the present organisation of social economy would no longer have any probability of existence. *But this limitation and the organisation of social economy are indissolubly bound up together.*[1]

In recent times two Socialist writers, in Germany and Austria, have treated the problem of population with considerable acumen, the Austrian Kautsky and the German Max Schippel, the intelligent director of the *Arbeiterbibliotek* of Berlin; Hertzka has hardly touched the question, and Bebel has written about it in a popular way with excessive levity.

Kautsky has added nothing new to what others have so often said before him. His book on the influence of the increase of population upon the advance of society[2] is, notwithstanding some correct observations, a book of slight scientific value.

Kautsky and the relations between Socialism and Malthusianism: Attempted concord.

Being both a Socialist and Malthusian, Kautsky vainly endeavours to demonstrate that there is not, nor can be, any difference between Malthusianism and Socialism. Convinced of a thesis contrary to that of the majority of Socialist writers, he does not at all believe that a better distribution of wealth could remedy the evils of over-population. And sometimes denying and at other times asserting the present excess of population over the means of subsistence, and the influence of the economic form over the birth-rate, he arrives at conclusions which are without either theoretic or practical interest.

[1] Schäffle : *op. cit.*
[2] K. Kautsky: *Der Einfluss der Volksvermehrung auf den Fortschritt der Gesellschaft*, Wien, 1880, p. 198.

Moreover, for some time, in all that he has written later than the publication of his book, he has changed his first opinions and entered almost entirely into the great current of Marx's teaching.

Max Schippel, a far more effective and safe writer, accepting

Max Schippel. largely the criticism of Rodbertus, boldly maintains that the evils which afflict society are nothing but the consequence of its condition. If a relative excess of population over the means of subsistence exist, we must look not to the exterior part of the phenomenon, but to the intrinsic causes which have

Examination of Schippel's teaching. produced the excess.[1] The capitalistic state of society, with all its defects and its very evil system of landed property, produces that improvidence of the popular classes, which is then the direct cause of the excessive increase of population. Salutary State interference, good legislation, can repair the evil by remedying its cause. Not even in Germany, where the phenomenon of population seems to excite so much anxiety, does a real and essential over-population exist, and even if it exists, we are compelled to allow that it results not from the decrease of productivity, but from its increase caused by technical development, which has lessened the price of goods, and deprived not a few working men of their situations, inevitably forcing them to habits of improvidence. When the masses shall have acquired greater power of acquisition, and the collective power be substituted for the salaried, it will cause the labouring men to partake more fully of the general revenues of the nation ; when crises and pauperism shall have been removed by better economic regulations, then also the phenomenon of over-population will disappear with the disappearance of the causes which produced it.

Doctor Hertzka, a very precise and subtle writer, utterly dis-

Doctor Hertzka and the optimist thesis. credits the present gravity of the problem of population, and frankly inclines to the optimistic thesis. "At present," he writes, "and for centuries, we must allow that the facility for satisfying wants, the raising of the general

---

[1] Max Schippel : *Das moderne Elend und die moderne Uebervölkerung*, Leipzig, 1883.

well-being, will increase with greater rapidity as the population becomes denser. Hence it would be a neglect of the immediate
duties of humanity to take precautions at present to hinder the
development of population, which will continue to   Hertzka and the pro-
be useful, and therefore necessary, during many   blem of population as
generations. Each epoch has its special duties, to   a problem of the future.
the fulfilling of which it should limit itself. Doubtless it is wise
and necessary to concern ourselves with the future ; but this is
true with the double condition of not neglecting the needs of the
present and the immediate future, and of being able to take
measures with that more distant future, which may be supposed
to be known in all the phases of its development. Now this is
not the case with what is called the policy of population (*Be-
völkerungs-politik*). We of to-day cannot hinder the future
population without acting against the interests of the immediate
future, and, on the other hand, it is absolutely useless to busy
ourselves with this matter instead of leaving it to future generations, who will understand what is necessary for them better than
the present generation, and will find the way of solving the problems which refer to them without our assistance. Nay, it is
quite certain that after several centuries our descendants will find
the policy with regard to population ˙which will be required by
their needs and by their situation only the more easily because
we have occupied ourselves less in solving it. And they will find
this solution all the more easily, if they shall have acquired a
more elevated intellectual culture, and this culture shall be the
more advanced if care be taken to remove whatever could impede
it. Each generation fulfils its duties towards the future the more
effectually in proportion as they extend the treasure of culture received from their predecessors." [1]

Hertzka denies, therefore, that political economy should occupy
itself with the phenomenon of population in the actual condition
of affairs.

In a scientific treatise it would not be worth while examining

[1] Th. Hertzka : *Die Gesetze der sozialen Entwickelung*, vol. ii., chap. i.,
p. 188.

Bebel and the Utopian tendency. the work and deductions of Bebel, who, writing for the masses, always arrives at most hasty and erroneous conclusions. Nevertheless, it is well to note his aversion to Malthus, whom he treats almost as violently as Marx does. But his criticism is poor, and his conclusions quite unwarranted. With the same Utopian tendency, which induces him to describe the society of the future in the most detailed way, he concludes, " In the socialistic settlement, according to which only it can be truly free and upon its natural foundation, humanity will go forward consciously in its development according to the laws of nature. Hitherto, humanity has always acted in ignorance of its proper laws, and hence unconsciously with regard to production, distribution and population ; in the society which is to be it will go forward with full consciousness of these laws and rules." [1]   This is ungrounded and absurd optimism.

Therefore, excepting some Socialist writers, naturally inclined **The aberrations of socialistic optimism.** to optimism, in view of the continual and dangerous increase of births, the majority of the German economists not only have not opposed the Malthusian teaching, but have not even thought of doing so. If some bold spirit has dared to connect the phenomenon of population with the economic surroundings, if someone has perceived that in our state of society the economic factor is much more influential than the biological one, he has nevertheless necessarily conformed to his surroundings, and accepted theories which had taken deep root. And as a **The tendency to economic pessimism in Germany.** remedy to the *Uebervölkerung* not only have they gone so far as to counsel the Malthusian moral restraint, that is to say abstention ; but even abortion has been legitimated ; nay even profound thinkers have wished that matrimony should become a real privilege of the richer classes; and they have had recourse to more immoral and degrading advice. Not long since Weinhold, a counsellor of the King of Saxony, seriously proposed the annual castration of a certain number of children of the popular classes. [2]

[1] Bebel : *Die Frau*, chap. xiii.
[2] See the *Revue socialiste* for February, 1892, p. 153.

We shall now see that the teaching of Malthus has had the same phases, and has been influenced by the same causes in England. Malthus was writing while a newer, a more powerful and stronger one was arising upon the ruins of the old industrial system, but the transition from one industrial form to another had rendered the phenomenon of over-population more threatening, and had weakened the confidence in the effects of social assistance. **The theory of population in England.** But the phenomenon of a disordered birth-rate, natural to a period of transition, was just ending when the fortunate parson of Haileybury died in 1834. Then began in England a long period during which the proportion of births was continually on the increase. The English birth-rate, which, in 1837, was 34 to a 1000, ascended with a rapid progress until it reached 35·5 in 1878. England and Wales, which, in 1821, had only 12,000,236 inhabitants, and in 1831 only 14,876,797, had not less than 27,499,000 in 1885, that is an increase of 111 for every 100. **Bases of the English economic theories.**

Had it not been for a law, which we shall study in the following book, and which Malthus did not at all foresee, after such a long period during which the birth-rate was so high, an exactly contrary phenomenon occurred, one which the rough and honest assertions of the Malthusians would be unable to explain.

While the means of subsistence had increased equally with and beyond the number of the population, the birth-rate suddenly grew stationary and then decreased. **Limitation of the birth-rate in Great Britain after 1878.** In England and Wales during 1878, the births were in a proportion of 36·5 for every 1000 inhabitants, in 1880 they were but 34·2, in 1884 they were 33·3, and, five years later, in 1889 they were as few as 30·5, a lower number than any hitherto reached in the present century.

The same phenomenon occurred in Scotland and in Ireland: the proportion of births in Scotland in 1878 was 34·3, and in 1888, 30·5, while in Ireland in the meantime it descended from 32·1 to 22·9.[1]

[1] *Cf.* Mille: *Le néomalthusianisme en Angleterre* in the *Revue des deux mondes* for December 15th, 1891.

Moreover, from 1878 downwards, that is to say, from the time of
the decline of the birth-rate in Great Britain until
now, the conditions of the United Kingdom have
been as prosperous as ever before.   The continual growth of commerce, the absence of sanguinary wars, the great increase in production, the development of institutions of public beneficence, were all
reasons which, according to Malthus, should raise the birth-rate,
which on the contrary, without any apparent cause, has diminished,
arousing all at once the fears of demographers and of statisticians,
who had hitherto believed in the danger of over-population,
and were suddenly compelled to study the menacing symptoms of
an opposite phenomenon.

The English writers on the problem of population can be,
therefore, classified in two great categories : those
who wrote between the work of Malthus and 1878,
and those who have written since.   The first, excepting only a
few bold writers who have not hesitated to connect the phenomenon of over-population with the great inequality of wealth, are
imbued with the spirit of Malthusianism, and, if they question the
two famous progressions, never dare to deny the fundamental
truth of the Malthusian teaching.   The others, finding themselves
face to face with a difficulty, which the great deficiencies of
Malthusianism are unable even to explain, gradually drift away
from the teachings and principles of the Rector of Haileybury.

Unless we reckon some isolated thinkers, such as Gray,[1] and
all the attacks made for a religious purpose, the
Malthusian theory met with no kind of opposition
in England from the beginning and for a long time.   Afterwards
Russel, Brougham, and Mackintosh accepted it blindly.   Even
theoricians of some worth, such as John Bird Summer, Francis
Place,[2] and several others, were both unable and unwilling even to
doubt about it, and laid it down as an irreputable canon.

[1] Gray's ideas were even better developed by G. Purves.   *The Principle
of Population and Production*, London, 1818.

[2] J. Bird Summer : *A Treatise on the Records of the Creator*, London,
1816; F. Place : *Illustration and Proofs of the Principle of Population*,
London, 1822.

Even the great Ricardo was content to simply observe that although, under the more favourable conditions it be Ricardo and Malthus; addition to the pessimistic thesis. probable that the power of generation will be exceeded by the power of production, this cannot be for long, the soil liable to cultivation being limited, and, moreover, of unequal fertility, every new part of capital invested will cause the relative quantity of the product to diminish, while the generative power will continue in full vigour.[1] To the Malthusian teaching, already imbued with pessimism, Ricardo therefore added a new dose of pessimism.

Mill does not in the least contest the law of Malthus, indeed all opposition to it seems to him to be affected with Mill, MacCulloch. Senior, and Cairnes followers of Malthus. sentimentality.[2] To Mill, the Malthusian precept seemed a real panacea, a prompt and certain remedy. Though ordinarily so moderate, so enamoured of good, and so sincerely democratic, he even goes so far as to say that no advance of public morality can be looked for until numerous families come to be regarded with the same contempt as drunkenness, and other corporal excesses. And although an adherent of the principles of the Manchester school, and adverse to Government interference, Mill does not hesitate to say that the moral obligation, not to have too many children, could, if the case called for it, be later changed into a legal obligation.[3] MacCulloch and Senior do not in the least modify anything that Malthus has stated.[4] Only MacCulloch, more sceptical and less empiric that Senior, timidly observes that if Malthus has established a partial truth he has not established an entire truth.[5] Cairnes more boldly declares that

---

[1] Ricardo: *Principles of Political Economy and Taxation* (edited by E. C. K. Gonner), London, 1891, pp. 47-49, 75, 400-403.

[2] J. S. Mill: *Principles of Political Economy,* book i., chap. x., sec. 2, and book ii., chap. xiii., sec. 2.

[3] Mill: *op. cit.,* book ii., chap. xiii. See also chapters xi. and xii.

[4] MacCulloch: *Principles of Political Economy,* i., 8 ; Senior: *Principles,* etc., propos. iii.

[5] MacCulloch: *Literature of Political Economy,* London, 1845 ; article, *Malthus.*

the principle of Malthusianism has revolutionised the study of social and industrial problems.[1]

Various intelligent theorists vainly attempted to oppose this The first opposition. strong current of Malthusianism. As early as 1830, one of them, Sadler, wished to make as the basis of the Sadler's theory. law of population the principle that the fecundity of a people is in direct ratio with the fertility of the earth. Although involved with many errors, Sadler's theory contained, as we shall afterwards see, a true and safe foundation. According to his view, the greater the density of a people with regard to the space inhabited, the less is its fecundity. But space has relation not only with extension but also with quality. Hence the greater the fertility of the soil, the greater the fecundity of the population, and *vice versa.*[2]

Thornton, foreseeing a principle destined to find favour at a Thornton and the fe- later day, stated it as his view, and justly, that if cundity of the rich. the world were only inhabited by proprietors, it would probably soon become unpopulated, through dearth of inhabitants.[3]

But these isolated voices, though they found some kind of echo, exercised scarcely any real influence upon the direction of the English economic science, which continued to form itself according to the errors and assumptions of the Malthusian theory.

But while the economic science, held within the narrow limits The biological views of a false teaching, abandoned objective research, about population in England. the studies of biologists and naturalists gave a new direction to the inquiries about population. Doubleday at first, then Darwin and Spencer, and lastly P. Geddes, were, in fact, displaying new horizons.

---

[1] Cairnes : *The Character and Logical Economy*, 2nd edit., London, 1875, p. 157.

[2] Sadler : *The Law of Population*, London, 1830, vol. ii., pp. 352, 353, and G. Ensor : *An Inquiry Concerning the Population of Nations*, London, 1818.

[3] Thornton : *Over-population and its Remedy*, London, 1846.

Doubleday, who believed that he had discovered the true law of population, did not discover a true law at all,   Doubleday.
nor, indeed, anything lasting; but he had the incontestable merit of having insisted upon the fact that the problem of population must be studied according to the needs of given states of society, and according to the greater or less degree of wealth distributed.

Whatever the reproductive capacity of men may be in Double-day's view, it finds a corrective in the abundance   Exposition of Double-
of nourishment.   In the actual state of society the   day's theory.
insufficient nourishment of the inferior classes produces an un-plethoric state, which is singularly favourable to the increase of a disordered generative capacity; while on the other hand plentiful food would make plethoric men more frequent, and in this state they are generally disinclined to rapid multiplication.[1] If the argument of Malthus consists precisely in the view that the means of subsistence are inadequate to the population, the contrary principle must be false without the necessity of examining it, since in order to check the evils deplored, it starts upon a false supposition, and would have that the food of all should not only be sufficient, but abundant, and hence declares, without any true foundation, that the production of the articles of food is sufficient to make all men plethoric.[2]

Darwin has expressly acknowledged that he perceived the principle of the struggle for life while casually   Darwin.
reading Malthus' book; but what Malthus judged a natural law of human society, Darwin made a general biological principle.

The vital competition between all the organic beings spread over the surface of the globe, is a fatal conse-   The law of vital com-
quence of their multiplication in geometrical ratio.   petition as a conse-
                                     quence of the Malthu-
This is the Malthusian law applied to the entire   sian hypothesis.
animal and vegetable kingdom. As more individuals come into existence than are able to maintain themselves in it, and as in

---

[1] Doubleday: *The True Law of Population shown to be connected with the Food of the People,* London, 1847.

[2] See Spencer's acute criticism of Doubleday: *Principles of Biology,* sec. 366; and Vanni: *op. cit.,* pp. 13, 14.

consequence, the struggle for the means of subsistence often occurs among them, if any being differ from the rest, in a way useful to itself, he will probably be chosen before the rest. Hence, it follows from the powerful laws of heredity, that every chosen variety will have a tendency to propagate its newly modified form. [1]

Thus Malthus' law, which, according to its originator, was one The struggle for life applicable to human society, became a universal
a universal law. law in the eyes of Darwin. And when later researches strengthened the weak basis of Malthusianism, the teaching of Darwin continued to repose upon a strong basis of biological researches, since the fundamental induction of Malthus extended to the whole of nature as an essential condition of the struggle for existence, remains an immovable truth. Regarding the human species, Darwin also believes that positive obstacles to population (sickness, hunger, war, infanticide) and prudent restraints (moral or restrictive of births), are also to be considered as special forms of natural or artificial selection. [2]

The Darwinian theory does not differ substantially from that Difference between of Malthus, from which it is derived. But what a
Malthus and Darwin. difference between the spirit of each ! To Malthus the pessimist, the disproportion between the population and the means of subsistence appears almost like a fateful curse, like a condemnation issued by destiny itself, as an evil and terrible fact. To Darwin, on the other hand, the disproportion seems to be the mainspring of progress, a beneficent factor of moral evolution.

Perhaps the formulas of Malthusianism are still invincible in Darwin partly avoids the eyes of the British naturalist ; but, after the
the extreme pessimism
of Malthus. historic hour which had originated the Malthusian pessimism, the same disproportion no longer seems threatening and terrible to Darwin's view.

But Herbert Spencer only has the merit of being the first to Spencer and the formulate a broad sociological theory of population,
sociological theory. a theory which, though we do not accept it with-

---

[1] Darwin : *Origin of Species.*
[2] *Ibid.*

out completion and modification, is still, in the history of theories on population, a marvellous monument of the acumen and perspicacity of the great English sociologist.

Doubleday's theory was, if we may so speak, a kindly and pleasing mistake. Charles Darwin's theory. of population was also defective and wanting in parts, and made the human struggle part of the general struggle of nature. Only with Spencer did the system of optimist individualism come to contain a theory of population, the consequences of which harmonise thoroughly with the premises.[1]

Every aggregate of living beings, says Spencer, forming an aggregate whose internal actions are adapted to counterbalance its external actions, it follows that **Examination of Spencer's theory.** the preservation of his movable equilibrium depends upon its development and the proper number of these actions ; the moveable equilibrium may be ruined when one of these actions is too great or too small, and through deficiency or need of some organic or inorganic cause in its surroundings. Every individual can adapt himself to these changeable influences in two ways : either directly or by producing new individuals, who will take the place of those whom the equilibrium has destroyed. Therefor, there exist forces preservative and destructive of the race. It being impossible that these two kinds of force should counterbalance each other, it is necessary that the equilibrium should re-establish itself in an orderly way.

There being two preservative forces of every animal group, namely, the inclination of every individual to self-preservation and to the production of other **Contrast between individuation and generation.** individuals, these faculties must vary in an inverse ratio ; the former must diminish when the second augments.

Generation constitutes a process of disintegration, and consequently a process the reverse of that of integration. Hence if we

[1] Concerning Spencer's views on population, see *A Theory of Population deduced from the General Law of Animal Fertility* in the *Westminster Review* for April, 1852 ; *First Principles*, sec. 82-88, 170-176; *Principles of Biology*, sec. 315-377 ; *Principles of Sociology*, sec. 272-277 ; *Study of Sociology*, chap. xiv.

apply the name of individuation to all the processes which complete and sustain the life of the individual, and the name of
generation to those which aid the formation and development of
new individuals, we see that individuation and generation are
necessarily antagonistic.

Observing the phenomena of unsexual generation, we discern
the presence of three evident truths : the larger organisms never reproduce themselves in the unsexual way, the smaller organisms reproduce themselves with the
greatest rapidity by this method, and between these two extremes
unsexual reproduction decreases while the size increases. Following the history of every plant and of every animal, we perceive
this physiological truth ; that while the general growth of the
individual proceeds rapidly, the reproductive organs remain im-
perfectly developed and inactive, while, on the contrary, the principle of reproduction indicates a decrease in the intensity of
growth, and becomes a cause of cessation.

The fundamental pro-positions of Spencer's theory.

Great fecundity is always attended by great mortality. Each
superior degree of organic evolution is accompanied by an inferior degree of fecundity. The
greater the genesis the less is the individuation and *vice versâ.*
The greater the differentiation of structure and functions, the
greater and more complex the organisation, the less is the power
of multiplication.

Individuation con-trary to genesis,

The individuals of each species, whose habits correspond the
most with the exigencies of their surroundings, are those which
survive the most easily. The survival of the fittest always brings
it about that superior species should continually replace the inferior species. And thus, if the most developed organism be,
absolutely speaking, the least fertile, it is, on the other hand,
relatively the most generative.

The same causes of increase and decrease of genesis, which
affect the animal species, also affect the human
species, notwithstanding that the inequality of
conditions among men, especially those dependent upon race, be
such as to make every comparison very difficult.

The biological theory also applicable to the human species.

Anyhow, it may be admitted that even with men abundant food is accompanied with an abundant generation and *vice versâ*. There is also reason to believe that the reproductive activity is weakened in proportion to the intensity of every muscular or nervous work. The fact that the most civilised societies are generally more numerous than the uncivilised races, although the genesis should be less among the former, does not overthrow the thesis at all, since the conditions of development are quite unequal, and it is to this inequality of conditions that this apparent anomaly is due.

In other words, to use a simple graphic demonstration, Spencer's theory may be summarised thus : if the

Graphic proof of
Spencer's theory.

A   C   B

line A B represent the aggregate of matter, that is, the sum of the organs and strength of a given individual, while A C shows the quantity devoted to individuation, and C B that devoted to generation, the inverse difference of A C and C B is evident. A total increase of energy (the line A B), as occurs in the strongest members of a species, who have also the largest power of reproduction, does not in any way modify the proportions we have spoken of. But if, on the other hand, the species be in course of evolution, the progress of individuation implies a certain economy, part of which may tend to arrest the decrease of the generation.

It being admitted, therefore, that fecundity of mankind is regulated by the very law of general multiplication, every new progress should be a progress towards The evolution of mankind should arrest and limit the birth-rates. the continual adaptation of the internal relations to the external relations. Now, looking at the future, we find that a wider adaptation of internal conditions to the external conditions, a greater harmony of actions, will produce a superior development of the intelligence and the sentiments.

In the past the abundance of population was the chief stimulus of progress, since, producing competition, it caused men to perfect themselves and make themselves Abundant population, the past cause of progress, will be limited by progress. more apt for the conflict. But, when the globe

will be entirely inhabited, when it will be cultivated in its inhabited facts to the highest degree, when intelligence and the
feelings suited to social life will be developed, then the abundance of population, having served its purpose, will gradually
cease. Towards this harmonious state of society, in which everyone will be adapted to the best of his proper function, many
social and organic changes are tending continually and with
mutual influences. This, the highest result of a perfectly
balanced population, will be only reached through a long process
of evolution, namely, that same universal progress which is displayed in the simplest inorganic action.

This is a summary of the general lines of Spencer's theory, the
defective parts of which we will examine in the following chapter,
with the assistance of sociological and statistical research : a
Essential truth of theory, partly erroneous, but containing such
Spencer's theory. essential truths as to make a complete theory of
population possible hereafter, which, after the exaggerated assertions of Malthus, accepted almost without discussion by
economic theorists, it was difficult if not impossible to formulate.

Spencer's theory has, however, found very slight favour with
economists; but on the other hand, sociologists and biologists have
not failed to give it the place due to it.[1]

The English economists, as we have seen, instead of rising
Antimalthusian reac- above, have always adapted themselves to the
tion in England. actual condition of the population. Malthus'
theory had originated like a spontaneous product of an alarming
and dangerous state of things ; but what was only a passing
phenomenon assumed a permanent and enduring character in the
eyes of the English economists. By preaching moral restraint
and the adoption of preventative means, they ended with creating
and authorising the immoral movement of the so-called Neo-
malthusian school.

---

[1] About the acceptance which Spencer's views have met with, *cf.* Vanni :
op. cit., p. 51, etc.

From 1798, that is the year when Malthus published his study, until 1878, the population of Great Britain con- Movement of the population of Great Britain tinued to increase in a very rapid proportion.[1] from 1798 to 1878.

Years.	Population.	INCREASE.	
		Total for the year.	And for per cent.
1801	16,237,300	—	—
1811	18,509,116	—	—
1821	21,272,187	—	1·37
1831	24,392,485	3,120,298	1·04
1841	27,057,923	2,665,438	0·25
1851	27,745,949	688,026	0·55
1861	29,321,288	1,577,349	0·82
1871	31,845,379	2,524,091	1·01

Until 1878, the annual increase of the population of Great Britain was unequalled and unsurpassed throughout Europe, with the exception of Germany [2] and of some small states, but slightly advanced in progress.

But, it is well to repeat here the number of births which in 1878 was 35·5 for 1000 inhabitants, decreased Limitation of the birth-rate in Great Britain. to 34·2 in 1880, to 33·3 in 1884, and 30·5 in 1889 : during the same ten years the Irish and Scotch birth-rates also diminished : thus the total number of births in the United Kingdom decreased in ten years from 33·3 to 29·6.[3]

This singular phenomenon, which contradicts all the dictates of classic economy with regard to population, found a strange coincidence in the campaign opened in 1877 by the so-called school of Neomalthusianism.

It was exactly in the year 1877, that is at the time when the birth-rate was greatest, that the famous atheist, The Neomalthusian School. Charles Bradlaugh, and Mrs. Annie Besant, began

[1] Block : *L'Europe politique et sociale*, Paris, 1869, pp., 404,405, and *Annuaire de l'économie politique*, 1852, Paris, 1852, p., 809, etc.

[2] See Marshall's statistical tables : *Principles of Economics*, London, 1891, pp. 248,249.

[3] Mille : *art. cit.*

their campaign in favour of Malthusian practices, a campaign
which found a great echo, since it raised to the rank of a principle
what had begun to be secretly practised.

Until then Malthusian practices and moral restraint had been
recommended by the upper classes only, and in
the interests of a conservative policy; hence,
they met with no very great acceptance. But
Bradlaugh was an atheist and a radical ;[1] Mrs. Besant was a
Socialist and atheist.[2] The acceptance of her theory, she told
her followers when speaking of Malthusianism, was absolutely
essential to the success of Socialism. It is quite intelligible why
the Neomalthusian campaign, when promoted by such advanced
persons, should have found in England generally and among the
middle classes in particular a greater favour and wider results
than the involved hypothesis and counsels of Stuart Mill and
Derby, and the numerous followers of the Malthusian school.

*Neomalthusian prac-
tices recommended by
English Socialists and
Radicals.*

The campaign in favour of Malthusian practices was opened by
Mrs. Besant and Bradlaugh with a little work on
the *Fruits of Philosophy*,[3] a work which, being held
immoral and condemned, was precisely on this account sold in
hundreds of thousands of copies. The *Fruits of Philosophy*, notwithstanding its full and pompous title, contains nothing but advice to young married people. After the noisy process, wihch
only served to diffuse the incriminated theory, Mrs. Besant with-
drew the bold book from sale, and published another book on the
law of population much larger, and endowed with a more scientific
appearance.[4] But not even does this mediocre book contain any-

*C. Bradlaugh and A.
Besant.*

---

[1] About Bradlaugh, his views and character, see the article, written in a
rather too Catholic light, by Reynaert : *M. Ch. Bradlaugh peint par lui
même* in the *Revue générale* for 1882, and Mr. C. Stephen's study entitled :
M. Bradlaugh and his Opponents in *The Fortnightly Review* for February,
1880.

[2] About Annie Besant, first an ardent Christian, then a Socialist, atheist
and Malthusian, see what W. T. Stead has written in an interesting
article in the *Review of Reviews* for October, 1871, pp., 349-367.

[3] London, 1878.

[4] Annie Besant : *The Law of Population*, London, 1878.

thing notable for the impartial searcher : Mrs. Besant, accepting the two famous progressions as an indisputable fact, builds upon them a vain structure of hypotheses and conjectures.

Anyhow, issued in 200,000 copies, reproduced in the newspapers, defended with ardour, the new publication did not delay in producing its effects, more especially among persons who had already begun to secretly practice what the Malthusians publicly advocated. Success of the Neo-malthusian propa-ganda.

So arose the Malthusian league, which, presided over by Doctor Drysdale, himself, author of a *brochure* on population,[1] and of several popular works, at once undertook the publication of a monthly review, *The Malthusian*, in order to spread the teaching of Malthus, *the divine pro-testant.* Several little treatises for a few pence each were also published. Adopting the methods of the religious societies, they went so far as to distribute in the streets *The Duties of Parents* by Drysdale, a treatise on *The Prosperity of the French Peasant*, and innumerable little works containing extracts from the writings of Mill, and of other authors in praise of a limited family. The Malthusian League in England.

This campaign, carried on with such ardour, naturally produced results within a very short time. Neo-malthusianism did not appeal to elevated instincts or noble feelings ; it was neither more nor less than a brutal affirmation of individual egoism. Well-conditioned working men, seeing in the absence or scarcity of children a means of putting an end to the difference between them and the lower middle class ; and these, knowing that they had to rely upon a small income, feared that a large family might reduce them to the condition of working men ; people who were independent, desirous of maintaining their social position ; all accepted it enthusiastically. Causes of the success attending the English Neomalthusians

These results did not delay in showing themselves. The birth-rate, which, until 1877, had been always on the increase, began, as I have said, to decrease from 1878 downwards ; marriages became fewer, and there occurred a The consequences of the Malthusian propa-ganda.

[1] Ch. R. Drysdale : *The Population Question according to Malthus and Mill*, London, 1878.

demographic phenomenon, which had appeared altogether un-
likely,[1] owing to the traditional fecundity of the people of Great
Britain.

Then the very apostles of the Neomalthusian practices appeared to be dismayed by the effects which their propaganda had
produced, and some of them even wished to withdraw. Mrs.
Annie Besant honestly declared that the experience of Neo-
malthusianism had convinced her that the practices suggested by the Malthusian league were
contrary to the interests of the nation as well as
to those of morality, that, while on the one hand they hindered
every development of the more elevated feelings, on the other
hand they weakened and unfitted the people of Great Britain for
the struggle of life.

Fatal influence of Malthusianism on the British people and civilisation.

A singular fact then took place, and one which is an evident
proof of the theory which I have already maintained, namely, that
the science of social economy, instead of foreseeing and penetrating beyond phenomena, has always followed them and confounded
them, even when transient, with the great natural laws. Thus
the English economists,[2] who until 1878 had hardly even discussed the teaching of Malthus, and were seized with a blind
enthusiasm for both the author and his theory, began to disagree
with it, and not unfrequently denounced it, and
attributed to the hypothesis only that modest
rank which belongs to it in the science of
economy.

Reaction of the Eng- lish economists to- wards Malthusianism after 1878.

W. Bagehot, among the first, accepting Spencer's views and
believing that the phenomenon of over-population
would disappear by means of evolution,[3] blamed
the inconclusiveness of the Malthusian theory, hitherto put for-

Recent English econo- mists.

---

[1] See the two articles by A. Lyttleton : *The Question of Population* in
The Economic Review for April and July, 1891.

[2] W. T. Stead : *art. cit.*, and Mille : *art. cit.*

[3] W. Bagehot : *Physics and Politics, or Thoughts on the Application of
the Principles of Natural Selection and Inheritance to Political Society*, book
iv.

ward as an indisputable truth.[1]   At the same time Doctor Farr, in a brilliant work, showed himself still more   Farr and Graham. averse and rebellious towards Malthus.[2]   William Graham, while raising doubts upon the theoretic truth of Malthusianism, further denies him every practical value with regard to the social problem.[3]   Without wishing to enter into the details of the question, Francis Galton justly observes that the teaching   Francis Galton. of Malthus has exercised a pernicious influence upon the race.[4] J. K. Ingram recognises that if Malthus has the   Ingram. merit of having forcibly drawn the public attention to a question, formerly insufficiently studied in its theoretical and practical aspects, he has, nevertheless, the blame of having exaggerated the consequences of his theory, and still more the nature and urgency of the dangers set forward.[5]   David G. Ritchie,   David G. Ritchie. studying with his accustomed warmth the relations between Malthusianism and Darwinism, inclines to the Spencerian hypothesis and refuses to allow Malthus' pessimistic conclusions.[6]   Alfred Marshall, the prince of modern English economists,   Marshall and the Malthusian hypothe- also admits without difficulty that the birth-rate   sis. differs in the different social classes, and is so much the greater in proportion as the wages due to the labouring classes is smaller, these being driven to become irregularly prolific.   But he thinks, notwithstanding, that the Malthusian theory is not only false, but erroneous in its formal part.[7]

[1] Malthus' study on *Population*, according to Bagehot "in its first form . . . was inconclusive as an argument, only it was based on true facts ; in its second form it was based on true facts, but it was inconclusive as an argument." W. Bagehot : *Economic Studies*, p. 37.

[2] Farr, in the *Journal of Statistical Society* for March, 1882.

[3] W. Graham : *The Social Problem in its Economical, Moral and Political Aspects*, London, 1888, pp., 432-448.

[4] Galton : *Hereditary Genius*, London, 1892, p. 343.

[5] J. K. Ingram : *History of Political Economy*, p. 112.

[6] David G. Ritchie : *Darwinism and Politics*, London, 1889, pp. 92-100.

[7] A. Marshall : *Principles of Economics*, pp. 229-249.   Marshall regrets (p. 234) that Malthus should have used the unhappy phrase about arithmetical and geometrical progressions in the first edition of his book.   But he forgets that Malthus has expressed the same idea almost with the same

E

Price, although he assigns Malthus a great place in the history
L. L. Price. of English economy, considers him chiefly as a
man who wrote for his age, and who generalised too much the
phenomena of that age.[1]   Keynes ingeniously shows that the
Keynes, Lyttleton, and Cannan. Darwinian theory was the result of historic circumstances.[2]   And about the historic character of
Malthusianism, A. Lyttleton [3] and Edwin Cannan [4] have insisted
with especial talent.

Henry Sidgwick, a good philosopher and brilliant economist, in
Sidgwick against Malthus. his *Elements of Politics* combats the Malthusian
methods not less strongly as evil and contrary to
the expansion and progress of humanity.[5]

Lastly, A. J. Ogilvie does not hesitate to declare Malthusian-
A. J. Ogilvy. ism false in its scientific essence, and, moreover,
baneful to civilisation and fatal to morality.   He expresses his
wish that the theory may perish, whatever support it may have
found among the learned, for it is essentially false, an obstacle to
discovering the true philosophy of life, etc.[6]

But how is it that Malthus' own country should differ so
widely from his teaching ?   Whence came so rapid and sudden a

terms even in the sixth edition. "It may safely be pronounced, therefore,
that population, when unchecked, goes on doubling itself every twenty-five
years, or increases in a geometrical ratio," and, "It may be fairly pronounced, therefore, that considering the present average state of the earth,
the means of subsistence, under circumstances the most favourable to
human industry, could not possibly be made to increase faster than in
arithmetical ratio," pp. 4, 5, 6.   It is not, therefore, as Marshall thought, a
question of an unhappy phrase but of an unhappy thought.

[1] L. L. Price : *A Short History of Political Economy in England from
Adam Smith to Arnold Toynbee*, London, 1891, pp. 35-60.

[2] John Neville Keynes : *The Scope and Method of Political Economy*,
London, 1891, p. 275.

[3] Arthur Lyttleton : *The Question of Population* in *The Economic Review*
for April and July, 1892.

[4] Edwin Cannan : *The Malthusian Anti-socialist Argument* in *The Economic Review* for January, 1892.

[5] H. Sidgwick : *The Elements of Politics*, London, 1891, pp. 302-306.

[6] A. J. Ogilvy : *Malthusianism* in the *Westminster Review* for September, 1891.

change of ideas in so few years? Where is the explanation for all this, unless we admit that theories, instead of dominating the historic phenomena of population, have never done other than follow them?

But if the strict dependence of the theory upon phenomena be evident when we study the history of demographic theories in Germany and England, this dependence will appear even greater now when we shall follow their development in France. France is now, as everyone knows, the country of Europe which has the weakest rate of annual increase. [1]

Theories of population in France.

Rate of annual increase in France.

				Annual Increase for 1000 Inhabitants.
1806	-	-	-	12·8
1821	-	-	-	3·3
1831	-	-	-	4·4
1841	-	-	-	4·1
1851	-	-	-	2·2
1861	-	-	-	6·9
1872	-	-	-	8·5
1881	-	-	-	4·1
1891	-	-	-	0·8

If the average of life has increased, the number of births has grown continually less, as appears from the following table :

Diminution of the French birth-rate.

Periods of Ten Years.					Annual Births for every 1000 Inhabitants.
1770-1780	-	-	-	-	380
1801-1810	-	-	-	-	325
1811-1820	-	-	-	-	316
1821-1830	-	-	-	-	309
1831-1840	-	-	-	-	289
1841-1850	-	-	-	-	294
1851-1860	-	-	-	-	267
1869-1880	-	-	-	-	245

[1] *Cf.* Block : *Annuaire de l'économie politique et de la statistique,* 1892, Paris, 1892, pp. 2, etc. ; De Foville : *La France économique,* Paris, 1890, chap. ii.

The annual increase of the population of France was very high
Say. in 1803, when J. B. Say published his classic
treatise on Political Economy. Hence, Say felt the same difficulty as did Malthus; and if, disfiguring the thought of Malthus,
he substituted the phrase " means of existence " [1] for the phrase
" means of subsistence," he neither added to or subtracted from
what Malthus had already said,[2] with the exception of this confusion of words.

" The institutions which are most favourable to the happiness
of humanity," Say says roughly, " are those which tend to multiply capital. It is just, therefore, to encourage men rather to be
economic than to have families." [3]

But, unfortunately, he could not foresee that France would
follow his advice beyond all anticipation, and in the future would
practice economy to excess.

But when Say wrote, the causes which later caused the aversion
from Malthus had not yet come into existence.

With the exception of Fourier, who developed an eccentric
Fourier. theory, according to which four obstacles oppose
excessive population in a well-organised state of society,[4] nearly
all economists, who have written about population between
1803 and 1848, have accepted the Malthusian thesis without
reserve.

Some vain endeavours to oppose the pessimistic current were
The first opposition. made from the beginning by such men as Moreau
de Jonnès [5] and Dupin.[6]

Led away by political passion, the writers of every shade of

---

[1] Concerning the difference between these two ideas of existence and subsistence, cf. Tracy : *Traité de la volonté*, Paris, 1818, chap. iv.

[2] J. B. Say : *Cours complet d' économie politique*, Paris, 1826, part vi.,
chap. vii.

[3] Say : *loc. cit.*

[4] Ch. Fourier : *Œuvres choisies* (edited by C. Gide), Paris, 1890,
p. 225.

[5] Moreau de Jonnès in the *Comptes-rendus* of the *Académie des sciences*,
Séance of October 2nd, 1843.

[6] Dupin : *Ibid.*, *Séance* for June 20th, 1836, vol. ii., p. 485.

thought were agreed in blaming any development given to public assistance, and in attributing the poverty and wretchedness of the working classes to their own fault. The legitimist noble [1] and the economist most enamoured of progress, proceeded in perfect agreement. Some, like Dunoyer, went so far as to use really violent language against the philanthropists, and against those who were induced by their natural goodness to endeavour to save from death so many beings imprudently brought into existence. [2]

About 1848, when the birth-rate had already begun to decrease, the Malthusian influence began to wane and a new direction began to make headway.

But the sad days of June had created a great mental depression, and a certain pessimism pervaded all. Then it was that a learned academician, [3] and writers of popular manuals, agreed in thinking that in view of so much poverty it was impossible to deny *que la population a pris les devants sur les aliments, les vêtements et les demeures.* [4]

But when the birth-rate grew less, and the statisticians perceived this, ideas began to change.

It was shortly afterwards, about 1848, that is, when the phenomenon which now attracts so much attention began to appear, that the opposition against Malthusianism grew strongest, and the economists who differed most widely in temperament and intellect, set themselves openly against Malthus. Not only profound demographists, like Guillard and Bertillon, not only men of radical tendencies, like Proudhon, but even apostles of the classic school, began to protest against Malthus' pessimistic deductions.

<small>Reaction against Malthusianism.</small>

[1] Duchâtel (Le Comte) : *De la charité*, Paris, 1829, p. 197.

[2] Dunoyer : *Mémoire sur les questions que la Révolution de Juillet à fait naître*, Paris, 1835, p. 175.

[3] *Tableau de la revolution seculaire des éléments de la population française due à la découverte de la vacine, presenté à l'Acad. des Sciences*, by Carnot : 20th November, 1848.

[4] Woloski et Fonteyraud : *Instructions sur l'Economie politique*, Paris, 1849.

And once perhaps for the only time, these two minds are found
Bastiat and Proudhon. in agreement.

Bastiat believes that population has a tendency to proportion
Bastiat.   itself to the means of existence, which far from
being regular and constant, are continually increasing with the
growth of population. If all the animals, led by a blind instinct,
tend to exceed the means of existence, man, on the contrary,
adapts himself to them, and they on their part grow even more
rapidly than the population.[1] Proudhon also, without attacking
Proudhon.   the law of population, is altogether of opinion
that between the industrial and generative faculties, between
labour and love, there exists an antagonism partly physiological,
and still more psychological, and infers that in future the improvement of feelings and ideas, in consequence of work, will exercise a
lessening and moderating influence upon the sexual instinct.[2]

Unquestionably, these are over hasty and often baseless conclusions, but they are of the greatest interest to anyone who
intends to study the changes of theories from the standpoint of
the influences exercised by surroundings.

Even in 1845, F. Le Play, the founder of the Catholic school
called after him, in the first edition of his *Réforme Sociale*, studying the decrease of the French birth-rate, partly abandoned the
Malthusian hypothesis, and attributed the phenomena of population to economic causes.[3]

Achilles Guillard, who gave a fatal blow to Malthusianism, was
A. Guillard.   also imbued with its spirit, but statistical inquiry
soon convinced him that instead of there being opposition between population and the means of subsistence, the former
always proportions itself to the latter. And in reality statistics
prove that the most productive countries are the most populous,

---

[1] Bastiat : *Harmonies économiques*, App. xiv. : *De la population.* The
16th chapter of the work, which speaks of population, is incomplete. The
part which we possess is devoted to an exposition of Malthusianism, and
Bastiat, as he even says himself, acts only as *reporteur*.

[2] P. J. Proudhon : *Système des contradictions économiques*, chap. xiii.

[3] F. Le Play : *La Réforme sociale en Europe*, Paris, 1845, vol. i., p. 74,
and 363 in the edition of 1867 ; see also *Les ouvriers Européens*, 1855, p. 141.

that the production of the means of subsistence increases at regular periods, that the population increases in the same proportion, and that, on the other hand, if the production of food decreases, the population decreases in proportion ; that if population, influenced by external causes, suddenly decreases, while the means of subsistence do not decrease, the enlarged birth-rate quickly supplies the need, that if some accidental influence hinders the development of work, the birth-rate decreases rapidly, and that in countries where the population increases, the increase is less in proportion as the density is greater.

Guillard, therefore, believed that births never exceed the number of men which a nation is capable of sup- Guillard's conclusions. porting, and that they are never over-numerous, unless when the average of life grows less or when the call for labour increases ; for, he adds, it is not land but labour which supplies food.[1]

This theory of Guillard, although having the germ of that optimistic fatalism, which, for fifty years, and chiefly in France after the Restoration, has influenced the spirit of the moral sciences, is yet one of the most powerful and correct theories ever set forth, and after it was later modified by Bertillon[2] it contributed not a little towards giving a direction to French demo- Bertillon. graphy.

Already an Italian of genius, Pellegrino Rossi, while living in France before the reaction against Malthusianism arose, had greatly limited the Malthusian theory. " The conclusion is evident," he said. Since men are unwilling to forego marriage, what Malthus called preventative obstacles must be substituted for repressive obstacles. [3]

Now the system did not altogether consist in this, and in taking a political character the classical theory moreover lost its essential character.

[1] Achille Guillard : *Éléments de statistique humaine ou démographic comparée*, Paris, 1855, chaps. iv., v.

[2] Bertillon : *Atlas de démographie figurée*, Paris, 1871.

[3] P. Rossi : *Essai sur la Population. Introduction* to the edition of 1845,

Against this influence, which was naturally and spontaneously caused by its surroundings, statisticians and economists made vain opposition, seeing in it the destruction both of Malthusianism and of one of the mainstays, if not indeed the chief one, of their individualist system of social nihilism. First, Quételet, in Belgium; then in France, Garnier, Courcelle-Seneuil, De Molinari, Block, Jourdan, Frederick Passy,[1] and several others, attempted to defend Malthusianism and to support a system upon which all the prejudices against social assistance were based. But the continual diminution of the French birth-rate, at first slight and changing but afterwards continual and dangerous, has had no effect but that of increasing the aversion to Malthusianism.

The defenders of Malthusianism in France.

Further, to show that economic research was always influenced by the needs and the opinions of the time, it may be well to recall those French economists who accepted Malthusianism at first, and then, when the French birth-rate diminished, rejected it with all the means in their power.

The causes of the success and failure of Malthusianism in France.

Wolowski who, in 1849, wrote with Fonteyraud the famous *Instruction pour le peuple*, which instigated them to Malthusianism, changes his opinions radically only a few years later. "Facts," he says, "should guide us in the discussion of economic questions." Now, when one studies the tendency of facts chiefly in our country, instead of regretting the great number of births one is led to notice the contrary. Those who think that nothing is more important nowadays than to induce the working classes to

---

[1] Quételet : *Du système social, et des lois qui le régissent*, Paris, 1848, book ii, sec. i. ; Garnier : *Du principe de population*, Paris, 1887 ; Courcelle-Seneuil : *Traité d'économie politique*, 3rd ed., Paris, 1891, book i., chap. v. ; De Molinari : *Questions d'économie politique*, Bruxelles, 1891, with an introduction by Garnier ; M. Block : *Les progrès de la science économique depuis Adam Smith*, Paris, 1890, chap. xx. ; Jourdan : *Cours analitique d'économie politique*, Paris, 1882, pp. 281, etc. ; F. Passy : *Le principe de la population, Malthus et sa doctrine*, Paris, 1868, and *Malthus et la véritable notion de l'assistance* in the *Séances et travaux de l'Académie des sciences morales et politiques* for February, 1892, etc.

greater prudence in marrying, are therefore singularly mistaken at present. It seems to me that the progress of population is the source, the scope and the sign of all progress."[1]

Not only is this an abandonment of the Malthusian theory, but it is a manifest return to the pre-Malthusian theories, to the ideas of Montesquieu, Rousseau and Filangieri.

Leonce de Louvergne, who, in 1865, was delighted at seeing the decline of the French birth-rate and had said that "the excess of population was the cause of poverty."[2] Eleven years later, in 1876, publicly asserted and declared "that experience proves that a numerical increase is perfectly reconcilable with increasing comfort."[3]

Nevertheless, some of the more timid economists, such as Baudrillart, not venturing to entirely abandon Malthusianism, declared it necessary to make an exception in the case of France.[4]

Other bolder economists frankly abandoned the Malthusian principles. And Legoyt, for instance, does not disdain to pass from one thesis to another in a very short time.[5]

Jacques Bertillon not only rejects Malthusianism but wishes at all costs that the legislature should intervene in order to increase the French birth-rate. In order to save France from the danger which is at hand it is necessary that fiscal and other laws be made, so that families having possessions should not have any evident interest in restricting the number of their births. In

---

[1] Wolowski in a meeting of the *Société d'économie politique* for Nov. 5, 1862.

[2] Leonce de Louvergne : *L'Agriculture et la Population*, Paris, 1865, p. 311.

[3] Quoted by Schoene : *op. cit.* p. 350.

[4] Baudrillart in the meeting of the *Société d'économie politique* for February 5th, 1873.

[5] Legoyt at first believed an abundant birth-rate to be dangerous (*Moniteur universel*, Feb. 4th, 1865) ; two years later, on the other hand, he was studying the limitation of the birth-rate (*Les nouvelles conditions d'accroissement de la nation française* in the *Journal des économistes* for August, 1867). See also his article in the *Révue Scientifique* for Sept. 18th, 1880.

a word, *it is necessary that the rearing up of a certain number of children* (three at least) *be considered as a kind of impost.*[1]

At present the French economists, almost without any difference

Aversion of the modern French economists to Malthus. of school or method, attack the premises and conclusions of Malthusianism, so severely falsified by the actual condition of France.

Y. Guyot and P. Cauwés attack Malthus without reserve.[2]

Y. Guyot and P. Cauwés. "It is now certain," says P. Leroy-Beaulieu, "that the teaching of Malthus has no application in our time, and that it cannot have any for at least two or three *Leroy-Beaulieu.* centuries, if not for longer still."[3] Ignorant, perhaps, of new biological and sociological discoveries, Leroy-Beaulieu is content to have recourse to statistical proofs. A. Ott, while admit- *A. Ott.* ting that, theoretically, Malthusianism may have some importance at a very distant period, thinks, nevertheless, that political economy cannot, and should not, give it serious attention. The question of a population that will overcrowd the whole world is so far away from us, that, if it ever really occur, it will be at a time which science can neither determine or foresee.[4] Charles Gide, after criticising Malthus' teaching with his accus- *Ch. Gide.* tomed skill, accepts the biological solution, and holds that the fecundity of the human species will grow gradually

[1] J. Bertillon : *La natalité en France et les moyens à employer pour la relever* in the *Revue de Sociologie* for January and February, 1893, p. 46.

[2] Yves Guyot: *La science économique,* Paris, 1881, pp. 185, etc. ; P. Cauwés : *Précis d'économie politique,* Paris, 1881, pp. 413, etc.

[3] P. Leroy-Beaulieu : *Précis d'économie politique,* Paris, 1868, p. 340. In another place he says : " Civilised society has nothing to fear from that increase which we may call normal . . . A country where the population is quite stationary, or even—and examples are not wanting—where the population decreases, is not, we believe, in a healthy and normal state : from a moral, political, and even from an economic point of view, it is in a morbid and lamentable condition." *De la colonisation chez les peuples modernes,* 4th edit., p. 676.

[4] A. Ott : *Traité d'économie sociale,* 2nd edit., Paris, 1892, vol. ii., sec. 172-175.

less in proportion as the intellectual and moral improvement of individuals increases.[1]

This aversion to the hasty and pessimistic conclusions drawn by Malthus has been, naturally, even greater among the sociologists, naturalists, and philosophers, than among the economists. In a way altogether different to that followed by Spencer, Jacoby, and De Candolle,[2] they have, however, arrived at very similar conclusions. De Candolle holds that there is unquestionably an evident opposition between the progress of the organisation and the increase of the race : Jacoby, studying the influence exercised by selection upon the progress of the human species, has shown that the great inequality of wealth, talent, and power have a depressing influence upon the individual and his descendants, and that, most of all, they cause sterility. Charles Richet, observing that the upper classes and those engaged in the higher functions of society are the least productive, holds it as a probable opinion that this is caused by their greater intellectual development.[3] Delaunay thinks that the birth-rate decreases with the increased development of a species, a race and a difference of race. This theory finds a counterpart even in human races, where the more advanced, by vigour of constitution, intelligence, and longevity, are precisely

Aversion of the French biologists to Malthusianism.

De Candolle.

Jacoby.

Ch. Richet.

Delaunay.

His teaching.

[1] Charles Gide : *Principes d'économie politique*, 3rd edit., Paris, 1891, pp. 348-351.

[2] Jacoby : *Etudes sur la sélection dans ses rapports avec l'hérédité chez l'homme* ; De Candolle : *Essai sur la sélection dans l'espèce humaine.*

[3] Ch. Richet : *L'accroissement de la population française* in the *Revue des deux mondes*, for April 1st and June 15th, 1882. In his recent prophecy concerning the world a hundred years hence (Charles Richet : *Dans cent ans*, Paris, 1892, chap. ii.), the talented physiologist, who directs the *Revue Scientifique*, thinks it very probable that the European races, whose territory is limited—with the exception of Russia—will decrease in number annually. Already, attentively following the birth-rate for the last twenty years, we see that the population of European countries has a tendency to become stationary, so that the example of France will be soon followed, and in Germany, England, and Italy, the increase will become gradually less rapid.

those which multiply the least. And what is true of particular individuals is true of races ; every development of body and mind, most of all any intellectual work, consume the generative power. This hypothesis seems to be confirmed by facts, if we compare the cultivated with the uncultivated classes, urban with rural populations, and the rich with the poor.[1] "The country is in peril," exclaims Léon Le Fort, and Raoul Frary calls it "the national danger."[2]

Even the physicians have attacked moral restraint, with a violence perhaps unequalled elsewhere. Bergeret Aversion of French physicians to Malthusianism. condemns every dishonesty in the generative action as an infanticide fatal to morality and civilisation. Amelin adds in a spirit of indignation : *La castration vant mieux, à tout prendre, qu'une prudence voisine de la pratique de l'avortement.*[3]

Brocca, vainly endeavoured with all his great authority to show that the prospective of a weak birth-rate could not but be reassuring and good.[4]

The fact now imposed itself, and all the prejudices of economic pessimism could not suffice to counteract its influence.

An excessive reaction was moreover inevitable, and it did not delay to appear in the most authoritative writers.

A well-known French sociologist, Letourneau, reaches un-Letourneau. founded exaggerations. "The close and continual relation between the production of food and the number of the population is now nothing else than a commonplace of statistics."[5]

Guyau, who has examined the relations between religion and Guyau. the fecundity of races with his accustomed im-

---

[1] G. Delaunay : *La fécondité* in the *Revue Scientifique* for October 3rd and 10th, 1885.

[2] L. Le Fort : *Des mouvements de la population en France* in the *Revue des deux mondes* for May 15th, 1867, and Raoul Frary : *Le Péril National.*

[3] *Cf.* Amelin : *Le libre échange absolu à l'intérieur et à la frontière*, p. 21 ; Bergeret : *Fraudes conjugales.*

[4] Brocca in the *Gazette des Hopitaux*, 1867, p. 202.

[5] Letourneau : *Science et matérialisme*, Paris, 1890, p. 249.

partiality, condemns Malthusianism as economically disastrous, morally dangerous, and fatal to civilisation.[1]

Fouillée, who has studied the problem of population from the point of view of public assistance, allows Spencer's   Fouillée. prevision as certain, and judges the day to be not far distant when the equilibrium will be finally established.[2]

Arsène Dumont has exposed a far more original theory in a work, wherein abundance of statistics is joined   Dumont and the theory of social attraction. with a width of observation and really admirable research.[3] He boldly denies to Malthusianism every theoretic worth, and every practical importance. Far from being regulated by the means of subsistence, the births on the contrary are most numerous in the poorest nations, provinces and classes. If rich nations, like England, have preserved the standard of births at the same level, this is caused by a persistence of the family spirit and of tradition. The more a nation becomes civilised, the more births diminish. Poverty, ignorance, coarseness, credulity in France, coincide almost always with a high birth-rate; while wealth, education, the decay of religious faith, go with a weak birth-rate. The most prolific French provinces are those which chiefly resist the attraction of central civilisation.

According to Dumont, the problem of population must be minutely studied, according to the demographical   Dumont and Malthusianism. history of each little village and a detailed study in different regions. What is the explanation afforded by the so-called great laws of Malthusianism? They are insufficient to explain the great facts of human history. What caused the great nations of antiquity, so rich and fertile in men, to disappear and begin to languish of *anémie* and consumption before the stranger came to give a new and strong life to a decayed civilisation?

[1] Guyau: *L'Irreligion de l'avenir*, Paris, 1887, 2nd edition, part ii., chap. vii.

[2] A. Fouillée : *La propriété sociale et la démocratie*, Paris, 1884, book ii., chap. iii.

[3] Arsène Dumont: *Dépopulation et civilisation. Étude démographique*, Paris, 1890, p. 520.

Malthusianism, with all its groundless and exaggerated principles, is unable to offer any explanation for all this.

The evil which menaces modern democracy is, according to The danger of modern Dumont, the more or less present peril of a limitademocracy. tion of the birth-rate.

In our democratic state of society everyone tends to raise himself above his actual condition. Each social molecule, guided by a fatal and irresistible instinct, having secured the means of existence, struggles to raise itself, impelled by a real force of social attraction. The greater this force of attraction is, the more the man feels the need of imposing upon himself those sacrifices and restrictions which will make him reach this the more speedily. The birth-rate is, therefore, in inverse ratio to social capillarity.

But despotism and the institution of social ranks, suppress or The birth-rate and the weaken this power; individualist democracy democratic individu- alist arrangement. favours it. When the individual is hindered in his personal progress, the power of expansion in the race gains by it, and men increase in number, being unable to increase in value.

Hence, individualist democracy exercises a totally different action to that which would be exercised by a socialist democracy; the latter, based upon the principle of equal worth of offices in the State, would produce a large birth-rate wherever it would be possible to apply it entirely. Democracy, suppressing all obstacles, habitually has for consequence an increase in the power of attraction. Given, therefore, the individualist democratic *régime*, the only classes to whom, in fact, if not by right, every advance is made impossible, such as miners and day-labourers, end by resigning themselves to their fate, and hence have large families.

Dumont's conclusions. Dumont's fundamental teaching can be summed up thus :—

(1) The progress of the birth-rate is in inverse ratio to social capillarity.

(2) The progress of an individual, either in personal worth or enjoyment, is in direct proportion to social capillarity.

(3) The development of the race is, on the other hand, in inverse ratio to individual development in worth or pleasures.

(4) The more brilliant a centre of culture is, the more it attracts, and the more it exercises attraction the more brilliant it becomes ; this is an effect which develops itself.

(5) The more considerable the attraction exercised is, the more suddenly are those overpowered who submit themselves to its influence. The plebeian sets before himself a higher ideal than the son of the rich man ; hence enjoyment becomes less accessible to him.

(6) Thus, democracy represents culture intensively, while the system of social inequalities represent it extensively.

This is, in general terms, the law to which the renowned demographer has given a strong foundation of historical and statistical proofs,[1] a law which, on account of its truthfulness and its originality, must be held as a great progress of demographic science. If, hitherto, the phenomenon of the birth-rate was only considered-in its relation to the actual greater or less economic progress of individuation, no one had considered it deeply with regard to the political and social constitution.

If the most satisfactory criticism of Malthus' broad statements have arisen in France during recent years, it is a *Causes of the new French demographic* fact which goes to prove the historic cause of *theories.* economic theories, which we have wished to analyse in this work. The continual diminution of the French birth-rate has gradually and necessarily led biologists, economists and social writers, to abandon all the prejudices and standards of Malthusianism.

And here the purpose of this the first part of my research concerning the historic causes of the economic theory of population would be attained, did I not feel the need of showing, at least in their main lines, the theories of Henry George and Tcoznicewsky, and those, even broader still, of Messedaglia, Loria, and Vanni.

[1] Besides the volume already quoted, which contains a wonderful abundance and originality of research, see also his study : *La Natalité dans les communes rurales en France* in the *Revue scientifique* for October 10th and 24th, 1891. See also work of Tarde : *Dépopulation et civilisation* in the *Études pénales et sociales*, Lyons, 1892, pp. 399-414.

Even a few years ago, the celebrated American economist, Francis Walker, characterised the attacks upon Malthus as the headless arrows of beginners in economics.[1] But the body of these beginners in America, of whom Carey[2] once formed part, has enriched itself within recent years, not merely with intelligent Socialists like Henry George, but with economists like Van Buren Denslow and Simon Patten.

Henry George believes that the misery and want generally

Henry George.   attributed to the excess of population to be really attributable, both as regards their existence and their permanence, not to the avarice of nature, but to the injustice of society. Those who come newly into the world do not call for more food than their predecessors, and they can produce much more. The productive power of a people is not to be measured by the articles necessary to life which it actually produces, but by the consumption of strength which it daily makes. The distribution of wealth necessitated by a great feast or the maintenance of an army is equivalent to a consumption of food of an equal value. When society will be better arranged and on the way to a state of equality, then only will cease the present dispersion of strength, and the constant and natural growth of population will tend to make men richer, not poorer.[3]

Van Buren Denslow holds that at present the problem of popu-

American economists and the theories on population.   lation has not assumed an acute form, and that it perhaps never will.[4] And Simon Patten, also accepting some principles of Malthusianism, then separates himself altogether from the general teaching, which he judges to be arbitrary and in opposition to facts.[5]

Another thoughtful American writer, Dr. J. S. Billings, studying the decay of the family in America, displays the most com-

---

[1] F. Walker : *Political Economy*, New York, 1883, p. 318.

[2] Carey : *Principles of Social Science*, Philadelphia, 1837-40.

[3] Henry George : *Progress and Poverty*, book ii., chap. iv.

[4] Van Buren Denslow : *Principles of the Economic Philosophy of Society, Government and Industry*, New York, pp. 230-33.

[5] Simon N. Patten : *The Premises of Political Economy*, Philadelphia, 1885, pp. 72-94.

plete aversion to Malthusianism, which he considers socially perilous.[1]

In a country like Russia, where the population is very seldom dense, and where there are hardly 17 inhabitants The theories of population in Russia. for every 100 *hectaires* of land, a country which, with the exception of the Scandinavian provinces, has the thinnest population in Europe, and which has, moreover, fallen a victim to the fever for expansion, the casual theories of Malthus have not found and cannot find favour. And it is precisely in Russia and Finland that two very learned writers, Tcernicewsky and Tallquist,[2] have opposed Malthusianism with the broadest, the most pleasing and keenest statistical confutation.

In Italy, where, as one of our clever writers has remarked, economic relations are very little noted, and The theory of population in Italy. assume an almost academic form, the economists have, hitherto, accepted Malthusianism almost without discussion. On the other hand, Messedaglia has disputed it, though only in part, while Achille Loria and Icilio Vanni have attacked it each in a different manner and with a different method.

After exposing and accepting in general the corollaries of Malthus, Messedaglia holds that " the whole Messedaglia. business of inquiry and the essence of the theory is simply to determine if, in practice, the equilibrium can be maintained by preventative obstacles only, or if repressive measures are always to be feared, or if there is nothing else to do but to await the ever-present scourge of famine and death." [3] Malthus' error, according to Messedaglia, was the supposing that the reproductive

[1] J. S. Billings : *The Limitation of the American Family* in the *Forum* for June, 1893.

[2] Tcernicewsky : *Osservazioni su la teoria di Malthus* in the *Biblioteca dell' Economista*, 3rd series ; J. V. Tallquist : *Recherches statistiques sur la tendance à une moindre fecondité des mariages*, Helsingfors, 1886.

[3] Messedaglia : *Della teorica della popolazione : I. Malthus e l'equilibrio della popolazione con le sussistenze*, Verona, 1850, p. 16. See also Messedaglia's other works : *Studi sulla popolazione*, in the 12th volume of the *Memorie dell' Istituto veneto*, 1886, and *La scienza e statistica della popolazione* in the *Archivio di statistica*, the second year, fasc. 3, Rome, 1877.

F

power is always and everywhere constant : the hypothesis, which is true, when it is a question of homogeneous populations and of limited periods, is absurd when it is held as the expression of an inevitable physiological necessity.

But if the geometrical increase of population be merely a biological hypothesis, the arithmetical increase of the means of subsistence is in no way to be proved. The productive capacity of the soil is limited, both economically and geographically; hence it may be stationary, it may progress slowly or rapidly, and thus be more or less powerful according to the various phases of economic development. In any case, Malthus, in supposing the arithmetical progress of the means of subsistences, formulated an hypothesis, which can be realised only under the most advantageous conditions.

The two progressions cannot be considered apart, and from the moment they are studied together, they cease to be independent, and the one tends to modify the terms of the other. Parallel with these two independent series, which represent the movement of increase in population and in food, Messedaglia puts a third, which represents the real impulse of increase which a population preserves when it is restrained by lack of food. The three series, developed in corresponding terms, are, therefore, as follows :— [1]

Messedaglia's progressions.

Hence, at the eighth point, the relation, instead of being 256 to 9, is 16 to 9.

1	2	4	8	16	32	64	128	256
1	2	3	4	5	6	7	8	9
1	2	4	6	8	10	12	14	16

Nevertheless, in spite of its attractiveness,[2] this hypothesis is not in any way borne out by facts, and, as we shall see later, though being far better than the Malthusian hypothesis, it also

[1] Messedaglia : *Della Teorica*, etc., pp. 54, 55.

[2] Loria has well shown the full importance of Messedaglia's hypothesis in his article entitled *Economics in Italy* published in the *Annals of the American Academy of Political and Social Science* of Philadelphia, 1891, No. 33, p. 68.

lacks the formula which will securely solve the complex and troublesome problem of population.

Achille Loria, first in a speech and later in his masterly *Analisi della proprietà capitalistica*,[1] has, above all others in Italy, shown the weak and defective aspects of the classic theory of population. He does not take the phenomenon of population to be natural and unceasing, but historical, and hence changeable in different ages. The poverty of our age is not a consequence of the fixed law of population, but a consequence of the actual degree of the density of the population, which last is nothing else but the necessary result of our economic constitution, and most of all of landed property, which artificially weakens the productiveness of land. But the economic phenomena of our social state are in turn derived from a previous increase of population, which has fixed, on the one hand, economic limits to agricultural production, and on the other hand, economic inducements to human generation. The actual excess of population and the poverty consequent upon it, are thus not a fixed occurrence, produced by the standing disproportion between production and the birth-rate, but an historic fact, which is combined with a certain degree of density of population at a given period of the social evolution. But Loria also inclines, almost unconsciously, towards an untenable economic fatalism. " The social system," he says, " is the result of the historical period in which we are living, and, as a fatal effect of facts foreign to the will of men, it cannot come to an end at the will of man, although he can and should endeavour to lessen its inevitable evil effects." [2]

Given the freedom of land, the increase of population is, in the opinion of Loria, in perfect correspondence with the growth of capital and of the means of subsistence. But without it, we have rent and the consequent inevitable excess of population, which is the result of the difference

A. Loria and his theory on population.

Population and the freedom of land.

[1] A. Loria: *La legge di popolazione e il sistema sociale*, Siena, 1882; *Analisi della proprietà capitalista*, Turin, 1889, vol. i., chap. v.

[2] Loria: *La legge di popolazione*, p. 60.

between the value of land which limits population and the value of labour which increases population.[1] And from this are derived as a fatal consequence, both wages and a marked division of society into two classes, the one rich, and hence provident and but slightly prolific, the other poor, and hence improvident and necessarily driven to a great multiplication. Excessive population is, therefore, nothing else but the result of the economic influences of the degree of occupation of land. "As the process of redistribution, made necessary by the cessation of the freedom of land, has for its last result an excessive capital, which injures production and is disastrously spent in speculation and crisis, so the process of population equally produced by the same cause, has for its last result an excessive population, which becomes lost in the voiceless ruins of poverty and degeneration."[2]

Such in general is Loria's pleasing theory, and if it also errs by too much neglect of the biological factor, and by being, as I have said, impregnated with an air of fatalism, which the brilliant Italian thinker does not always succeed in escaping, it is none the less one of the most profound and satisfactory theories on population which have been hitherto exposed.

Icilio Vanni, who has dealt with this complex and awful pro-

1. Vanni.   blem of population with admirable depth and capacity, also accepting Spencer's biological theory, has endeavoured to complete it where defective, and chiefly from the social point of view. Hence, applying the law of universal proportion to the principle of population, he has arrived at this con-

The law of universal proportion.   clusion : "If the total be such that the units composing it deliberately succeed in adjusting their number to the means of subsistence, either by restricting their number or by increasing the abundance of the latter, we shall have an equilibrium which is due to human causes, social and historic, there being always, however, certain regular variations in the amount of increase. If, on the other hand, the equalising

---

[1] Loria : *Analisi della proprietà capitalista*, vol. i., p. 687.
[2] Loria : *Analisi*, etc., vol. i., p. 693.

power which consists in prevention cease to operate, the equalising power of repression takes its place, causing oscillations which are the more perceptible in proportion as the impulse to the equalising balance was strong."[1] Having faith in historic heredity, as a factor in the foresight exercised in procreation, in the teachings of psychology and in progress, Vanni is not blind to the fact that until the social evolution shall have definitely gained its due proportion, there will always be a tendency in the population to exceed the means of subsistence.

I should have to speak of many other Italian authors [2] in the present short treatise on the principle of population, were it not that my purpose is simply to show the historic causes which have given rise to the various economic theories concerning population, and not to analyse in detail all the theories which I have hitherto exposed.

The reader who has followed me through this lengthy, but not uninteresting research, will be, I trust, convinced   Conclusion.
of the truth of what I have asserted. I have chiefly wished to set in relief the following cardinal points, which will serve to make the way clear for the research of the true law of population.

1. The Malthusian theory was nothing else but a passing political theory, a protest of conservative individualism against the faith placed in human perfectibility by economic radicalism.

2. The success of Malthusianism was due less to the truths which it upheld than to the interests which it defended.

3. The followers of the philosophy of poverty followed and follow, with regard to population, a direction opposed to the followers of the philosophy of wealth.

4. Countries which have a high birth-rate still follow Malthusianism ; those in which the birth-rate is weak reject it.

---

[1] Vanni : *op. cit.*, p. 47.

[2] While omitting many works of Italian writers, it is necessary to mention Majorana, Virgili, Colajanni, Zorli, Lebrecht, etc., and especially two very brilliant and profound authors, the illustrious Professor C. F. Ferraris, and Professor De Johannis.

5. Malthusianism, originated and received enthusiastically at a time when the beginning of a new economic era had produced grave demographic disturbances, was impeded or limited, when the continual increase of the birth-rate in every civilised country began to gradually decline.

6. All those who have written critically about population have been influenced either by their surroundings or by their judgments in social matters; and hence not only have they not judged the phenomenon of population from a higher point of view, but they have blindly submitted to it.

Economic research is always dangerous and difficult; so much the more difficult is an objective study of the laws of population. Nevertheless, the light gained from what we have so far said will help to make clearer, less arduous and perilous a path of which we may say :

> Quale per incertam lunam sub luce maligna
> Est iter in silvis.

BOOK II.

Now that we have shown under what economic, demographic, and social influénces the many theories on population have been formed, it only remains for us to study which laws of population are really confirmed by objective and impartial research.

Summary of the Theories on Population.

The most important and original theories hitherto advocated may be summed up thus :—

ORIGINATORS.	THEORIES.		PRACTICAL CONCLUSION.	
Bodin, Süssmilch, and the predecessors of Malthus.	Every increase of population is a good. There is no disproportion between population and the means of subsistence.		The State should encourage the increase of population.	
Malthus (1798).	The increase tends to exceed the means of subsistence.	But it finds : (a) positive, (b) negative, obstacles.	To avoid (a), adopt (b).	
Darwin (1859).	Id.	Hence the struggle for existence: (a) natural selection, (b) artificial selection.	Both lead to evolution.	*Laissez-faire,* that is, avoid (b) for the good of the species.
Spencer (1852-66).	The rate of multiplication varies in inverse ratio to that of individuation.	Id.	Id.	Individualise.
Guillard (1855).	The production of men tends to set itself in proportion to the production of the means of subsistence.		*Laissez-faire.*	

ORIGINATORS.	THEORIES.	PRACTICAL CONCLUSION.
Marx (1859).	Each economic phase has its special law of population. The actual capitalist system naturally produces over-population.	Collectivism.
Loria (1882).	Population is strictly bound up with the social system, and then the social system is strictly bound up with land.	The economic evolution is fatal : the more extreme shocks must be made less painful.
Dumont (1890).	Population does not tend to exceed the means of existence. The birth-rate is in inverse ratio to social capillarity.	Socialise.

These theories are so various, discordant, and different from each other, both in their theoretic premises and practical consequences, that it is impossible not to discern under each of them not so much broad and objective observation as the direct influence of the surroundings in which the writer lived and the political theories which he professed. Hence the two systems which form the philosophy of riches and the philosophy of poverty both find, and perhaps more in the question of population than elsewhere, intelligent and pleasing theorists.

And what appears still more clearly is the continual and increasing abandonment of Malthus' scientific and political system. Even between Darwin, who, though admitting the increase of the means of subsistence to be unequal to that of population, thinks, nevertheless, that this disproportion is a continual benefit for the progress of the species, and, therefore, dissents from Malthus' saddening conclusions to Spencer, who, starting from a biological principle, believes that the progress of evolution contains the certain remedy for abnormal increase of population, there is an immense progress. And when Guillard discovers the laws of the necessary proportion between population and food ; when Marx discovers the intimate connection between economic circumstances and a disordered birth-rate ; when Loria assigns the present excess of population not to natural

Gradual abandonment of the Malthusian hypothesis.

causes but to the capitalist order of society and the system of landed property ; when, finally Dumont exposes the law of social capillarity and demonstrates that the danger of an advanced state of society is not in any way a great and disordered birthrate, but, on the contrary, a cessation of births the Malthusian theory, which once appeared as firm as a granite rock, against which all the systems conceived by the philosophy of poverty must fall to pieces, suddenly fails like the political system which gave rise to it. And of this vast idea which seemed to have formed the solution of the mystery of human poverty, of this thought, from which the whole social science seemed to have inherited a blindly fatalist character, of this terrible theory which condemned suffering humanity to an unending inequality, there will perhaps remain nothing more than a memory, just as there is hardly a memory left of other theories, impregnated with the same fatalism and the same pessimism, and set up in the past in defence of political systems which are now no more. Far from being the foundation of the political and economic systems of the future, it appears to the unprejudiced student as nothing more than a passing theory, produced by an historical circumstance now very remote from us.

The strongest defence yet made of the two famous progressions of Malthus, consists in the assertion, that, contain- **The experience of centuries.** ing an essential fund of truth, they are erroneous in form, since excogitated by Malthus at a time when the science of statistics was in its infancy, they could not but be based upon a weak support of statistical proofs.

However can objections be made to Malthus? asked Burdett in astonishment. It would require a thousand years **Burdett's defence.** to refute him. And Ferrara,[1] repeating Burdett's poor jest, delights in it as a powerful argument.

Nevertheless, it was not necessary to wait a thousand years in order to refute Malthus, nor to look to the future for proofs which the past afforded abundantly. Malthus supposed that, in favourable conditions, population doubled every 25 years : we can now

[1] Ferrara : *op. cit.*

maintain, as the least favourable hypothesis, that the doubling of the population in the past has been, even in the view of Malthus, only once every hundred years.

The population of Europe in 1800, that is, when Malthus conceived his terrible law, was about 176 millions.[1] Now, if the Rector of Haileybury had calculated a doubling of the population every hundred years he would have arrived at the following absurd result :—

Absurd consequences of the Malthusian hypothesis.

Population of Europe in 1800	-	-	-	176,000,000
„ „ „ 1700	-	-	-	88,000,000
„ „ „ 1600	-	-	-	44,000,000
„ „ „ 1500	-	-	-	22,000,000
„ „ „ 1400	-	-	-	11,000,000
„ „ „ 1300	-	-	-	5,500,000
„ „ „ 1200	-	-	-	2,250,000
„ „ „ 1100	-	-	-	1,175,000
„ „ „ 1000	-	-	-	587,500

And, following the progress still further backwards, he would perhaps have found but *one solitary inhabitant* of the earth in the time of our Saviour, and the history of the Old Testament would have seemed to him nothing else than a strange fable invented by extravagant minds.[2]

Even supposing that the world were inhabited by only a 1000 individuals 4000 years before the time of Malthus, and granting,

---

[1] Levasseur : *Statistique de la superficie et de la population des contrées de la terre*, 1ᵉʳᵉ partie, table 29.

[2] Voltaire, who was dead before Malthus wrote, had ridiculed the so-called geometrical progression in his *Dictionnaire philosophique.* "The population," he said, "has tripled itself since the era of Charlemagne. I say tripled, and this is much. *The human race does not multiply according to geometrical progression.* All the calculations made about this pretended multiplication are absurb. If a family of men or of monkeys multiplied in this way, the earth would have been long since incapable of supplying them with food. It is like the Fates, who were always spinning and cutting. It has been entirely busied with births and deaths."

for the sake of argument, that the population doubled itself once in a century, Malthus should have found, in his day, 1400 milliards of men upon the earth, that is to say, about 1000 times more than its actual population.

But now that statistics have made such great progress, and the comparison between the population and the means Comparisons between population and the of subsistence in a fixed period of time is no longer means of subsistence. based upon hypotheses, but upon concrete and certain data, in a science of observation it is no longer possible to give the name of law to a theory like that of Malthus, which is in complete disagreement with facts. As our century has been free from the wars, pestilences, and famines which have afflicted other ages, population has increased as it never did before, and, nevertheless, the production of the means of subsistence has far exceeded the increase of men.

Statistical study shows us that, in every civilised country of modern Europe, even in the periods of disordered Increase of population in the 19th century. birth-rate, which have characterised the nineteenth century, the means of subsistence have always exceeded the population, and that the unproductive consumption on the one side and pauperism on the other, increasing with fatal progress, are nothing else but a necessary consequence of the vitiated form of the distribution of wealth, and not of the excessive increase or fecundity of the human species.

The countries where perfection of statistical material and the abundance of research have made the comparison easiest and most certain, have given the recent Malthusians the most complete and severe falsification.

In prolific England, even between 1600 and 1800, that is in a period when a succession of discord and war, and the birth of a new phase of economy, ought to have impeded production, it has, on the contrary, increased much more rapidly than the population.[1]

---

[1] I have compiled the following table upon data furnished by Cunningham : *The statement of the Malthusian Principle* in *Macmillan's Magazine* for December, 1883, and from those given by Giffen: *The Growth of Capital*, pp. 73-110.

POPULATION AND WEALTH IN ENGLAND.

Year.	Population.	National Wealth.	Wealth according to each inhabitant.
	Millions.	Millions Sterling.	£.
1600	4½	100	22
1680	5½	250	46
1690	5½	320	58
1720	6½	370	57
1750	7	500	71
1800	9	1,500	167

Nor has the relation been less encouraging in the present century when the birth-rate has assumed such menacing proportions.[1]

Year.	Population.	National Wealth.	Wealth according to each inhabitant.
	Millions.	Millions Sterling.	£.
1812	17	2,700	160
1822	21	2,500	120
1833	25	3,600	144
1845	28	4,000	143
1865	30	6,000	200
1875	33	8,500	260
1887	37	10,000	270

In France the national wealth has grown much more rapidly
Population and wealth in France. than the population, even when unsuccessful wars and a spendthrift policy have, for a long time, threatened to arrest or reduce the annual capitalisation of the rich and powerful nation.[2]   The population of France, which some-

---

[1] Giffen : *loc. cit.*; Cunningham : *op. cit.*, p. 699.

[2] On the valuations of the national wealth of France at different epochs, see De Foville : *La France économique*, Paris, 1890, chap. xxxii., and see also the conference of the same author on *La fortune de la France.*

what exceeded twenty-four millions towards the end of the last century, was more than thirty-eight millions in 1891.[1] But the production of grain, which Lavoisier calculated in 1789 to be about thirty-one millions of *hectolitres* reached a hundred and nineteen and a half millions in 1890.[2]

The average consumption of corn in France for every inhabitant[3]

In 1821,   ... *hectolitres*, 1·53

„ 1862,   ...   „   1·85

„ 1872,   ...   „   2·11

„ 1888,   ...   „   2·70

The consumption of other kinds of food increased not less rapidly : the consumption of meat, which was seventeen *kilogrammes* a year for each inhabitant in 1788 had, on the contrary, a century later, in 1888, reached 30·360 *kilogrammes.*[4]

In the United States of America, that is, in.the country which suggested to Malthus his terrible law of population, the same phenomenon has occurred and still occurs.[5]

Population and wealth in America.

Years.	Total of Wealth.	Wealth for each inhabitant.
	Milliards of Francs.	Francs.
1790	3,7	955
1810	7,5	1,035
1830	13,3	1,030
1850	35,8	1,540
1860	80,8	2,565
1870	128,7	3,340
1880	212,8	4,210
1888	350,?	?

[1] Schoene: *op. cit.*, p. 216 ; Block : *Annuaire de l'économie politique pour* 1892, p. 1.

[2] Schoene : *op. cit.*, p. 405.

[3] Block : *Statistique de la France*, ii., 389, *Tableaux statistiques du Ministère de l'Agriculture.*

[4] *Tableaux*, etc.

[5] De Foville : *op. cit.*, p. 523.

Notwithstanding the great density of population in Belgium, the medium of consumption has rapidly increased, even among the working classes.

Population and wealth in Belgium.

Articles of food consumed by the Belgian working man, calculated according to months :—

		1853.	1886.	1891.
Bread	kil.	15·920	17·677	20·770
Potatoes	,,	22·573	21·966	17·866
Meat and bacon	,,	757	1·627	1·828
Butter and fat	,,	875	1·233	1·246

Therefore the Belgian working man at present consumes 4·850 kil. more bread than in 1883 ; the consumption of meat has increased by 1·071 kil.; that of butter and fat by 371 grammes. The consumption of potatoes has decreased, while the consumption of bread and of substances rich in fat and in albumen has notably increased.[1]

We could, moreover, demonstrate without difficulty that all statistical reports concur in showing that in every country, which has passed from the agricultural period into the phase of industrial and commercial civilisation, the increase of population has followed the increase of the means of subsistence.

The greatest mistake which Malthus made was in placing the law of population outside of man and not in man. The greater the riches of a country, the greater can be the population ; but the population *always has an organic and virtual tendency* to adapt itself to the means of subsistence.

Organic and virtual tendency to adaptation.

The most thickly populated countries are, in fact, either those where the national wealth is very great, or where needs are very slight. Thus, while the frugal population of China has multiplied most rapidly by reason of their frugality, the peoples of Europe, compelled by climate and habit, to a more expensive and substan-

[1] A. Julin : *Une enquête en Belgique sur les salaires, les prix et les budgets ouvriers* in the *Réforme Sociale* for November 16, 1892, p. 761.

tial manner of food, have unconsciously limited their fecundity. But there is an organic and virtual tendency in human nature itself, which hinders the population from increasing beyond certain given limits, and which causes it to continually adapt itself to the means of subsistence.

Famine, massacres, wars of extermination, far from being caused by an excess of population, are hardly ever anything else than the effect of vitiated social organisation. And the virtual tendency to which I have referred, is so strong and general, Relation between the number of marriages, that even Malthusian statisticians have uncon- the birth-rate and the price of articles of sciously recognised it. Even in 1847, Quételet food. pointed out a singular relation between the price of grain and the number of marriages ; later almost all statisticians perceived this relation, and Bela Weisz even went so far as to give it a solid basis of statistical proofs.[1] "It is clear," said Guillard, "that the twofold production of corn and of men has proceeded in a parallel proportion, and with perceptibly equal measure. In two-thirds of a century, owing to clearing, drying, or some improvement in the division of land, and afterwards owing to cultivation, the production of corn has increased at about 49 per cent., and from this cause alone, notwithstanding so many obstacles of every kind, epidemics, sanguinary wars, and not less murderous poverty, the population has increased in the same proportion."[2]

Only a few years ago Hector Denis, in a learned memoir, showed that the number of marriages in Belgium has followed the increase and decrease of the prices of coal.[3] If the research were further prosecuted, there is no doubt that it would quite clearly appear that *the production of men virtually tends to proportion itself to the production of the means of subsistence.*

[1] Bela Weisz : *Die Ehe-Frequenz in ihrer Abhängigkeit von den Getreidpreisen* in *Statistiche Monatschrift*, Wien, 1879. See also Villermé in the *Journal des économistes* for 1843, vol. vi. ; Buckle : *Histoire de la civilisation en Angleterre*, vol. i., chap. i., etc.

[2] Guillard : *Éléments de statistique humaine*, Paris, 1855.

[3] H. Denis : *Recherches sur la matrimonialité en Belgique. De ses rapports avec les prix du blé et de la houille* in the *Bulletin de la Société d'Anthropologie*, vol. i., 1883.

Generally speaking, the countries which have a great mortality *Relation between births and deaths.* have also a great birth-rate and *vice versa ;* we may almost say that death calls for life, and that there is something unconscious and fatal in this vicissitude of things.

Wars, famines, and epidemics, are generally succeeded by years of a very high birth-rate.

In France in the two years preceding 1870, the birth-rate was only 28·5 ; but after the very high death-rate produced by the war and the small-pox of 1870-71, the birth-rate rose in 1872, and for some years following remained at 26·7.

In Prussia, while for the two years preceding 1870 the birth-rate was 39, it increased and remained at 41·5 for the three succeeding years.[1]

When the despotic French sovereign cynically said that a Parisian night was sufficient to fill up the vacancies of his army, he spoke a fact, from the social point of view, and he expressed, moreover, a profound demographic truth.

In 1868, Finland suffered from a terrible scarcity, which increased the death-rate ; but a remarkable fecundity during many years filled up the gaps.[2]

The parallelism between the births and deaths is, therefore, so evident that no one can venture to question it.

The peoples who increase most rapidly either follow the increase *The peoples who increase most rapidly* of production (England, Germany and Belgium) or adapt themselves to a smaller consumption made possible to them by their ethnical character and surroundings (China).

The famines of the past, which seemed to Malthus to be the *Famines in the past and the economic order.* terrible penalty inflicted by nature upon those who attempted to do it violence by wishing to sit at the banquet of life, when all the places were taken, were caused, as we have already said, by the insufficient market and

[1] *Cf.* Bertillon : *art. cit.*, p. 37.
[2] Bertillon : article, *Finlande* in the *Dictionnaire encyclopédique des sciences médicales.*

the economic order, and not by natural causes. In France, under the old régime, in periods of great distress, regions where men perished of hunger, bordered upon others where there was a menace of a superabundance of grain. Even where means of communication were not wanting, the internal duties very frequently caused the crops of one province to be insufficient, and caused deaths and atrocious suffering, while in another they rotted in the granaries, and by their cheapness were the cause of much more evil than good.[1]

The extreme localisation of the sale of grain, as we have said, caused death in one province, while in another, their abundance caused ruin. The rural population of France, at a time when it was not as numerous by one-third as at present, in periods of bad harvests was often obliged to live upon roots and herbs.[2]

But even then the form of social constitution caused a number of births not above the economic capacity of the country.

The less advanced nations, and the classes which are least elevated, when overcome with discouragement, *The peoples who allow themselves to be extinguished.* and when they do not believe that their abasement and wretchedness will end, allow themselves to perish of slow *anemia* rather than increase a race or class, in whose future they have no faith or hope.

Already, long before the days of Malthus, the Marquis d'Argenson noted this singular fact in his memoirs : *Some observations of d'Argenson.* " In this country parts where I live, I heard it said that the population and marriage are quite dying out on all sides. In my parish, where there is little passion, there are more than thirty young men and women who have been already marriageable for some time ; they never marry and they do not even think of it. If others prompt them to it, they all make one reply, that it is not worth bringing into the world other unfortunates as miserable as they themselves."[3]

---

[1] Taine : *Les origines de la France contemporaine*, tom. i., *L'ancien Regime.*

[2] Van der Smissen : *op. cit.*, p. 249.

[3] D'Argenson : *Journal et Mémoires*, published by Rathery, vol. ii., p. 322.

The intervention of positive or destructive measures is, therefore, not only unnecessary, but has never been necessary in order to proportion a people or race to its means of subsistence and to its commerce. We shall afterwards see that if there has at any time been an excess of population, owing to given economic causes, the birth-rate has, in every case, simply followed the continual and increasing movement of the production of the means of subsistence for the most part, and that, as often as the population of a country has halted in its increase, the cause of this cessation should be much rather sought for in reasons of political and social kind, than in reasons of an economic kind.

Moreover, there is nothing vaguer than the word, *means of subsistence,* which many demographers and statisticians have used so much and so badly.

Civilisation and the means off subsistence.

The quantity of the means of subsistence necessary for the life and progress of each species varies greatly according to the race, and differs very much in the same race according to the greater or lesser degree of civilisation arrived at, and according to the various systems of distribution of wealth.

If, by means of subsistence, we mean not only what is closely bound up with the needs of alimentation, but the total of the things necessary to an individual in a given degree of civilisation, we see that no other word has a more varied and variable signification.

What is meant by means of subsistence.

Even in the question of alimentation we must admit that our ancestors had far fewer wants than we have, and that they lived much more poorly than we. The satires of Juvenal, so full of exaggeration and rhetoric, and the poems and histories of very unimpartial Roman writers, have hitherto caused the belief that the rich classes of Roman society were made up of greedy *gourmands.* On the contrary, Renan says that the ancients were of quite an extraordinary frugality, one which we can only imitate and realise with difficulty.[1]

---

[1] Renan : *Marc-Aurèle et la fin du monde antique.*

Putting aside abstemious emperors, like Marcus Aurelius, for whose nourishment a few vegetables sufficed,[1] *The means of subsistence in antiquity.* even the richer classes were satisfied with a food which would be readily rejected by a common man in an advanced state of society.

Horace, who has been handed down to posterity as one who enjoyed life, had very moderate tastes.

> " Vivitur parvo bene cui paternum
> Splendet in mensa tenui salinum." [2]

The articles of food mentioned by Horace were very simple :

> " Inde domum me
> Ad porri et ciceris refero laganique catinum." [3]

And he says elsewhere :

> " O quando faba Pythagorae cognata simulque
> Unctu satis pingui ponentur oluscula lardo." [4]

A few vegetables cooked with fat supplied him with healthy and nourishing food. *Frugality of the ancients.*

The food of the lower classes and of slaves was such as would satisfy no working man of to-day.[5]   In ancient Rome, even the soldiers, who were exposed to great fatigues, and who had to march great distances, subsisted on a food greatly inferior both in quality and quantity to that of modern soldiers.[6]

---

[1] *Ibid.*   [2] Horace : *Carmina*, ii., 16.

[3] Horace : *Satyrae*, i., 6 ; v., 115.   [4] Horace : *Satyrae*, ii., 6 ; v., 63.

[5] Wheat, when boiled *(puls pulmentum)*, or in the form of bread, was the principal food of a Roman. A. Bouché-Leclercq : *Manuel des Institutions Romaines*, Paris, 1886, p. 224. Cato, who was a great usurer and wary creditor (Deloume: *Les manieurs d'argent a Rome*, Paris, 1890, p. 81), tells us that the Romans gave to their slaves as their only food, an amount of bread weighing about 1·300 grammes. Piret : *Traité d'économie rurale*, Brussels, 1890, vol. ii., p. 247.

[6] *Cf.* K. A. Souklar : *Ueber die Heeres Verwaltung der alten Römer in Frieden und Krieg*, Innsbruck, 1848, and Langen: *Ueber die Heeres Verpflegung der Römer in letzten Jahrh der Republik*, vol. i. *(Programm der Gymnasium in Brieg, 1878.)*

What is now thought indispensable was a luxury a century
Luxury in antiquity. ago ; the shirt, which not even a countryman of
our day could dispense with, was at a time, not so remote from
ours, so rare an object as to cause the loss of his crown to a
Swedish king, who hoped to preserve his own though disguised as
a rustic.[1]

Our ancestors made long journeys on foot, and often went to
labour in distant regions, leading a life of poverty in the countries
through which they passed.[2] Now even an ordinary working-
man goes by *omnibus* from one quarter of a city to another. In
the sixteenth century, Slaney, an English author, speaking on
Rural Expenditure, was indignant at seeing oak wasted in building, whereas willow-boughs had been previously used. "Formerly,
houses were built of willow-boughs, but the men were men of
oak ; now the contrary is the case." The chronicle of Hollinshed
deplores that the refinement of his contemporaries (1577) goes so
far as to make them build chimneys, instead of letting the smoke
go where it would, and even to replace wooden vases by others of
clay.[3] Luther relates that during his youth even the richest of
his friends only drank water.

A few centuries ago there was neither tobacco, coffee or sugar ;
The standard of life in alcoholic substances were almost unknown ; they
the past. are now articles of popular consumption, of which
few can afford to deprive themselves. Nay, so far have they
penetrated into the wants of the people, that, as Bela Weisz has
demonstrated, in countries where the standard of life is very high,
at every increase in the price of grain, it is observed that the
people make restrictions rather in the consumption of articles of
primary necessity than in that of the superfluous articles.[4]

[1] Laveleye : *Le luxe*, Verviers, 1887, chap. iv.

[2] *Cf.* Laveleye : *Le luxe*, pp. 13, 14 ; Roscher : *Die Grundlagen der
Nationalökonomie*, iv., 2 ; Nitti : *L'ora presente*, Turin, Roux and comp.,
1893.

[3] On this point see the interesting monographs on the life of working
men in the middle ages, and in the sixteenth, seventeenth and eighteenth
centuries which have been published in the *Réforme Sociale* of Paris.

[4] Bela Weisz : *art. cit.*

If the changes between epoch and epoch are so fundamental, the differences between different races of men are still more so ; while the poor inhabitant of the desert of Kalakari, even though compelled to struggle with the asperity of the climate and the unclemency of the situation, periodically supports long parts and lives upon very little ; [1] while many tens of millions of the inhabitants of India scarcely even eat vegetable substances, and deprive themselves of all animal food ; [2] while in China a little rice is sufficient to nourish an adult working man; [3] in Europe, and in more civilised countries, even a man who performs but little work is obliged to spend much more in regard to his food.

The great inequality of riches—though, on the one hand, it compels the masses of the people to live poorly, on the other hand, encourages unproductive consumption and raises the standard of food of the wealthier classes—has brought it about that the upper classes in every civilised country eat more than is necessary, and even beyond what their constitution can bear without harm. The art of enjoyment, in so individualist a society as ours, as a renowned German moralist has observed, never goes below the level of champagne and oysters. [4] A French physiologist, Charles Richet, in replying to Tolstoï, who, with his artistic insight, had already perceived the dangers of such excessive food, [5] asserted that physiologists have exactly measured the food necessary to a man, and have found that for a day of twenty-four hours 125 grammes of flesh, 300 grammes of bread, 300 grammes of potatoes, and 50 grammes of butter and cheese

The distribution of wealth and the problem of the means of subsistence.

The food of modern peoples.

[1] Zaborouski : *L'avenir des races humaines* in the *Revue scientifique* for December 17th, 1892.

[2] L. Theureau : *L'alimentation dans l'Inde* in the *Revue scientifique* for September 17th, 1892.

[3] Piret : *loc. cit.*

[4] T. H. Ziegler : *Die sociale Frage eine sittliche Frage*, chap. iii.

[5] L. Tolstoï : *Notre alimentation* in the *Revue scientifique* for August 20th, 1892. Voltaire had already said (in *L'Homme aux quarante écus*) that if the average of life was to be prolonged men must eat less.

suffice for an adult. This amount of food is physiologically adapted to every man in ordinary conditions. Nevertheless, observes Richet with regret, every day each of us exceeds this limit to the great detriment of his health.[1]

Hufeland has said that the majority of men eat more than necessity calls for, and the practice of making children eat more than is needful causes them to lose in early childhood the instinct which tells them when they have had sufficient.[2]

The problem of population must be chiefly considered from the Population and the social system. standpoint of the distribution of wealth with which it is strictly bound up. We can assert that *a country* which, in the actual form of economic constitution, is capable of sustaining a certain number of individuals, could sustain a much greater number when the economic form is changed in the direction of a wider distribution of the wealth produced. Against this truth, essential to anyone who would thoroughly grasp the phenomenon of population, some theorists have ventured to raise arguments, which do not well sustain even the slightest scrutiny.

" The millionaire," writes Block, " does not consume an entire The classic thesis. ox, or a hundredweight of bread ; and if he pays their weight in gold for a dish of Chinese birds' nests, no one need be jealous of it. The main point is that he can only consume the ration of a single man, so that there are others for other men, for those who can gain them in the first place, and next for the sick and incapable." [3]

A long process of reasoning is not necessary to demonstrate the Fallacy of the classic thesis. fallacy and puerility of this thesis. It may be unnecessary to know what is the nutritive power of the food of the richer classes ; it may even be that luxurious food is either slightly nutritive or altogether hurtful.

---

[1] C. Richet: *L'alimentation et le luxe* in the *Revue scientifique* for September 24th, 1892.

[2] Hufeland : *Macrobiotik*, part ii., chap. xii.

[3] Block : *L'Europe politique et sociale*, 2nd edit., Paris, 1893, pp. 304, 305.

But a dish of Chinese birds' nests, if it contains nutritive elements inferior to those contained in a *chilo* of flesh-meat, costs a great deal, and its price is, at least in great part, in relation to the efforts made to find and carry it. What is true of luxury in general may be said of luxurious living in particular. A rare dish, like a rare lace, generally represents a greater or less amount of time, and their social utility does not compensate for the effort necessary for its production.

As we have already seen, it has been abundantly proved that one of the most imperious laws of society, the law ᵁⁿᵖʳᵒᵈᵘᶜᵗⁱᵛᵉ ᵉˣᵖᵉⁿˢᵉ which has been the chief cause of progress, but ᵃⁿᵈ ᵗʰᵉ ˡᵃʷ ᵒᶠ ⁱᵐⁱᵗᵃᵗⁱᵒⁿ. which very often is one of the chief causes of decadence, is the law of imitation.[1] When the upper classes abandon themselves to luxury, the working classes are compelled to imitate their example, making an ill practice of unproductive consumption. A strictly individualist order of things, in a state of society which is in advanced economic phases, and where wealth is almost the only, or at least the most influential, real cause of competition, necessarily leads not only to luxury, but to an ostentation of luxury. Useless or parasitical industries, which are engendered by the exaggerations of luxury which invade all classes, daily produce an enormous dispersion of energy and strength.

Thus, in our state of society, the term *means of subsistence* has come to express not only the total of natural ᵀʰᵉ ᵐᵉᵃⁿˢ ᵒᶠ ˢᵘᵇˢⁱˢᵗ⁻ needs, but a total of artificial needs originated by ᵉⁿᶜᵉ ⁱⁿ ᵗʰᵉ ᵃᶜᵗᵘᵃˡ ˢᵗᵃᵗᵉ ᵒᶠ ˢᵒᶜⁱᵉᵗʸ. given economic surroundings, and hence very changeable needs, and such as will change in passing from a strictly individualist economic phase to a phase of ordered and intelligent social co-operation.

Now a large part of these industrial efforts are originated by the need of providing not the necessaries of life, but its superfluities, and often what is simply evil. As a truthful writer has said : " Industry which is both an economist and an industrialist, finding customers chiefly among the rich, necessarily applies itself

---

[1] *Cf.* Tarde : *Les lois de l'imitation*, Paris, 1890.

in great measure to producing objects of luxury, leaving unsatisfied many needs of primary necessity ; so that our economic system prepares exquisite and often hurtful delicacies for the rich, and does not succeed in procuring beds for all the citizens." [1]

The luxury of the society of to-day is far less the expression of a strong desire for enjoyment than the assertion of economic superiority ; fashion, which is its widest manifestation, has become what Jhering calls a hunt after class vanity. [2]

Luxury and the means of subsistence.

I do not wish to enter here upon the question, already so often discussed, as to whether luxury be productive or unproductive from an economic point of view, or licit or illicit from an ethical point of view.

It is well, however, to make note of at least one fact. The rich burgesses of the Middle Ages made the front of their houses simple, and reserved rich and costly decorations for the interior of their apartments. It was a laudable custom, and avoided much enmity and many rancours.

But in our day the opposite custom obtains ; and the luxury of the wealthy classes is hardly anything else but the expression of a need of self-assertion rather than of enjoyment. [3]

Now it must be remembered that luxury has a singular effect upon men's minds. For if the physiology of an individual, his character, habits, and general conception of life be revealed in each of his actions, each of his actions on the other hand reacts upon his entire person. [4] And this is so true that there is not a single

The increase of luxury and the development of unproductive expenses as a necessary consequence of the capitalist order of things.

---

[1] E. Lepetit: *Del Socialismo*, p. 185. See also Tscernicewsky : *Osservazioni critiche su talune dottrine economiche di Stuart Mill*, chap. ii. of the *Biblioteca dell' Economista*, 3rd series.

[2] Jhering : *Der Zweck in Recht*, 2nd edit., vol. ii., p. 238.

[3] Nitti : *L'ora presente*, pp. 27-30.

[4] This thesis has been very well proved by T. H. Ziegler : *Sittliches Sein und sittliches Werden*, p. 83, etc. *Cf.* also C. W. Kambli : *Der luxus nach seiner sittlichen und sozialen Bedeutung*, St. Gall, 1890, a somewhat disordered but interesting work, and F. A. Lange : *Die Arbeiterfrage*, 3rd edit., 1875, chap. iii. : *Glück und Glückseligkeit*.

action which can be considered as morally indifferent, and which is without social consequences.

The luxury of our modern society not only begets envy, but an unhealthy emulation, which even takes possession of those who are not in a position to share in it. Hence there is a contest of vanity, an acute rivalry, which fictitiously raises the standard of life and menaces even the existence of society by begetting in all a deep sense of misery.[1] Naturally, and in consequence of that terrible law of imitation from which no society is exempt, the popular class does not succeed in escaping the force of the contagion. And progressing in wealth, it feels much less the need of participating in the ideal goods of intellectual progress and culture, than that of imitating the richer classes in unproductive and dangerous expenses, in the expenses which increase vanity and inflame the senses.

It is sufficient to examine the family accounts of working men to see that the example of the upper classes is dangerous to them, and exercises a very evil influence upon the conditions of existence and upon morality.

Mr. Gould, who has directed American inquiry towards the conditions of labour in Europe and in the United States of America, and who has succeeded in establishing exact data upon the amount gained *Family accounts of the working classes and unproductive expenses.* and spent by each family of the labouring class, has abundantly proved that even among the labouring classes of modern society unproductive consumption occupies a large place.[2]

Summing up some of the data furnished by Gould, we find that in the families of men employed in the coal industry wages and expense are thus distributed :

[1] Ziegler: *Die soziale Frage eine sittliche Frage*, chap. vi.

[2] See the summary of the inquiry made by E. R. L. Gould himself : *The Social Condition of Labour*, in the acts of the *John Hopkin's University.*

ACCOUNTS OF THE FAMILIES OF MEN EMPLOYED IN THE COAL INDUSTRY.

Nations.	Annual Income of Families.	Lodging.	Food.	Clothing.	Books and Newspapers.	Alcoholic Drinks.	Tobacco.	Other Expenses.	Total of Expenses.	Remainder.
United States	2.751,50	305,95	1.187,20	560,50	26,50	90,45	46,50	406,45	2.623,55	127,95
Great Britain	2.476,25	237,50	1.231,75	331,50	20,35	113,30	53,95	298,30	2.286,60	189,65
Belgium.....	2.132,75	94,80	1.091,30	314,15	6,90	132,50	26,95	190,20	1.856,80	275,95
Germany.....	1.957,45	193,20	968,—	328,60	13,85	57,40	19,30	266,60	1.846,95	110,50

ACCOUNTS OF THE FAMILIES OF MEN EMPLOYED IN THE IRON INDUSTRY.

Nations.	Annual Income of the Family.	Lodging.	Food.	Clothing.	Books and Newspapers.	Alcoholic Drinks.	Tobacco.	Other Expenses.	Total of Expenses.	Remainder.
United States	3.920,55	536,65	1.406,05	619,40	41,25	125,50	65,85	562,80	3.357,50	563,05
Great Britain	2.599,95	266,35	1.130,40	478,80	29,20	103,85	63,65	331,10	2.403,35	196,60
France......	2.323,70	154,90	979,20	445,55	14,75	233,65	26,30	151,10	2.005,45	318,25
Belgium.....	1.796,85	171,15	825,00	417,25	16,85	92,85	28,65	215,50	1.767,25	29,60
Germany....	1.411,00	88,45	737,80	274,75	12,20	73,90	20,25	232,95	1.440,30	—

ACCOUNTS OF THE FAMILIES OF MEN EMPLOYED IN THE STEEL INDUSTRY.

Nations.	Annual Income of Family.	Lodging.	Food.	Clothing.	Books and Newspapers.	Alcoholic Drinks.	Tobacco.	Other Expenses.	Total of Expenses.	Remainder.
United States	3.317,80	432,20	1.270,90	550,45	33,30	132,75	52,40	345,50	2.817,30	500,30
Great Britain	2.945,65	241,55	1.370—	483,60	30,20	169,20	66—	293,55	2.654,10	291,55
Germany (East)	1.250,65	43,50	641,45	238,90	9,65	52,20	21,40	253,85	1.260,95	—

If we were to examine the very numerous monographs on the family which Le Play and his numerous disciples Prevalence and increase of productive expenses. published, we would see at once how much unproductive and hurtful consumption has increased.[1] And, on the other hand, the studies of demographers and sociologists, to which we have referred, show that this kind of consumption has now become so necessary, has so deeply penetrated into our habits, that when the price of the most necessary articles of food is raised, the popular class restricts rather the consumption of the latter than of the former.

Even a century ago social life was much less complex and difficult than it now is, and even the wealthier classes ordinarily dispensed with what now seem indispensable to the working classes.[2]

In the richer countries, such as the United States of America, such useless and pernicious consumption now far Prevalence of useless or hurtful consumption over the consumption of necessaries in the richer countries. exceeds the consumption of necessaries. According to an American journal, *The Manufacturer and Builder*, the sums expended in the United States in 1885 for certain articles of use, in comparison with the expenses of the moral order, were balanced thus:[3]

Drinks:	900 millions of dollars.
Tobacco:	600 millions of dollars.
Bread:	800 millions of dollars.
Meat:	303 millions of dollars.
Iron and steel:	290 millions of dollars.
Wood for building:	223 millions of dollars.
Cotton stuffs:	210 millions of dollars.
Shoemaking:	190 millions of dollars.
Sugar and molasses:	158 millions of dollars.
Public instruction:	85 millions of dollars.
Missions at home and abroad:	5 millions of dollars.

[1] *Cf.* Block: *op. cit.; cf.* also Cheysson and Toque. *Les budgets comparés de cent monographies de familles*, etc., Rome, 1890; and most of all the official Belgian publication: *Salaires et budgets ouvriers en Belgique au mois D'Avril, 1891*, Brussels, 1892, p. 578.

[2] Nitti: *L'ora presente; loc. cit.*, Turin, 1893.

[3] Quoted by Block: *op. cit.*

In every civilised country, sugar, alcohol, tobacco, and coffee were articles of luxury until the beginning of the second half of this century, but they are now articles of the most common use.[1]

Moreover, with a few exceptions, the quantity of the substances most necessary for life consumed, if measured for each individual, has almost doubled itself in our day[2]

In a state of advanced civilisation, therefore, the term, *means of subsistence*, assumes, as we have shown, a very wide meaning. The means of subsistence of which we have need continually vary with the progress of civilisation. And they vary, moreover, and in a greater degree, according to the existing social order and the systems of distribution of wealth.

Extreme changeableness of needs.

The food of all the richer classes of our day has become infinitely superior to the food of past ages. It is impossible to conceive how much we now eat for simple luxury.

If it is true on the one hand that primitive man had nearly the same physiological needs as the man in an advanced state of society, and that the former consumed almost the very same quantity of azote, carbon and hydrogen, it is true on the other hand that our food is greater and more abundant, and that we eat many things either through *gourmandise* or habit, and not to satisfy physiological needs.[3]

Luxurious food.

And this need of luxurious food spreads from the middle classes to the labouring classes, which, especially in great cities, are

---

[1] Block: *op. cit.*, chap. xi.

[2] *Cf.* James Caird : *General View of British Agriculture* in the *Journal of the Royal Agricultural Society of England*, vol. xiv. part ii., p. 35 ; Piret : *Traité d'économie rurale*, vol. ii., book iv., chap. ii.

[3] A french physiologist says : "Compare the food of a rich Parisian *bourgeois* of 1891 with that of a French peasant of the seventeenth century, or of a contemporary *moujik* or of an Indian or an Arab, and it will be seen that all, or almost all, the food of the *bourgeois* is luxurious : white bread, meat, fresh vegetables, wine and coffee ; these are articles of food which he could dispense with without any danger of death by hunger. But he is accustomed to luxury, and this *recherché* food has become indispensable to him." Charles Richet : *Dans cent ans*, Paris, 1892, pp. 147, 148.

drawn by the fatal law of imitation to sacrifice the need of nourishing substances to the desire for more tasteful food. Richet says : All the inhabitants of cities are great eaters in comparison with the inhabitants of the country, and the country people of our day eat more and better than their ancestors. The necessity for well-being and comfort increases continually, and it is a fatal progress. When a step has been taken in advance, there is no possibility of receding.[1]

The density of population possible to a country, and compatible with the production of the means of subsistence, varies therefore according to the economic condition which the country in question has reached.

Levasseur, calculating upon land of medium fertility, and studying the density of population in relation to civilisation, has proved that we can divide the historic periods of population into five great phases.[2]

In the first state, that is, during the *barbaric period*, the population is necessarily slight. Being obliged to live by hunting, barbarous populations are necessarily less dense, and this is still more true if the countries which they inhabit have a cold or torrid climate. Thus, among the Esquimaux, Nordenskiöld has found two inhabitants for every hundred *kilomètres*, q. e., and in the province of Amazonas in Brazil there are only three inhabitants for every hundred *kilomètres* q.

In the *pastoral period* the same territory can support a greater number of men, but it can only support very few. Hence, in the steppes of Kirghisi, there is but one inhabitant for every *kilomètre* q., and in the three provinces of Turkestan from 0·5 to 2·7 for every *kilomètre* q.

In the *period of agricultural civilisation* human development has much smaller obstacles, and the density of population in favourable conditions may reach forty inhabitants for every *kilomètre* q.

[1] Richet : *op. cit.*, pp. 148, 149.

[2] Levasseur : *Les causes et les limites de la population dans le monde* in *Séances et travaux de l'Académie de sciences morales et politiques*, May, 1892.

In the *period of industrial civilisation* active exchange between the cities and the country, and progress in the methods of cultivation, gives the soil a real but artificial fertility, and allow of a population four times superior to that of the preceding period—160 inhabitants for each *kilomètre* q.

In the *period of commercial civilisation*, that is to say, at an economic period, which, owing to the activity of the exchanges, allows of the importation of a large number of articles of food for industrial products, the density is almost unlimited, and entire states, both in modern and in ancient history, have existed on very limited territories.

These observations of Levasseur, which are substantially true,

Consequences of Levasseur's theory. show us that the earth could even maintain a population infinitely superior to the actual one. The countries of the world which have entered into the phase of commercial civilisation are very few ; many are still in the phase of industrial civilisation, and still more are in the period of agricultural civilisation, while entire continents still largely belong to the barbarous and pastoral periods.

It is well to note here that the automatic excess of population, which occurs in the three primitive periods, the barbarous, pastoral, and the agricultural, and also, although in a slighter degree, in the fourth, has been the greatest cause of human progress, since it has compelled entire populations to either undergo a transformation or to decay, and it has forced the primitive civilisation to leave the static period and to enter upon the dynamic period.[1] But as humanity became civilised, and as the last two phases succeeded to the three earlier, so the production of men has always proportioned itself to the production of the means of subsistence.

There could not, therefore, be a greater mistake than the belief that population is regulated by fatal laws external to mankind,

[1] All ancient histories demonstrate that the law of population acted with great severity in the first periods of mankind, originating war, emigration and transformation. In the 13th chapter of Genesis we find an instance of this.

and to consider fecundity as solely dependant upon natural causes.

Predictions with regard to population, at least those hitherto made by the followers and adversaries of Malthus, are not, nor can be, anything more than hypo- Predictions about population. thesis, based upon extremely changeable and changing data, and vainly seeking to make the future clear.

Nothing, therefore, is more absurd than such conjectures. The increase of population constitutes a phenomenon, the limits of which it is difficult to determine, a phenomenon strictly bound up with intellectual and economic progress, and having the chief cause of its changes in the continual vicissitudes of economic phases.

Walpole thought that towards the end of the sixteenth century England had a population of slightly less than Walpole's calculation. five millions, and towards the end of the seventeenth, six millions. The eighteenth century added 2,800,000 souls, and made the population 8,873,000. But the first forty-five years of the nineteenth century' gave an increase of five millions. Hence, while the annual increase was 10,000 persons in the seventeenth century, and 28,000 in the eighteenth century, it was 180,000 persons from 1807 to 1846.[1]

Had any one, says Dr. Bertillon, sought to forecast the time when the population of France would be doubled, Bertillon's calculation. making his calculation between 1821 and 1831, he would have calculated a period of 101 years ; if, on the contrary, between 1845 and 1857, using not less exact data, he would have predicted a period of 314 years.[2]

There are nations in Europe which, for a long time, have had an annual increase of more than nine for a thou- Error of the demographic hypothesis. sand inhabitants (Denmark, Russia, Germany, Greece, Holland and England) ; there are others (Norway and Belgium) which have an increase of eight, and others which have an increase of seven (Italy and the Austrian Empire). Now the empirics would have us believe that the first have an increase in

[1] Walpole : *History of England*, vol. vi., p. 339.
[2] Bertillon in the *Encyclopédie d'hygiène*, vol. i., p. 140.

77 years, the second in 87, the third in 95.   Yet could this ever be true ?

And now a short-sighted demographist could judge from the same calculations how many years hence France and Ireland are destined to disappear, unless they be invaded by foreign nations.

The birth-rate is subject to laws which were utterly unknown The laws of population. to Malthus and the Malthusians.   We have seen nations enter upon a period of great civilisation, become rich, have a very dense population, and then suddenly become unpopulous and decadent from a slow *anemia*.   And on the other hand we have seen nations which long remained in a state of slight civilisation, become rapidly populated and the centres of a new civilisation under the influences of external causes.   Many ancient states civilised came to an end not by invasions or war, but solely by a cessation of the birth-rate.

Malthus' law explains nothing just as it comprehends nothing. Bound by rigid formulas which are belied by history and demography, it is incapable of explaining not only the mystery of poverty but the alternate reverses of human civilisation.

As we shall afterwards see, population, like every natural phenomenon, is subject to general laws which it is impossible to violate.   Thus, statistical examination shows that the birth-rate scarcely ever goes below 20 births for a 100 inhabitants, and scarcely ever beyond 50.

But all the oscillations which occur between 20 and 50, are but necessary results not of a biologically fatal law, but of economic and social laws, which vary with the change of civilisation and of economic constitution.

If we prescind from an ethical fact and study the causes which Causes which produce the development and limitation of population. most strongly influence population, we shall see that these last can be summarised in three great categories :—

(1) Psychical and moral causes :
    (*a*) Religion.
    (*b*) Morality.
    (*c*) Esthetics.

(2) Social causes :
    (*a*) Political organisatiou.
    (*b*) Social divisions.

(3) Economic causes :
    (*a*) The distribution of wealth.

The causes of a psychical order, although at first sight they appear to be of slight importance, exercise a perpetual and unceasing influence upon population, which is only the greater because it appears to be less. A strictly individualist state of society, where the wealthy classes are ruled by the strictest egotism, and the inferior classes drawn by their evil example, is a state of society in which the social duty of fecundity cannot be scrupulously fulfilled. When individual idealism and the want of solidarity impel each individual to place all his ideality in himself, population must necessarily be affected by it.

Morality is one of the least studied but most important demographic factors. In reality the question of the de-   *Morality and the development of population of France is purely and simply a* population. question of morality.[1] Thus spoke Guyau, one of the most profound intellects produced by modern France.

And a truthful observer, Doctor Rochard, in his treatise on social hygiene, justly observes : "A family of five or six children was once an ordinary thing; now it is regarded as a veritable affliction. The unhappy parents are blamed ; the fact is regretted, and this is worse ; they are laughed at, and this is worst of all ; and this is the reason why the upper classes are failing." [2]

There are two ways of making money in a nation which is in a state of advanced progress :

(1) Working much and producing much so that the production exceed the consumption.

(2) Consuming the least possible and working the least possible.

Every nation which has an egoistical morality tends much rather to the second system than to the first.   *Literary influences.*

[1] Guyau : *L'irréligion de l'avenir*, Paris, 1887, p. 276.
[2] J. Rochard : *Traité d'hygiène sociale*, p. 322.

Notwithstanding all the persecutions and troubles which it has been condemned to suffer for centuries, the little Jewish people has maintained itself, and has increased simply because it has always considered marriage as the first duty of mankind, and because it has maintained and still maintains the family ideal.[1]

Putting aside economic causes, which we shall elsewhere examine, no one will deny that the literature of England and France has exercised different influences upon the development of both peoples.

English literature has never attacked the family ideal; even the least optimist novelists, the most dissatisfied

English literature and the family ideal.

poets, have never striven to destroy the familiar poetry of home, sweet home. Poets, comic writers and novelists have, on the contrary, delighted in describing numerous families. The house full of children is one of the most beautiful ideals of life in English novels.

A French demographic writer relates that two or three years ago *Friend Fritz* was being represented in a very aristocratic London theatre. When the Rabbin pronounced his eloquent tirade against bachelors, the whole audience enthusiastically rose to their feet, and began to loudly applaud.[2]

On the other hand, more especially in the second half of our century, French literature, which is a reflection of

French literature induces to the single state.

the morality of the dominant class, has been fatal to the spirit of family unity. Plays, novels, and poetry, being imbued with a spirit of individual idealism, have not ceased to instil the subtle poison of egotism into the public mind. In a great deal of quite recent French literature, husband is almost a synonym for a deceived man, wife almost always a synonym for an adulteress, and the friend who deceives almost always a synonym for a man of spirit. It is sufficient to read the most popular novels and to hear the best known plays to conclude that,

---

[1] Voltaire ; *Dictionnaire philosophique*, under the word *Mariage*, has quite seized this truth.

[2] Mille : *Le néo-malthusianisme en Angleterre* in the *Revue des deux mondes* for December 15, 1891.

according to the prevalent morality, marriage is an evil affair which must be avoided, or if incurred at all, then as late as possible, and a numerous offspring is an absolute evil which must be hindered at any cost.

The reader may remember how, in the *Francillon* of the younger Dumas, one of the most successful dramas of the day, two women of the aristocracy, Countess Francine de Riverolles and Baroness Theresa Smith, speak of their children : The family ideal in the French theatre.

Thérèse—Et tu n'as qu'un enfant ?
Francine—Combien veux—tu que j'en aie ?   Je ne suis mariée que depuis un an, dix mois et sept jours, je ne peux pas en avoir cinq comme toi.
Thérèse—Dont deux jumeaux.
Francine—Quelle horreur !   Et tu les a tous nourris ?
Thérèse—Tous.
Francine—Même les jumeaux.
Thérèse—Même les jumeaux.
Francine—Miséricorde !

And an intelligent demographer, recalling the impression which this scene of *Francillon* always has upon the French public, adds : " Whoever has assisted at the play knows that the audience is in sympathy with it.   It assents to the thought of the young French wife, Francine : *Cinq enfants, dont deux jumeaux, quelle horreur ! Et la mere les a nourris tous, meme les jumeaux, miséricorde ! Francine only says what everyone thinks.*" [1]

And in one of Zola's recent novels, *Le Docteur Pascal*, there is a young woman, Clotilde, who unconsciously en- Reaction against this tendency of French literature. tertains an aversion for that arid and sterile literature which neither understands, nor feels, nor loves maternity.   "*Mais surtout, son continuel étonnement, sa continuelle indignation étaient de voir que, dans les romans d'amour, on ne se préoccupe jamais de l'enfant. Il n'y était pas même prévu, et quand, par hasard, il tombait au milieu des aventures du cœur, c'était un catastrophe, une stupeur et un embarras considérable. Jamais les*

[1] Van der Smissen : *op. cit.*, p. 393.

amants, corsqu'ils s'abandonnaient aux bras l'un de l'autre, ne sem-blaient se douter qu'ils faisient œuvre de vie et qu'un enfant allait naître. Cependant, ses études d'histoire naturelle lui avaient montré que le fruit était l'unique souci de la nature."

In face of this fact even the Conservative schools become alarmed. "*Les enfants,*" says the Viscount de Vogüé with sorrow, "*on a quelquefois, cela arrive encore.*"[1]

The influence of religion upon the birth-rate is not less evident, and forms part of the very large and complex cate-gory of influences belonging to the psychical and moral order.

Religion and the birth-rate.

The scope of every religion is that of fixing the soul upon a dis-tant object: personal salvation. Nevertheless, this unity of ideal scope has succeeded in creating strong connections between very different ethical groups, and in giving a broad idea of social duties even to primitive populations.[2] On the other hand, religion in-duces the belief of a providential intervention, and impels races to fecundity, and there is no people more disposed to solidarity than a very fertile people.

The great fecundity of the Jews was largely a consequence of their religion, which abhorred virginity, and of which the heroes were men of numerous families and abundant offspring.[3]

But in all the idealist religions, and chiefly in the Christian religion, individual idealism, in the periods of the greatest religious fervour, always originates a tendency towards the contemplative life, and hence a relative infecundity.

The idealist religions and the birth-rate.

If we study the Gospel we see that matrimony is no longer, as in the Old Testament, the great means of propagating the species;

---

[1] De Vogüé in the *Reveu des deux mondes* for December 1st, 1889, p. 189.

[2] About the enormous influences exercised by religion upon the birth-rate among ancient peoples, see the book by Fustel de Coulanges : *La cité antique,* 12th edit., p. 90, etc. Sumner Maine, in *Ancient Law,* arrives at the same conclusions.

Cf. Voltaire : *loc. cit.*

if the paternal authority be still held in great honour it is only because it is the earthly representative of the Divine Power.[1]

In the first Epistle of St. Paul to the Corinthians we clearly perceive the sympathy of the Apostle for those who preserve chastity, and are rather bent upon peopling the kingdoms of Heaven than those of earth.

If occasionally, as in the Epistle to Timothy, St. Paul wishes that young widows should marry, have children, become mothers of families, and give no occasion of evil-speaking to the enemy,[2] he is chiefly moved by this last desire, by the wish to avoid sin and scandal.

All the primitive Christian sects, those which carried their idealism furthest, abhorred matrimony; the Manicheans utterly condemned it, the Encratists, the Docetists, the Marcionites, all recommended chastity.

When Christianity arose, oliganthrophy had already shown itself in Greece and in Rome, and economic and social causes continually led more and more to demographic oliganthropy, hence Christianity was disposed to exercise its influence, which limited fecundity.[3] The vacancies which occurred later were speedily filled up by the invasions of the barbarians.

It is true that Christianity has honoured and sanctified matrimony, but it has preferred chastity.[4] The apostles, the saints, the men whom the Churches venerate, have been nearly all chaste, and, in every case, have only reached perfection when they had attained chastity.

Christianity and the birth-rate.

When Aurelius Augustin was still wavering between the im-

---

[1] Schœne : *op. cit.*, chap. v.

[2] 1 Epistle to Timothy, v. 14. Moreover, Paul clearly shows his preference of the state of chastity. See the 1 Epistle to the Corinthians. Indeed, Malthus cites him on his own behalf (book iv., chap. ii) and even a Catholic economist believes the Malthusian moral restraint is to be found in germ in the exhortations of St. Paul (Villeneuve-Bargemont: *Histoire de l'Economie politique des anciens et des modernes*, Paris, 1842, tom. i., 247).

[3] *Cf.* Bucher : *Die Hufslande der unfreienarbeiter*, 1874, chap. iv.

[4] *Cf.* Backouse and Tylor : *Storia della chiesa primitiva fino alla morte di Costantino* (Italian trans.), Rome, 1890, pp. 113 and foll.

pulses of his ardent African nature and Christian asceticism, he felt that he could never attain perfection without chastity. And with wonderful sincerity, not having the courage of seeking it at once, he begged for it in a prayer which has become celebrated : " O Lord, give me chastity and continence, but not at once." [1]

The greatest of the disciples of Christ, he whom Renan has almost ventured to compare to the sublime Teacher Himself, and who, at least, may be considered as the greatest and the purest of Christians, never looked at a woman without a real emotion, as an instrument of sin. The proximity of one caused him alarm. The weak, he used to say, suffer shipwreck ; even the strong lose something on her account. Unless a man be well tried, contact with woman is difficult to escape from, just as it is difficult to walk on coals without burning the soles of one's feet. The proximity of women was compared by him to a sweet poison mixed with honey, which overcame even the saints. [2]

In all lives of the saints, the most meritorious actions and those most generally praised refer to chastity and the resistance to the temptations of the flesh.

The expansive soul of St. Francis only found the ideal comfort proper to a strict and austere life in spiritual relations with a virgin, Clare of Assisi.

But one day the saint perceived that Clare's virgin companions were saddened because they had not seen him for a long time, and he thought too human a desire was manifested in this sadness.

Even an apostle had observed, many centuries before that, at the mystical meetings when the Christians exchanged kisses, there were men and women who repeatedly kissed, as though finding pleasure in it.

Francis, therefore, was saddened at this, and he spoke not a word. After a lengthy prayer, he asked for some ashes and drew a circle around. Silence weighed upon the virgin nuns. Francis

---

[1] See Barzellotti : *Santi, solitari e filosofi*, 2nd edit., Bologna, 1886, p. 20.

[2] See A. Bournet : *Saint Francois d'Assise*, Lyons, 1893, p. 86. See also Karl Hase : *Franz von Assisi*, Leipzig, 1856 ; Taine : *Voyage en Italie*, Paris, 1876, 3rd edit., tom. ii.

rose and said to them : "Let us recite the *Miserere mei Deus.*"
When it was over he got up and went away without speaking a
word.[1]

And there is hardly a single Christian hero who has not resisted the flesh as did Francis. The most elect, the greatest,
condemned themselves to the severe and mortifying chastity of a
life-time.[2]

To show that Christianity, by causing individual idealism,
stimulated to chastity, it is sufficient to observe how, even in our
own day, the minds which are most imbued with the Christian
spirit, such as Leo Tolstoï, still experience a real repulsion, not only
for sensuality, but also for the practice of matrimony, and they
have for their ideal type a state of chastity.[3]

But Christianity, and later, Catholicism, losing its primitive
ascetic fervour, adapted themselves to places and times.[4] With
the disappearance of mysticism, the Christian religion was, and is
still, among modern peoples, a stimulus to fecundity. Indeed, not
unfrequently among the poor, a belief in providential aid leads to
the contracting of matrimony, and the avoidance of celibacy and
fornication.

Hence the economists like Mill and Garnier, who are most
devoted to Malthusianism, display every possible Catholicism according
aversion to Catholicism. Garnier says that the to Mill and Dunoyer.
fatal and *blameworthy* impulse to increase the population is largely
caused by Catholic writers, by Casuists, and by means of the Con-
fessional.[5] Mill, on his part, recognises that the influence of the
Catholic clergy is always in *direct proportion with the development*

---

[1] Bournet : *op. cit.*, pp. 87, 88.

[2] About the ideas of the first Christians on celibacy and chastity, see
Backouse and Tylor : *op. cit.*, pp. 116, 117.

[3] See Tolstoï : *La sonnade à Kreutzer, Le salut est en vous* and *Marchez
pendant que vous avez la lumière.* Tolstoï attributes all the evils of our
society to egoism and sensual love.

[4] *Cf.* Schœne : *loc. cit.*

[5] Garnier : *Principe de Population,* p. 494, See the polemic against
Casuists in the appendix,

of the population, and thinks that Catholic priests must advise matrimony in order to prevent a dissolute life, and fornication.[1]

Some demographists have recently rejected these ideas of Mill, Garnier, and of the followers of the Malthusian school generally. Indeed, Arsène Dumont believes that Catholicism has an op-

Catholicism opposed to a large birth-rate. posite influence in our day. "Can there be," he asks, "a more dangerous book from a social point of view than the *Imitation of Christ?* The solitary reverie, the interminable dialogue with a phantom, not only unnerve a man and put him in an unhealthy torpor, but they inflate his pride and inspire him with a transcendental contempt for the active life, the warm and happy natural expansions, the beneficent family affections, the care of public interests, the functions of a father and a citizen. This is the true quintessence of Catholicism, the *maximum* of its kind; for, if matrimony and the active life are permitted as an inevitable necessity, the ideal is always the life of monks and nuns, the isolated individual, in every case the idle celibate; since the supreme model whom men are called to imitate is a man-God without fatherland, property, regular profession, family, wife, or children, while the model proposed to women is a virgin. . . ."[2]

Now, there is truth in all this, and yet there is evident ex-

Catholicism, individual idealism, and the birth-rate. aggeration.[3] Unquestionably, Catholicism impels to individual idealism; but if this influence be very great in a population whose religious spirit is very strong, and was at one time able to depopulate entire regions, in later times it has exercised very little influence. And in modern nations, on the contrary, especially in agricultural countries,

[1] Mill : *Principles,* book i., chaps. vii., xiii.

[2] A. Dumont : *Dépopulation et civilisation,* Paris, 1890, p. 350, 351.

[3] Dumont even reaches such exaggerations as the following : "The habitual relations between young people of both sexes are the most efficacious remedy against drunkenness, clericalism, and the increase of illegitimacy." And he moreover asserts : "Christianity, become Catholicism, and afterwards Clericalism, is the most perfect instrument for unnerving mankind that the perverse spirit of evil and darkness has ever invented," *op. cit.,* p. 509.

Catholicism, by inspiring a faith in providential help, has always usefully influenced fecundity.

On the other hand, in the countries where Catholicism has lost ground either in the number of believers or in the force of faith, this has occurred far less because of the diffusion of a strong and serene social faith, than because of the diffusion of egotistical sentiments, and a vague feeling of pessimism which has largely penetrated the mass of the people. And this, increasing the causes of individual idealism, according to the state of men's minds, has produced an increased infecundity even in Catholic countries.

Now, if religion in general be a demographical factor of great importance, each religion acts differently, according to its spirit and tendencies.

How can a Jewish woman become resigned to perpetual chastity, when she can still believe or hope that the future Messias may be the fruit of her womb?

Granted equal conditions, according to all the results of statistical inquiry, a group of Israelites, we may be quite sure, is much more prolific than a given number of Protestants, just as a given number of Protestants is more prolific than a number of Catholics.

From 1851 to 1864, the 123,625,000 Catholics in Europe have had an annual increase of 0·48 per 100; the 52,212,000 Protestants have had an increase of 0·98 per 100, and the Jews an increase of 1·53 per 100; figures _{The increase of Catholics, Protestants, and Jews.} which are relatively about in the same proportion as 1 to 2, and to 3·3.[1]

It is impossible to ignore the fact that, among all the religions of civilised peoples, Catholicism is the least favourable to fecundity, and that, in the times of its greatest power, it has nearly always produced a weak birth-rate as its necessary consequence.[2] Doctor

---

[1] See the communication of Doctor Lagneau for February 17, 1885, published in the acts of the *Académiè de Médecine* of Paris.

[2] See the statistical demonstration made by Dumont, *op. cit.*, chap. xviii. There is, moreover, no stronger influence to individual idealism than

Bertillon has given a statistical basis to this dangerous influence of Catholicism on the birth-rate.[1]

For some time, more especially after the studies of Marx, Hertzberg, and Loria, the economic interpretation of history has suffered evident exaggerations. The influence of the moral or religious factors upon social life have been either ignored or subordinated to purely economic causes. And if we even accept the economic interpretation of history, and believe that morality, law, and politics be dependent upon the economic structure, we find that this essentially true thesis is only such within certain limits.

For example, certain economic causes brought about the Protestant Reformation; but, on the other hand, the moral and religious ideals which sprang from the reform have powerfully contributed to the modification of the economic constitution of society. In this way the effect becomes a cause in turn, and even reacts upon the facts which gave rise to it.

Hence to ignore the influences of religion upon the birth-rate would be absurd, just as it would be still more absurd to deny the influence of morality.

We can assert that every system of morality which leads to individualism is contrary to a great fecundity of race, and that, on the other hand, every system of morality, which has as a fundamental principle social solidarity and mutual assistance are favourable to a large birth-rate. Now the systems of morality of modern nations have generally no other basis than the strictest individualism. Catholic morality recommends isolation and ascetic egotism; Jacobin morality sees no other chance of salvation than in the freedom of the individual from every social bond; the so-called pessimist morality, erroneous in interpreting the struggle for existence, is not less strictly individualist than the preceding.

Systems of morality and the birth-rate.

Catholic education. " The question of salvation," said Mgr. Freppel, " is a *personal affair, and it little matters that the family or the city suffer injury therefrom.*" Freppel : *Saint Cyprien*, p. 52.
[1] See Bertillon's studies in the *Revue d'anthropologie* for 1877, and in the *Revue de Sociologie, art. cit.*, pp. 31, 32.

For many years a pessimistic tendency has been diffused throughout social economy, and this has singularly in- Economic pessimism and the birth-rate. fluenced morality and has helped to depress many fertile energies. Besides the Malthusian law, the value of which, from a pessimist point of view, we have already examined, the so-called law of diminishing profits, which asserts that, in the future, more intense human labour will be repaid by an inferior fertility in the earth; the so-called law of the wages-fund and other supposed economic laws, which science has long since proved to be fallacious, have helped to make morality and economy almost altogether pessimistic.[1]

Many economists are accustomed to consider poverty as a leaven of civilisation, as something fatal and necessary. Economic pessimism and its social action. One of the economists held most in honour in recent times, Cournot, speaks in this sense with an unjustifiable severity, which recalls some of the most tragic passages of Malthus—" If social solidarity were extended as these preachers wish, who have sprung up on all sides, and who altogether differ in this argument, the strongest, the most hard-working, the most provident, the most moral part of the population would have to struggle in order to maintain a parasitical population, which is often lacking in these very qualities, and who, it is very much to be feared, would transmit a part of its hereditary vices to future generations."[2]

Now this despairing pessimism, which considers poverty as both fatal and inevitable, has exercised a most dangerous influence upon the conditions of existence in our social life. If poverty be really necessary, then perhaps the will to do good is not vain, nor every effort to find a remedy condemned beforehand.[3]

Pessimist morality impelling to individualist idealism and extinguishing every fertile energy is, therefore, singu- Pessimism leads to the extinction of the larly contrary to increase of population. species.

Is not Hartmann's great dream that of the extinction of the

---

[1] *Cf.* Renouvier : *loc. cit. ;* Bonar : *loc. cit. ;* Fouillée : *loc. cit.*

[2] Cournot : *Revue sommaire de la science économique,* p. 288.

[3] Ziegler : *op. cit.,* chap. iii.

species ? When humanity will be convinced that sorrow only is positive, when it will see all the vainness of its efforts, when it will feel all the reality of its terrible fate, then flowers will be no longer cut to adorn the cradles of the newly-born, but only for the weaving of funeral garlands. Then men will love without begetting children, and they will resolve to follow that fatal process which will lead to the extinction of the entire species.[1]

Hence, all the classes which have undergone or undergo the historical pessimistic phase, all the classes which have made dogmas of the postulates of pessimistic morality, struck by individual idealism, do not tend to reproduction, or tend but very slightly.

Luxury, social divisions, the very number of marriages yearly in **Fecundity and the moral sentiments.** a State, greatly depend upon the morality and moral sentiments diffused among the people. A people without the feeling of social solidarity is indisposed to make sacrifices for the good of collectivity, and has a tendency to consider reproduction not as a duty towards the species, but as an evil from which, to be at least in great part, independent. The Chinese are perhaps the most populous nation, because they possess a morality which impels them to an extreme solidarity, and which, depriving the individual of all importance, makes family and race the objects of importance.[2]

Although morality should itself be considered as the result of the real and ideal needs of collectivity, it reacts in turn upon this last, by directly influencing social relations. Even aesthetic ideality feels its influence directly or indirectly.

Every aesthetic refinement, having luxury for its result, and **The birth-rate and luxury.** propagating itself in a democratic society from the highest to the lowest classes, in virtue of the law of imitation, always increases individual idealism, which

[1] About Hartmann and his conclusions from a social point of view see Franck : *La philosophie de l'inconscient* in the *Journal des savants* for 1877 ; Haym : *Die Hartmann'sche Philosophie des Unbewussten* in *Preussische Jahrbücher* for 1873, fasc. 31 ; T. Reinach : *La morale de Hartman* in the *Revue Philosophique* for 1879, fasc. 7 ; and J. Sully : *Hartmann's Philosophy of the inconscious* in the *Fortnightly Review*, 1876, fasc. 20.

[2] See the study by Simon in the *Nouvelle Revue* for March 15, 1883.

compels every member of a highly-civilised society to impose upon himself, in the interests of egotism, all the privations which his social environment calls for.[1]

This truth, which is essential for the students of the question of population, is apparent not only in men, who Æsthetic idealism and daily sacrifice more and more to the care of their the birth-rate. persons the fruits of their labour, because desirous of maintaining themselves in a superior æsthetic sphere ; but above all in women, who continually sacrifice more and more the social duty of bearing and nursing children to the preservation of beauty and grace. A century ago, even among the richer classes, a mother who gave her children to be nursed by another was a mere solitary exception. Now the refinements in the æsthetic sphere impel more and more to individual egotism, and even the feeling of maternity begins to grow less.[2] In the sixteenth century a very well-known poet, Tansillo, wrote a short poem, *La balia*, deploring that mothers of the aristocracy gave their children to be nursed by women of low social degree. Now, there is not a mother of the middle class, in easy circumstances, who being able to do so, does not voluntarily renounce the duties of maternity.

In past ages æsthetic idealism was, at least, more human, more elevated, and more healthy. The painters of the Æsthetic idealism in Renaissance have handed down figures of healthy the past. and strong women ; even the Madonnas were for the most part portraits of mothers with full breasts and strong bodies, with a baby on their arm or around their neck. The types of the women painted by Rubens, Rembrandt, Titian, and even Raphael, are types of healthy and robust women, under whose naked bosoms runs a sound and vigorous blood.

[1] A. Dumont has very well studied the influence of idealism upon the birth-rate, *op. cit.*, chaps. xiv.-xvii.

[2] Dumont has noted that even in country parts, when the inhabitants begin to copy the customs of the city, the birth-rate feels the effect. "When, on the contrary, it is observed that the local habits of a district become bad, and rapidly begin to resemble those of the cities, it is almost certain that the civil marriage registers will show a decreasing birth-rate," *op. cit.*, p. 339.

Nowadays, æsthetic idealism delights in weak and morbid types; The actual æsthetic just as the women in novels are generally hysteri-
idealism. cal and nervous, the figures which modern art loves
are mostly figures of women which display an incapacity for
maternity, and such as must be the mothers of weak and delicate
children.

Individual idealism, the refinements in the æsthetic sphere,
while they inflame the senses, destroy the broader and more elevated feelings. Adam Smith, who combined the acumen of a
psychologist with the profundity of an economist, has observed
that luxury, though inflaming the passions, would seem to weaken
and often destroy the power of generation.[1]

And Quesnay, always so acute and pleasing, had, even in his day,
attributed the infecundity of certain classes in France to the
" désordres du luxe, dont on se dédommage malheureusement par
une économie sur la propagation." [2]

But if the influences of psychical and moral factors be so great
Influences of the and evident in regulating the birth-rate of a
political form upon
population. country, the influence of the political factor is still
more evident.

A country where the difference between classes forms a really
insurmountable barrier affords an instance where the law of social
capillarity has no influence at all, or acts but weakly. On the
other hand, a country which has a democratic organisation, but
where there are, at the same time, great inequalities of fortune,
and wealth is the only basis of distinction, affords an instance
where the law of social capillarity acts with most intensity.

When, in short, the political constitution is such that an individual, born in an inferior class, is compelled to die there, this
individual has not, nor can have, any wish to raise his social position, nor does he feel the need of making any sacrifice, nor in any
way restraining the prolific instinct. Wherever, on the contrary,
the constitution levels every barrier between the different classes
of society, and makes it possible for each individual to better his

[1] Smith : *The Wealth of Nations,* book i., chap. x.
[2] Quesnay : word *Grain* in the *Encyclopédie.*

position, but at the same time allows and fixes an economic inequality, the law of social capillarity develops itself with all possible force and causes a weak birth-rate.

When, therefore, there is no impediment, every man tends to raise his social position, and to make the sacrifices which his elevation calls for. "We never see the great proprietor make his sons farmers, nor a farmer make his day-labourers," says Sismondi ; "we do not see the great merchant destine his children to become lesser merchants, nor these last destine their children to become artisans, nor the artisans make their own children work by the day. Notwithstanding the frequency of revolutions, which injure the national fortune, and daily oblige a rich family to become poor while maintaining its former conditions, nothing is so rare as that families should voluntarily descend from one condition to another." [1]

The law of social capillarity.

Therefore until class distinctions and rigid monarchies make it impossible or very difficult for a man to pass the barrier which separates him from another class, the phenomenon of oliganthropy never occurs. But when democracy brings it about that every citizen can better his condition, and, at the same time, maintains profound economic inequalities, the birth-rate will quickly feel the effects, and diminish rapidly.

Ancient states were able to last a long time and develop, when they had rigorous and authoritative monarchies, or democracies based upon a relative economic equality.

But, on the contrary, when popular democracy or Cæsarian democracy are in possession of states which have maintained great inequalities in the economic order, the phenomenon of oliganthropy has never delayed in appearing.

Laveleye truly says : "Democratic institutions have never given men rest except when, as in Switzerland and in primitive times, manners are simple and conditions very equal." [2]

Even ancient authors perceived this profound truth. Polybius

---

[1] Sismondi : *Principes d'économie politique*, ch. ii., p. 164.

[2] Laveleye : *De la propriété et de ses formes primitives*, 1891, 4th edit., p. 362.

says : " Let us cite this decrease of population, this scarcity of
men which now makes itself felt throughout the whole of Greece,
which leaves our cities deserted, our country parts uncultivated,
though continual wars and such scourges as pestilence have not
exhausted our strength." [1]   And Plutarch, likewise distressed by
the fewness of men in his country, adds with regret, that in his
days Greece could not furnish the 3000 hoplites, which even little
Megara once sent to the battle of Platea. [2]

India, which is perhaps the most prolific country, is oppressed
The high birth-rate in by the most terrible political tyranny.   The
India.
Indians have not only an unbending social hier-
archy, but this hierarchy is based upon the belief that it is willed
by God Himself. [3]   And, notwithstanding the tendency of Bud-
dhism to fuse the castes, [4] India still remains tenaciously attached
to its ancient *régime.*

It being absolutely impossible for a man of an inferior caste,
although endowed with genius and making the greatest endeavours,
to raise himself to another caste, the birth-rate is naturally most
abundant.

An entire religious and civil system of laws compels the Indian
to fecundity, and to increase his own caste.   The religious books
of India (*Narada*) contain a severe command to parents to find a
husband for their daughters, almost as soon as they have arrived
at the age of womanhood ; if they did not do so, their crime would
be equal to infanticide.   If the wife has no children, the Indian
repudiates her ; if, on the other hand, the husband is incapable of
having children, the wife takes a brother or relative of the husband. [5]

---

[1] Polybius : book xxxviii., pp. 4, 79.

[2] Plutarch : *De defectu oraculorum,* chap. viii.   See also on this question the very interesting book by Karl Bücher : *Die Aufslande der un-
freinen arbeiter,* 1874, chap. iv.

[3] Barthélemy Saint-Hilaire : *La législation indoue,* in the *Journal des
savants,* February, 1889.

[4] Saint-Hilaire : *Les livres sacrés de l'Orient* in the *Journal des savants,*
December, 1888.

[5] About these dispositions of the Code of Manou, see L. Theureau :
L'alimentation dans l'Inde, in the *Revue scientifique,* September, 17, 1892.

Hence it is that, putting aside ethnical and economic causes, the density of population in India is very great, and that some regions are really menaced with over-population.

The Chinese, who have also a very great birth-rate and a population which often, and in many places, assumes *Chinese fecundity and the absence of capillarity in China.* threatening forms, have no castes, but have a domestic organisation which hinders capillarity. The family is a very well-established institution ; there is not a poor Chinese who does not know the history of his ancestors for several centuries, there is not one who does not count among his ancestors nobles and heroes on the one part, and weak characters and labourers on the other. Even Montesquieu, while studying the facts of population, had perceived that the great birth-rate in China was attributable to the political and family organisation, " if China contains so prodigious a population, it is merely the outcome of a certain manner of thinking ; for if the children regard their parents as gods, and respect them as such during their human life ; if they honour them after their death by sacrifices, in which, they believe, that their souls, annihilated by the Tyen, assume a new life, *everyone is led to increase his family, which is so submissive in this life and so necessary in the other.*"[1] Every Chinese may reach the most elevated position, but a series of exceedingly difficult examinations form a barrier only to be passed with difficulty, and always limits him to his family. "The Chinese family," says a writer of that country, "may be compared to a civil society in which every member participates fully in every privilege. All its members are obliged to help each other and to live in common. It is a species of religious order, subject to fixed rules ; all the resources are gathered into one, and all the contributions are made by each without distinction of greater or less. The family is subjected to a *régime* of equality and fraternity."[2]

[1] Montesquieu : *Lettres persanes*, letter 119.

[2] See the study of Tcheng-Ki-Tong in the *Revue des deux mondes*, May 15, 1884. Also see the study of Eugène Simon in the *Nouvelle Revue*, March 15, 1883. The state of Chinese society is such as to compel to stability, and to prevent the passing from the static to the dynamic phase.

Such a domestic order allows tranquillity in his position to every Chinese ; he has no desire of raising himself, and he never even thinks of leaving the community where he was born.

Hence, this absence of social capillarity produces a very high birth-rate.

After all that has been said we can affirm that a *great birth-rate*

Necessary antagonism between the increase of the birth-rate and the development of social capillarity. *cannot exist except in countries where the pheno-menon of social capillarity is wanting, or but very weakly felt. Countries which have an absolute régime, or which eliminate or moderate the phenomenon of social capillarity, have hence, under equal conditions, a much greater birth-rate than countries which have a democratic régime.*

But the influences of the psychical-moral order, and the in-

Population and the economic factors. fluences of the political order, are but very slight compared to influences of an economic kind. In-deed, we know what is the importance of the economic factor, and how the psychical-moral phenomena and the political form feel its influence, and daily suffer its irresistible effect.

But in primitive communities, and as long as land was free, there was no disproportion between the population and the means of subsistence, since the earth was able to maintain new-comers, or caused a less abundant birth-rate. The equilibrium was there-fore never disturbed, or, if it were occasionally disturbed, it soon re-established itself. [1]

But when the land ceased to be free, and with this ceased the

Systematic excess of population in the capitalist phase. system of slavery, capital, seeing itself menaced, was obliged to use every possible means to cause a systematic excess of population. " But," says Loria, " when the earth ceases to be free, the new members of the population de-pend for their subsistence upon the good-will of the capitalist class, that is to say, upon the increase of profit, which it consents to distribute, under the form of food, among the other class. But, until profit is raised, these increases of profit, which are spent in food, are sufficient to maintain the new members of the popula-tion, but must be divided into two parts, one of which keeps the

[1] *Cf.* Loria : *op. cit.,* vol. i., pp. 615-620.

workers, the other the mendicants, since these last are necessary to capital, in order to guarantee the continuance of the *minimum* salary and of profit ; hence, there is formed a systematic excess of population not over food but over capital. When, on the other hand, the rate of profit decreases, an excessive population is no longer necessary to guarantee the persistence of the capitalist economy, and hence the increases of profit, which are,converted into food, may be entirely employed in the demand of labour. But if this increase of profit which is employed in the demand of labour be insufficient to absorb the entire population, an excess of population over capital is formed ; and if the capitalist class be really disposed, through a spirit of charity, to employ in the maintaining of the excessive population a part of its profit, but such, that it is insufficient to maintain the entire excessive population, there is an excess of population both over capital and the means of subsistence. Now this result does not delay in appearing. Indeed, on the one hand, wages and the minimum of profit, produced by the cessation of the freedom of the land, by the limiting production and productive accumulation, diminish the quantity of profits, which can be employed in the demand of labour, and that which can be employed in alms ; while wages also produced by the cessation of the freedom of land, causing a great fecundity, causes the population to soon exceed the limits of accumulation or of the means of subsistence, and thus produces the formation of an automatic excess of population. Nevertheless, this, which Malthus thought to be the only form The historic cause of the actual form of population. of excessive population, and which he considered as perpetual phenomenon, produced by the unchangeable disproportion between population and production, appears to us to be nothing but the last stage of a long and laborious demographic development, and as the result of an essentially historic cause, the cessation of the freedom of land ; which, on the one part, begetting by means of the wages an economic limitation of country production, and on the other part, by means of salary and its oscillations, an economic stimulus to human generation, has as a necessary effect poverty and the excess of population. And as revenue is nothing else than the value of land in itself, and is nothing else than the value of wages for labour, so we may say that the systematic excess of population is produced by the difference between the value of land limiting production, and the value of labour stimulating the population."[1]

The essential truth of this theory of Loria, to which I would

Marx and Loria. only add a few restrictions, will appear an evident consequence to anyone who has followed the movement of population during the various economic phases. Marx had already clearly foreseen it, when he showed the necessity which weighs upon every capitalist organisation, at the risk of perishing, of producing a systematic excess of population.[2] Were it not that, denying that an automatic excess exists, and asserting that the excess of population is caused simply by the influence of technical capital, the theory of Marx, essentially true, nevertheless remained erroneous and deficient.

The historical process by which capital has caused the

Population and the struggle for the persistence of profit. systematic excess of population was already known to the best theorists, but they did not realise its intrinsic cause.

Now the intrinsic cause which drove the capitalist class to originate by every means and every expedient, the rapid and abundant birth-rate of the wage-earning classes, is simply the necessity of securing the persistence of profit. Indeed, we see that when the wages are above the *minimum*, and the persistence of profit is endangered, the capitalist class devises every means, and tries every way to impel the wage-earners to a great fecundity.[3] They leave nothing untried ; advice, inducements, and even corruption of manners are resorted to. And that which finally drives the wage-earner to this is the utter impossibility of a provident life, and the need of finding in

---

[1] Loria : *op. cit.*, pp. 686, 687.

[2] Marx : *Das Kapital*, i., 645 and foll.

[3] See the very full historical and theoretical proofs which Loria has furnished in defence of this essential truth : *op. cit.*, vol. i., pp. 615-693, and vol. ii., pp. 380-416.

the work of women and children a margin to compensate for the decrease of the wages of adults.

Thus we see that at times, and in countries where property is greatly subdivided, there is almost a proportion between the births and deaths, and the quota of annual increase is, in every case, very slight.[1]

But when the permanence of profit is menaced by this proportion, the capitalist class restricts the demand for work and occasions pauperism, and hence the abundant and disordered birth-rate, which is its fatal consequence. Phases of the struggle for the permanence of profit. Hence we see why, at times, when there existed a proportion between population and the means of existence, nay, even when these last exceeded the former, pauperism, nevertheless, existed and spread. This is the explanation of the mystery about which the disciples of Malthus were in doubt and uncertainty.

" But," says Loria, " at the moment when a population, even if increasing in equal or less proportion with the means of subsistence, has caused the cessation of the freedom of land, this occasions profit, and with it necessarily produces, by means of the perfect equilibrium between men and the means of subsistence, a systematically excessive population ; while, moreover, begetting revenue restrictive of production, the minimum of profit, limiting accumulation and wages, an incentive to fecundity, brings as its last effect the regular excess of population. Hence the growth of population is a necessary but insufficient cause of the excess of population, which only takes place when the increase of population produces the cessation of the freedom of land, and this originates powerful economic influences, that is, profit causing systematic excess, and wages, revenue, and the minimum of profit, which lead to the regular excess of population, while if the growth of population did not hinder the freedom of land, or if this did not produce the designed economic influences, this would be unable to create an excessive population. All which is equivalent to saying that excessive population is not the result of the growth of population,

---

[1] *Cf.* Sismondi : *Etudes sur l'Économie Politique,* i., 90 ; Ch. Smith : *Three Tracts on Corn Trade,* 259 ; Loria : *op. cit.,* vol. ii., p. 394.

but of economic influences concerned with the occupation of land." [1]

Even at the dawn of the present capitalist era, nay, chiefly at its dawn, the causes which were to produce the systematic excess of population showed themselves very forcibly. For centuries workmen had enjoyed a relative tranquillity, even when their condition was poor, by means of union and economic organisation, they were sure of not falling into pauperism. But when the perfection of technical industry destroyed the little local industries, when corporations were abolished and the *régime* of industrial liberty prevailed, the workman was compelled to seek the means of subsistence in employment of his productive forces, by exchanging his work for wages. Being utterly defenceless and unorganised, they were very often obliged to accept such low wages that the next lowest degree was economic death. At that time the means of communication were but few and badly developed; while, in the meantime, the capitalist, by means of his superior position, being able to provide himself with men even outside of the local market, every change of place was certainly difficult, if not impossible, to the workingman. Under the pressure of competition the working day reached its *maximum* and wages reached the *minimum*. And when the wages of the adult no longer sufficed for the needs of the family the factory began to fatally attract women and children.[2] It was a terrible inducement to a disordered and abundant birth-rate.

The beginnings of the capitalist phase and the excess of population.

In England, where this economic process developed more intensely than elsewhere, the factories were invaded by children even from the beginning of the century; 10, 20, 25 children for every adult worker became a normal proportion; in Lancashire the proportion of children to adults was 55 to 1; in Dumbarton 60 to 1.[3] It was not the scarcity of adult workers which led the employers to this tremen-

The factories employ women and children.

[1] Loria : *op. cit.*, i., 690, 691.

[2] De Molinari : *Les bourses du travail*, Paris, 1893, chap. vi.

[3] Howell : *The Conflicts of Capital and Labour*, 2nd edit., London, 1890, pp. 97, 98, 101-9, 236-9,

dous child massacre; nay, while the graceful bodies of the children were being exhausted, adults remained unemployed, and sought labour in vain. The mere employment of child-labour secures employers a saving of a third in the wages. Fielden exclaims in alarm : "The profit of capital is compared with the death of a child, our industrial prosperity is based upon infanticide."[1] Of 4,000 children employed in the English factories at the beginning of the century, only 600 reached the age of 30 ; the use of the children's frames went so far that there occurred something which antiquity never saw and which is still rare in our day—the suicide of children.[2]

In England, as in every industrial country, the wages of women and children supplemented the insufficient wages of the adult. Then the labouring class, compelled *Necessary improvidence of the popular classes.* by necessity, abandoned that prudent foresight which it had maintained for centuries, and multiplied itself without bounds and without order.

Senior, the defender of classic economy and the enemy of labour legislation, is overcome by the sight of the sale, suffering, and death of children, and obliged to confess that the commissions of inquiry have reported horrors which seem to belong to some distant age.[3]

Pitt, the English minister, the same who riveted the fetters of Irish servitude, answering the employers who sought protection, cruelly told them to employ children. It was only a few years later that Sir Robert Peel, the father of the great minister, raised the merciful cry : *Save the children.*

But when the laws forbid child-labour, which menaces the decay of the race, the employers have already attained their end : the reduction of the wages of adults. The inspectors[4] of English

<hr/>

[1] Fielden : *The Curse of the Factory System*, p. 15.

[2] Loria : *op. cit.*, vol. ii., chap. ii., sec. 2. This period of the industrial civilisation of England has been splendidly illustrated by Cunningham : *op. cit.*, chap. xxi.

[3] Senior, quoted by Marx (French edit., roy.), p. 212.

[4] C. van Overbergh : *Les inspecteurs du travail dans les fabriques et les ateliers*, Brussels, 1893, p. 21,

factories observe that, when this reduction has been obtained, child-labour is less sought for.

The very economists who are most favourable to individualist **The wages of children operates as a stimulus to fecundity.** exaggerations and the Malthusian thesis, are compelled to recognise that the abundant and disordered birth-rate can only be attributed to the mode of action employed by capital. "The workers," says Molinari, "found themselves in the power of a number of contractors, always less, in proportion as manufacture grew, and wages soon fell below the level necessary to supply the needs of a family. The supplement of resources procured by the labour of children operated as a new encouragement to the increase of the working population."[1]

And Rogers frankly confesses that the rapid increase of population in England, between 1740 and 1780, was due to the increasing call for manufacturing workers, and especially for young men.[2]

Now without any further examination of the process by means **Inconsistency of the classic theory.** of which capital has succeeded in producing first a systematic excess and, later, an automatic excess, it is well to note here that, admitting the direct and deep influence of the economic form upon population, the scope of the work of Malthus is here deficient. We have already seen that the classic theory had no other purpose than to attribute the discomfort of the working classes to their own improvidence ; we shall now see that the moral restraint which was hoped to be a remedy to the evil has no thorough efficacy. Hence, since the foundation of Malthusianism is insufficient, the foundation of the political economy of Malthusianism falls also, since it based itself upon the supposition that the population might be subjected to the individual will of the members of society. This is where the practical scope of Malthusianism falls short, since the system only desired to justify the actual state of things, and to attribute the poverty and the abundant birth-rate not to the vitiated way in which

---

[1] De Molinari : *op. cit.*, p. 59.
[2] Rogers ; *Six Centuries of Work and Wages*, London, 1884, p. 407.

wealth was distributed, but to the blindness of the poor and wage-earning class.

Nay, more, a strong scientific law stands in the way of the practical deductions of the Malthusian school and of economic individualism. According to this law *the birth-rate is determined by the economic form.* In a country where the inequality of wealth is very great, and there exists a large class of wage-earners, the birth-rate tends to be disordered and abundant ; on the contrary, in a country where social wealth is greatly subdivided, and the number of small possessors large, the birth-rate tends to be slight.

It is a long time since intelligent economists perceived that the richer classes have an aversion to rapid multiplica- The economic causes tion. A good English economist has said that if which restrict fecundity. the world were only inhabited by proprietors, it would probably become depopulated for want of inhabitants.[1]

Modern society has destroyed the causes of civil inequality which the laws had sanctioned for centuries, but it has, at the same time, made more easy the growth of economic inequality. Thus, while economic inequality has increased, and the intolerance of poverty has increased with it, aristocratic prejudice has remained as a relic of the former state of society. The struggle for existence is assuming a form which it never had before ; and as a struggle is more ferocious between the species which most resemble each other and have, therefore, the same needs, so the struggle is more intense in a society like ours where all have the same aspirations to wealth, and tend, with equal ardour, to raise themselves in the economic sphere.

Ancient states of society had a conception of virtue which connected it with strength ; *vir, vis, virtus,* really Unproductive capital and the aversion to expressed at bottom one simple conception of manual labour. strength. But, since our struggle is essentially economic, even our conception of virtue is economic. We say a *man of worth* and *a man of value,* etc.

According to the prevalent morality that once existed, the horror

---

[1] Thornton ; *Over-population and its Remedy,* London, 1846, p. 119,

of society was the becoming a vile or an unworthy man, now it is the becoming a poor man.

All the efforts of the capitalist class, in whose hands rests almost the whole of political power, are in the present state of society actuated by the need and instinct of self-preservation.

When, therefore, wages tend to increase and the workers have the chance and sometimes even the hope of ease, the capitalist class, seeing itself menaced, tends to change a great part of capital from productive into unproductive. Led in these tactics by the fatal instinct which guides every organism, just as every institution, to save itself, it gives a powerful impulse to the expansion of unproductive capital. And thus is originated and grows an entire parasitical class whose only scope is to crystallise wages and to secure the permanence of profit. The development of exchange, the enormous increase of intermediate classes, risky and useless speculations, the spreading of banking capital, are all consequences of one single cause.[1]

These economic relations end by directly influencing the ethical

Effect of the development of unproductive capital upon the feelings and morality. sentiments; as the richest and most powerful class is precisely that which speculates upon unproductive capital, labour daily loses its former nobleness. The idealist theory of happiness, in which we believe and which every society must believe in, at the risk of ruin, considers labour as the most precious part of human existence, as the securest means of developing and preserving the best faculties of man.[2] On the contrary, among the rich and unproductive classes there is not only a growing aversion for manual labour, but for every productive labour, and, through the law of imitation, this aversion passes from the rich to the working classes. The movement for the increase of wages and the reduction of the hours of labour is certainly based upon a very useful and fruitful principle. Recent economic inquiries have, in fact, proved and set beyond doubt that a great productiveness always corresponds with higher wages

[1] Loria : *op. cit.*, vol. i., chap. iv., secs. 3 5 ; and vol, ii,, chap. v., sec. 1 of part i.

[2] Ziegler : *op. cit.*, conclusion,

and shorter days of labour,[1] and it is, moreover, a good thing that the need and desire of sharing the intellectual benefits of civilisation should penetrate deeply into the masses of the people. But this movement, which is so largely true and good, is influenced by the already common idea that labour is essentially a penalty. Hence, some of the Utopians of the Collectivist school abandon themselves to the dangerous and immoral illusion that in the future, given different forms of social organisation, it will only be necessary to work two or three hours a day,[2] and that the *minimum* of labour is necessarily identical with the *maximum* of pleasure.

In ancient society the humiliation of poverty was not as great as it is in modern society : the worker compelled to live continually in a corner of the earth, and confined most often within the narrow limits of a corporation, had neither the desire or the power of bettering his condition. Poverty was neither disturbed or offended by the disdainful wealth of those who had succeeded in making a fortune. In short, poverty was in no way dishonourable ; nay, it was rather a misfortune than a disgrace in the eyes of the public and in the general esteem.

But now there is only one social distinction : wealth. Never were the psychological value of money and its Psychological value of power of acquisition so great as in our society, wealth. which claims its authority in the name of democratic principles. Hence it appears why all tend to raise themselves in the economic sphere, and how some who have succeeded in reaching a position, of whatever kind, seek to the best of their power never to lose it,

[1] See the magnificent study by Lujo Brentano : *Les rapports entre le salaire, la durée du travail et sa productivité* in the *Revue d'économie politique*, April, 1893 ; and Nitti : *I problemi del lavoro*, prolusion to the lectures on Political Economy, delivered on the 7th December, 1893, in the University of Naples. Rome, 1893.

[2] Lafargue : *Le droit à la paresse*, Paris, 1883. In *Looking Backward*, Bellamy speaks of a day of four hours' work. Even Stiegler believes that, if Collectivism be established, the labour of each day will not exceed three hours. *Cf.* Nitti : *Il primo maggio e l' agitazione per le 8 ore di lavoro* in the *Scuola positiva*, I. year, No. 2.

and consider the hypothesis of becoming proletaires and of having to live by manual labour as the most fatal and awful.

The desire of advancing, or at least of maintaining, oneself in the economic sphere which has been reached, has the effect of causing men, who possess a degree of wealth, to make the greatest sacrifices for its preservation. And as individual egotism continually grows, these sacrifices generally destroy or limit fecundity.

The solution of the problem of population is precisely this, Poverty and wealth as whether poverty or wealth be the cause of abundant demographic factors. fecundity. Laveleye says : "Everything is summed up in the question whether discomfort or ease lead to an increase of the population."[1]

And we must examine this point attentively. Agrarian inquiry in France has established that proprietors, and chiefly small proprietors, have an aversion to fecundity, and a tendency to accept Malthusian practices, while, on the other hand, only the working class, or those who are without property, remain devoted to the social duty of having children.[2] "In certain communes," says a French writer, "the names *brother* and *sister* are hardly any longer in use; the primogenitive, abolished in 1789, has been replaced by unigeniture."[3] And Guyau, who was the *angelical doctor* of the new philosophy, recognised that French sterility is much rather an economic than a physiological phenomenon.[4]

The small proprietor perfectly understands that his having Small proprietorship children will necessitate sacrifices; and these an obstacle to an abundant birth-rate. sacrifices may perhaps mean that he should one day sell what he possesses and divide it among his children. And, with the prevalent morality, he fears nothing more than a social descent, and he prefers to curtail his family than his property. Hence late marriages, sterility, and unigeniture prevail and tend to continually increase among the classes that have property.[5]

[1] Laveleye : *Le socialisme contemporain*, 5th edit., p. 69.
[2] Guyau : *op. cit.*, p. 274.
[3] Toubeau : *La repartition des imports*, tom. ii.
[4] Guyau : *op. cit.*, p. 281.
[5] *Cf.* Mortara : *I doveri della proprietd fondiaria e la questione sociale.*

M. Baudrillart, a French economist, studying the country population of Poitou, says that during an excursion, he came to speak with his guide about the unfruitfulness of the marriages in that district: "My guide explained it to me, without blaming it very much as it seemed to me, by the fear of diminishing comfort and mutilating the family inheritance. It was simply a confirmation of what I already knew."[1]

This weak birth-rate of the proprietor classes, desirous of escaping what an Italian writer calls the economic horror,[2] namely, the fall from their present social condition to a lower one, is a universal phenomenon, the existence of which it is very easy to ascertain. It is not only in slightly prolific and Jacobin France that the rich have few children, but in the most prolific countries in the world, nay, in the classic country of a disordered and abundant birth-rate, the phenomenon occurs with equal precision and equal intensity.[3] *Weak birth-rate among the proprietor-classes.*

The limitation of the French birth-rate has raised a great deal of discussion during late years. Some hasty economists[4] and physicians ignorant of demographic laws[5] have attempted to ascribe it to the slight fecundity of the French race. Both have forgotten that this very race, which has now become sterile, was able to recuperate itself rapidly after the wars of the fifteenth

Rome, 1885, p. 38 and foll.; Sartori: *Grande e piccola coltivazione delle terre,* Milan, 1891, pp. 81-84; Loria: *La legge di popolazione ed il sistema sociale,* p. 15 and foll.; etc. In the French agrarian inquiry of 1867, M. Hubert-Delisle made the following attestation: "When once the cultivators acquire slight possessions, they are unwilling that they should be afterwards divided, and they try to have only one child, so that there may be no division." Oettingen (*Moralstatistik,* Erlangen, p. 281) has shown all the dangers and moral perils of the French infecundity. For a contrary opinion see Tallquist: *op. cit.,* pp. 17, 50.

[1] Baudrillart: *La population agricole du Poitou* in the *Comptes-rendus de l'Académie des sciences morales et politiques,* 1887, tom. i., p. 173.

[2] Mortara: *loc. cit.*

[3] Sumner-Maine: *Early History of Institut,* p. 335.

[4] Leroy-Beaulieu in the *Journal des Débats,* September 9, 1890.

[5] Hardy in the *Bulletin de l'Académie de Médicine,* 1890, vol. xxiv., p. 693.

and eighteenth centuries; was able, in less than three quarters of a century, from 1715 to 1789, to increase from eighteen to twenty-six millions, and in France, in Canada, in Algiers, and in distant countries where there is no impediment to the birth-rate, to become very prolific.[1]

Therefore the cause is very different, and hundreds of writers have already detected it.

A clever French economist says : " The most probable causes of our insufficient birth-rate are economic and moral causes, the difficulties of living, the desire of comfort and luxury ; the same causes which lead to a diminution of marriages and which tell, moreover, upon the birth-rate." [2]

The causes of French sterility.

And the French physician who has given most study to the demographic phenomenon, and the statistician who has studied it most, carrying his investigation through the history of centuries, both agree with the economist in thinking that the influences restrictive of fecundity in modern France are simply of an economic kind ; and they are the increased need of comfort and the diffusion of small property.[3]

Small proprietors are driven to provident infecundity by the desire not to fall into a lower social condition. And among the rich all the conditions of life lead to infecundity. Softness and nervousness cause a degeneration of feeling, changeableness of passions, frequent adulteries.

For a great part of the classes which form the so-called *elite*, adultery is a real social necessity ; they very often consider conjugal fidelity as a *bourgeois* virtue, which disqualifies those who practice it ; while for the lower classes naturally more chaste and temperate, prostitution is an economic necessity. The rich woman feels the duties of maternity very slightly or hardly at all. To have many children would

Infecundity of the rich classes.

---

[1] C. Richet in the *Revue des deux mondes*, June 1, 1882.

[2] Cauwés: *Cours d'économie politique*, 3rd edit., vol. ii., p. 36.

[3] Lagneau in the *Bulletin de l'Académie de médecine*, 1890, vol. xxiii., p. 659 and foll., and vol. xxiv., pp. 129, 130 ; Levasseur : *op. cit.*, vol. iii., p. 158 and foll.

mean that she should renounce every æsthetic ideal, perhaps luxury, perhaps even wealth. Hence her feeling of maternity is absorbed by the continual search of pleasure, the rage for enjoyment, the desire of intense sensations.

Corruption, ease, refinement of manners, abuse of æsthetic ideals, cause a very weak birth-rate among the richest classes; foresight and the love of property compel the small proprietor to carefully follow the neo-Malthusian practices.[1]

A man that enjoys a certain ease, more especially if he have it without having won it, makes his ideal of life a very expensive one, since he sacrifices very much to ostentation. A too numerous family, and hence children to be brought up, new duties to be taken up, appear a real calamity in his eyes.[2]

Ease as a cause restrictive of fecundity.

On the contrary, the wage-earner who lives inexpensively, who is soon exhausted, has, like all who are socially weak, need of union; the wage-earner to whom a child becomes capital, has every interest to become a parent. Moreover, given the actual organisation, as Wirchow has well observed, there remain for the people no other pleasures than those of the sense and the excitements of alcoholic drinks.

"The fact is," says Loria, "that the worker of to-day is led by two motives to an improvident fecundity. On the one hand, he

---

[1] Courcelle-Seneuil : *Liberté et socialisme*, p. 246.

[2] Doctor Bertillon cites some curious facts in support of his theory, according to which property has the effect of lessening the births. In the 21 French departments which have fewer proprietors (177 for 1,000 inhabitants) the average of births is 28·1 ; while on the other hand in the 30 departments which have a larger number the average of births is 24·7. *Cf.* Vacher in the *Économiste français*, Oct. 14, 1876 ; and the same for April 7, 1877. "This," says Guyau, "is the cause of the reasoning made by parents nowadays, altogether different to that once made, ' to create an influential family I need only transmit the capital which I have amassed while dividing it the least possible, that is to say, to make my family as small as possible.' Capital, *in its egotistical form, is, therefore, an enemy of population, since it is opposed to division, and since the multiplication of men is always more or less a division of wealth,*" Guyau : *op. cit.*, p. 267.

K

very soon arrives at the ultimate limit of his aspirations, the apex of his career, hence every effort of ulterior improvement, and, indeed, every idea of foresight is completely thrown aside ; while on the other hand, the possibility of employing children in factories leads to the idea of increasing the income of his family by increasing the number of his children."[1]

There is, therefore, but one class which has an abundant birth-rate, without check or limit, and it is the class of those who possess nothing, and who have neither the hope nor the chance of bettering their social condition. Impelled by the capitalist class to a great fecundity, and to secure the permanence of profit, devoted to the practice of matrimony, little given to adultery, the wage-earning class is the only one which abandons itself heedlessly and without trouble to the duty of reproduction.

Abundant birth-rate among the poor.

The process by which capital causes the excess of population, and the causes which drive it in this direction, are quite manifest. The graver economic inequalities become, the more largely the working class is multiplied. It is true that the law of social capillarity is a natural law, and that all who occupy low positions are fatally drawn by the desire to ascend ; but it is also true that the intensity of this effort to rise, and hence the greater or less number of sacrifices to rise, are measured by the desire and not by the possibility. Hence the lower the rank of the people and its impossibility of bettering itself, and its impossibility of a social ascent, its want of foresight and fecundity are necessarily so much the greater. " Those who, like beggars, have absolutely nothing," said Montesquieu, " have many children. It is because they are in the same position as a new nation : it costs the father nothing to teach his trade to his children, and they being born are even the instruments of his trade. Such people, in a rich or superstitious country, increase because they do not bear the burden of society, but they are themselves the burden of society."[2]

Causes which limit or destroy the effects of social capillarity.

[1] Loria : *La popolazione*, etc., p. 74.
Montesquieu : *Esprit des lois*, book xxiii , chap. xi.

Loria truly says : " The nature of this method of capital is quite clear from the fact that, hardly has it permanently *The function of capital in the new phase of demography.* reduced the wages of adults to a *minimum*, than the capitalist suddenly abandons it, and at the same time the brutal violence ceases, because adult labour is replaced by less expensive work. This fact, inexplicable, if we consider the employment by capital of women and children as a desire for greater profit, becomes reasonable if we look upon the process as a form of the struggle of capital for the conquest of superfluous labour, or for its own permanence, a struggle which is evidently without a reason, when wages are reduced to a *minimum*. But when, with the growth of population, the price of labour is raised though wages remain at a *minimum*, the employment of women and children becomes more general and energetic, but changing its nature radically, it no longer exists as a process of lowering wages, but as a process of lowering labour, which is performed by substituting cheaper workers for adults. Thus the employment of women and children begins as a means of lowering wages, then, when this has reached a *minimum*, it suddenly stops, and finally reappears more vigorously, as a means of lowering the price of labour, when the degree of limitation to the productivity of the soil raises it." [1]

This fact is quite evident, because the wages of women are always inferior to the wages of men, even if the thing produced be equal.

Malthusian economists, like John Stuart Mill, have vainly endeavoured to attribute this inferiority to custom and to the fewness of women's needs. The reasons will not bear the slightest criticism, and are not worth examination. [2]

The work of women, like that of children, is only maintained in order to lower wages and to artificially stimulate the birth-rate of the wage-earning classes.

The most diligent inquirers are now agreed in reporting that

---

[1] Loria : *op. cit.*, vol. i., pp. 290, 291.

[2] *Cf.* Sidney Webb: *The Alleged Differences in the Wages of Men and Women*, in the *Economic Journal* for December, 1891.

the working classes would gain very much from the moral point of view, and would lose very little from the economic point of view, if the work of women *in manufactories* were suppressed.[1]

Carroll D. Wright, when director of the office of Labour Statistics in Boston, had already concluded, after accurate research, that the increase of wages contributed by women to the needs of the family is so slight that it is her interest to remain at home, rather than to go to work.[2]

And the recent Belgian inquiry on wages has only more strongly confirmed Wright's conclusions.[3]

The employment of women and children had no purpose from the beginning except that of lowering wages; it was only later that it helped to lower the price of labour. The demographic phenomenon of an abundant and disordered birth-rate simply was, and is still, its inevitable consequence. The simple removal of children and women from manufactories—a removal which we believe must take place sooner or later, by means of legislation—could not, therefore, but act usefully upon the birth-rate.

But some have objected against what has been hitherto said about fecundity in relation to poverty and wealth, that the history of the past serves to demonstrate the contrary. And indeed why was it, that under the old system, when the dominant classes were as great in power and riches as they were limited in number, that the inhabitants of generation increased so slowly? If poverty be a help to the country, why did the poor increase so little during so many centuries?

Economic and social causes of the weak birth-rate in ancient and mediæval times.

It is here necessary to distinguish between a state of relative poverty and a state of extreme poverty. The extremely poor, when weakened by hunger, when

Extreme poverty and the birth-rate.

---

[1] *Cf.* A. Julin : *Une enquête en Belgique sur les salaires, les prix et les budgets ouvriers*, in the *Réforme Sociale*, November 1, 1892, pp. 683, 684.

[2] *Sixth Annual Report of the Bureau of Statistics of Labour*, Boston, 1875, *Summary of Results*, p. 384.

[3] See the official publication : *Salaires et budgets ouvriers en Belgique au mois d'avril*, 1891, Bruxelles, 1892.

they have no hope of resuscitation, not unfrequently abandon themselves to extreme misery. They await death, and believe, like the famished peasants who made answer to d'Argenson, "*que ce n'est pos la peine de faire des malheureux comme eux.*" [1] And if they have children, they are so weak and incapable that the first hardships of poverty kill them, and originate the dreadful infant mortality of the poorer classes.

When a class or a society abandons itself to despair through extreme poverty, either because injured by the great wealth of others, or because overcome by a too rigid rule, then it is no longer fertile, and it lets death overtake it.

This is why slaves, often much better fed than the working-men of our time, are generally unprolific, and, notwith- Birth-rate among standing the inducements of their masters, multi- slaves, and its causes. ply slightly and ill. [2]

Many ancient wars of conquest were remotely caused by the sterility of the slaves. In the ancient economic state, especially in certain nations, slaves were almost the only class that attended to agriculture and industry. And, as the slaves, necessarily unprolific, multiplied themselves but very slightly, there was the irresistible need in the ancient civilisation of providing new arms. And as commerce alone very often proved insufficient for the needs of production, war became an inevitable necessity.

The slaves of modern colonies are not less sterile than the slaves of antiquity; the masters vainly endeavour to impel and to excite them to fecundity. A sense of discouragement pervades them and causes a weak birth-rate, even though they be well fed. [3]

---

[1] D'Argenson : *loc. cit. Cf.* also Schœne : *op. cit.*, chap. x.

[2] When, however, slaves were completely resigned and well fed they were extremely prolific. See Baudrillart : *La question de population en France au dix-huitième siècle*, p. 4.

[3] On the fecundity of slaves in antiquity and in modern colonies, see Dureau de la Malle : *Examen des causes générales qui chez les Grecs et les Romains devaient s'opposer au développement de la population* in the acts of the *Académie des inscriptions*, 1842, xiv. 318 ; Tucker : *Progress of the United States*, New York, 1843, pp. 58-63, 120, etc.

In the Middle Ages, when slaves were replaced by serfs, the
Infecundity of serfs in the Middle Ages. condition of those last was really much better, and
fecundity spontaneously increased. And thus
there arose almost everywhere laws which restricted the marriages
of serfs ; while they experienced still more fully the economic law
which creates a proportion between a weak birth-rate and slight
possessions. But when their conditions were improved, and their
comfort increased, and they became real land-owners, they necessarily had a very weak birth-rate, and each serf had rarely more
than two children. Thus the population of the Middle Ages increased but slightly, and for entire epochs in rich regions it was
almost stationary.[1]

The same effect occurred among the workers as among the proprietors : the economic constitution greatly limited fecundity.[2]

According to the statutes of most cities, Italian and foreign, it
The ancient industrial organisation restricted fecundity. was very difficult to become a master (*magister*)
before the age of twenty-five ; many who were
incapable or unfit never attained the rank. And as it was almost
without example that a working-man, not yet a master or in-
scribed in a corporation, should marry, marriages were always
retarded.[3]

In countries like France, where the corporations had a long and
Effects of the corpora-tions on the birth-rate. tenacious life, we see the worker compelled to a
régime which necessarily restricted fecundity. He
began work, not as in modern industry, at a tender age, but when
his constitution had become strong. His *apprenticeship* was always long ; at Paris it was eight years, elsewhere it was even
longer. He did not generally become a master before the age of
twenty-five or thirty ; and during this delay he was forbidden to
lead an irregular life, every kind of irregularity and licence being

---

[1] *Cf.* Guillard : *op. cit.*, p. 39 ; Thornton : *Over-population*, pp. 126-28.
Rumelin : *Reden und Aufsätze*, p. 315 ; Lamprecht : *Deutsches Wirth-
schaftsleben im Mittelaler*, 1886, p. 1156, etc.

[2] *Cf.* Sismondi : *Nouveaux Principes d'économie politique*, book iv., chap.
ix.

[3] Sismondi : *loc. cit.*

forbidden him. The corporation very often refused to receive young men who kept women; the Parisian manufacturers absolutely excluded anyone who lived with a dishonest woman; *qui tiegne sa meschine au chans ne à l'ostel.* The Paris corporation of weavers in 1281 regulated the expulsion from their body of any dissolute person, *qui entretient sa putain au chans.* The labour of women was only beginning; it was not, as now, either perilous to the future of the race, or dangerous to morality. On the contrary, the working-man who wished to introduce a woman into the workshop had to prove *par bons temoins ou par créabilité de Sainté Eglise, que il a espousé la fame.*

Our long working days, which depress energy and often develop a morbid sexual excitability, were almost unknown. Work always ceased at 2 P.M. on Saturdays, and the worker generally enjoyed a long rest every week. If faith is to be placed in the testimony of contemporary chronicles, we must admit that the working class generally dressed better than now; and their food was unquestionably more healthy and plentiful.[1]

This is the sum of the life which, throughout the Middle Ages and down to the seventeenth century, exercised a Causes which formerly restricted the birth-rate. powerful influence restrictive of fecundity, and made impossible the essentially modern phenomenon of an abundant and disordered birth-rate.

And what is the case nowadays?

In country parts the small proprietors almost everywhere grow daily ess, while the body of wage-earners Causes which excessively raised the birth-rate in our day. increase. The system of the cultivation of land, the systems of impost, the influence of banking capital, continually cause the disappearance of small farms, and of the old systems of contract. The blind and inevitable link which for centuries bound man to the land begins to disappear; the peasant The modern peasant necessarily prolific. is, moreover, often obliged to abandon it, and he abandons it without regret. The continual exodus of the country

---

[1] *Cf.* Alfred Franklin : *La Vie privée d'autrefois*, chap. ii.: *L'ouvrier;* and Hubert Valleroux : *Les Corporations d'arts et métiers et les Syndicats professionels en France et à l'étranger*, pp. 42 and foll.

population towards the cities is a fact everywhere occurring, and with perilous intensity.

As the peasant gradually sinks to the condition of a mere wage-earner, he loses that prudent foresight which the mediæval farmers maintained for centuries, and generates recklessly, impelled by the need of supplementing his own insufficient wages by the wages of his children.

What occurs among industrial workers is still graver. In the **The modern worker and his fecundity.** Middle Ages the economic constitution led to a limitation of numbers; while in modern times it impels them to a rapid multiplication. The long working days of 12, 14, and 15 hours make their intellectual improvement impossible, and compel them to seek their sole enjoyments in those of the senses. Compelled to work for many hours, in places heated to a great temperature, often promiscuously with women; obliged to live upon substances which, if insufficient for nutrition, frequently cause a permanent excitability; persuaded that no endeavour will better their position, they are necessarily impelled to a great fecundity. Add to this that the premature acceptance of children in workshops leads the parents to believe that a large family is much rather a good than an evil, even with respect to family comfort.

A state of extreme poverty or of great distress is unquestionably contrary to the impulse to an elevated birth-rate. But if, on the other hand, social wealth be sufficiently developed, the lowest class is necessarily led to rapid reproduction. As in animal struggles parasitical species are deeply injured by the disappearance or decrease of the species upon whom they subsist, so when the struggle for the permanence of profit occurs, capital, like a parasitical species, compels the workers to abundant fertility by means of a process, which is perceivable to the onlooker.

This truth, which is essential to anyone who wishes to study **Birth-rate among rich and poor.** the demographic phenomenon, was noticed by the economists of the past. Some of them went so far as to study the relation between the historic oscillations in the process of the distribution of wealth and the demographic phenomenon.

The decrease in the number of small farms of from ten to fifteen acres has been observed by an English economist of Disappearance of the small farms a stimulus to fecundity. the eighteenth century as a great stimulus to fecundity. In fact, the children of the small proprietor made it a duty to maintain the rank of their economic condition, and, far from marrying in youth, they remained many years in service until their savings, with a slight help from friends, made their purchase of a small holding possible. But now, such remuneration is so rare that few wage-earners seek to save anything of their wages. But although they make little or no economics for the future, they generally marry at an earlier age than formerly, and naturally very soon fall into poverty. . . . Marriages of the lower classes are very rarely restrained by prudential motives. Hence there is such an increase of population, that not only is the value of work diminished, but in many districts old people and children are unable to find employment.[1]

Even before Malthus' pessimistic work saw the light, Adam Smith recognised that "poverty is a stimulus to generation."[2] And Barton affirmed that the lower the social rank, the less foresight necessarily is, and he believed that a state of poverty is generally accompanied by a great want of foresight.[3]

And the Romans, many centuries before, with wonderful demographic intuition, had designated poor working-men as *proletarii.*

After the researches of Quéletet in Brussels, Farr in London, Scwabe in Berlin, Villermé and Benoison de Châteauneuf in Paris, it is no longer possible to doubt that the *maximum* of births takes place among the poorer class, and that poverty itself is an irresistible inducement to an abundant and disordered birth-rate.

H. Passy has demonstrated, with great statistical precision, that

[1] *Reason of Increase of Poor Rates*, pp. 11, 12, quoted by Loria : *op. cit.,* vol. ii., p. 399.

[2] Adam Smith : *An Inquiry into the Nature and Causes of the Wealth of Nations,* edit. prepared by E. Belfort Bax, London, 1887, vol. i., p. 80.

[3] Barton : *Agricultural Labour,* 30, 32, 33. See Legoyt's study in the *Revue scientifique*, September 4, 1880.

the cities of France with the weakest birth-rate are those inhabited by *bourgeois.*

On the other hand, the cities which have a high birth-rate are manufacturing cities or seaports, where the working population is very considerable.

According to the same author, in the four *arrondissements* of Paris which are inhabited by rich families, there are not 1·97 births for every marriage. In the four *arrondissements* inhabited by the poorest class the births are as many as 2·86. Between the second elegant and rich *arrondissement* and the twelfth, which is exclusively composed of working-men, the difference is 1·87 to 3·24, that is 73 per cent.[1]

Birth-rate of rich and poor in Paris.

Cheysson, a French statistician and follower of Le Play, asserts that, after a minute demographical study of the Parisian *quartiers,* the average birth-rate of the poor *quartiers* was 28 for every 1000, while it was hardly 20 for every 1000 in the richer *quartiers.*[2]

According to a recent calculation, the birth-rate of Paris is hardly 22 in a 1000 in the *quartiers* of the Louvre, the Bourse, and the Opèra; it is as much as 17 in that of Passy, and in the most spendthrift, that of the Champs d'Elysée, it is 16·4. On the other hand, there are as many as 30 for every 1000 in those of Popincourt, Gobelin, Vaugirard, and Buttes Chaumont, and it reaches 38·8 in the *quartier de l'observatoire,* where the poor population resides.[3]

In their last census of Paris there was found an enormous number of unprolific families in the elegant *quartier* of the Place Vendôme; on the other hand, in the popular *quartier* of Epinettes, there were found more families with more than four children than unprolific families.[4]

---

[1] See the careful study by H. Passy in the *Mémoires de l'Académie des sciences morales et politiqué's,* 1839, 2nd series, vol. ii., pp. 288 and foll.

[2] Cheysson in the *Journal de la société de statistique,* 1883, p. 457. About Le Play's criteria of replenishing the deficiencies of the population of France, see *La Réforme Sociale,* 1867, pp. 328 and 427.

See the *Die Neue Zeit* of Stuttgart, 1893, No. 35.

Turquan in the *Revue scientifique,* January 12, 1889.

The department of the Seine-Inférieure, which exhibits the strange phenomenon of quite a prolific demographic island surrounded by unprolific departments, has a very high birth-rate. Yet it has a very poor industrial *prolétariat* formed of men whom poverty and fatigue has very much reduced, and which supplies an enormous number of recruits unfit for military service: 47 unfit for every 100 conscripts.[1]

Demographic examination of two French departments, the one prolific and the other unprolific.

On the other hand, the department of Tarn-et-Garonne supplies the most complete contrast with the preceding; having no industrial *prolétariat*, and scarcely any paupers, it has a very low birth-rate. In the *arrondissement* of Montauban the average birth-rate is 22, while the average for all France, at the same period, was 24.[2]

An acute French observer says: "The richer a commune, the more fertile its soil; the more widely spread its comfort, the fewer births occur. And in the most privileged points, in the rich country of Tarn and Aveyron, on the hills where the cultivation of fruit-bearing trees is a source of wealth to the inhabitant, the birth-rate is weakest, being only 16 or 17 for every 1000.[3]

The most unprolific parts of France are Normandy and the Garonne, which are very rich and prosperous; the most prolific is the poor and sterile province of Brittany.

Chervin has even shown that the law which connects riches with sterility, holds good not only in vast regions but also in small isolated centres. Thus in the department of Lot-et—Garonne, rich in crops and poor in men, the richest *cantons* are the least prolific. And, moreover, in rich centres the richest men are the least prolific.[4]

On the contrary, in parts where anxiety for the future does not

[1] Chervin in the bulletin of the *Association française pour l'avancement des sciences* for 1885.

[2] Dumont: *op. cit.*, p. 81.

[3] Guirand in the *Revue scientifique*, November, 1888.

[4] *See* the study made by Chervin in the *Bulletin de la Société d'Anthropologie* for 1891.

exist and the form of economic organisation allows a general diffusion of comfort, the birth-rate is fairly high.[1]

In general, however, we must agree with Bertillon that " the French birth-rate is reduced by the voluntary sterility of families, having small possessions (such families are exceptionally numerous in France), because these families foresee that to have but one child is a certain means of preserving their wealth, while, on the other hand, to have more than two children, is a certain way of losing what they have."[2]

What occurs in France occurs everywhere.

At London the birth-rate of the poor quarters is 35 for 1000 Birth-rate of rich and inhabitants; while, on the other hand, it is 25 in poor in London. the rich quarter of Saint-George. [3]

I have attempted to carry out in Naples the same researches Researches upon the as other statisticians and demographers have made birth-rate among rich and poor in for Paris and London, and my calculations, based Naples. upon personal examination and data furnished me by the Municipal Office of Statistics, have amply confirmed my anticipations.

It is well, however, to remark that there is not at Naples as in many other cities, a clear division of popular quarters from aristocratic and middle class quarters.

We may, nevertheless, hold it as certain that seven quarters of the city (S. Ferdinando, Chiaia, San Giuseppe, Monte-Calvario, Stella, and San Carlo all'Arena) are mostly inhabited by the richer and middle class, and by the better class of working-men. Five other quarters (Vicaria, S. Lorenzo, Mercato, Pendino, and Porto) are mostly inhabited by the lower *bourgeoisie* and the common people. Then there are two villages (Miano and Fuorigrotta), the population of which are almost exclusively of the working class.

And at Naples as elsewhere the birth-rate is much greater among the poor than among the rich.

---

[1] *See* Bertillon : *art. cit.*, pp. 27-30.

[2] Bertillon: *art. cit.*, p. 46.

[3] Stallard : *On the Relation between Health and Wages* in the *Journal of Soc. Arts*, December 4, 1867, quoted by Loria : *op. cit.*, vol. ii., p. 400

BIRTH-RATE IN THE DIFFERENT QUARTERS OF NAPLES FOR EVERY 1000 INHABITANTS.

QUARTERS CHIEFLY INHABITED BY THE RICHER CLASSES.

	1881.	1882.	1883.	1884.	1885.	1886.	1887.	1888.	1889.	1890.	1891.	1892.
San Ferdinando	27·2	26·5	25·9	27·9	24·9	27·3	26·8	25·7	25·3	24·6	24·3	24·6
Chiaia	28·2	28·0	26·3	29·9	27·7	28·1	31·2	28·9	31·3	30·0	30·5	32·4
San Giuseppe	27·4	26·0	25·9	26·6	23·8	23·8	24·8	25·0	24·2	24·6	29·8	24·8
Monte-Calvario	29·5	27·6	27·3	30·4	27·9	28·3	29·8	27·8	28·7	28·0	28·7	25·8
Arvocata	31·4	28·1	31·7	31·5	29·6	31·1	31·9	29·6	33·6	29·5	30·2	27·8
Stella	30·2	29·1	29·8	32·3	31·2	31·3	32·4	32·1	33·3	32·6	32·3	29·5
San Carlo all'Arena	31·3	29·3	31·2	35·5	32·1	34·9	34·4	33·5	34·0	36·2	37·1	36·1

QUARTERS CHIEFLY INHABITED BY THE POORER CLASSES.

	1881.	1882.	1883.	1884.	1885.	1886.	1887.	1888.	1889.	1890.	1891.	1892.
Vicaria	33·9	33·0	31·1	36·0	32·3	35·6	37·6	38·1	43·1	39·6	42·7	40·7
San Lorenzo	49·8	48·2	42·8	46·0	43·8	41·2	41·1	38·2	40·8	39·4	40·7	41·4
Mercato	36·0	36·3	34·7	38·1	34·9	36·6	38·2	36·0	39·4	34·8	38·5	39·3
Pendino	37·2	35·6	36·0	35·3	30·9	35·5	36·7	36·3	36·0	29·5	31·4	26·8
Porto	34·6	32·9	33·2	32·7	31·2	32·8	37·0	34·4	34·8	30·5	29·0	24·4

VILLAGES CHIEFLY INHABITED BY WORKING MEN.

	1881.	1882.	1883.	1884.	1885.	1886.	1887.	1888.	1889.	1890.	1891.	1892.
Fuorigrotta	39·7	36·3	43·2	45·8	49·5	42·0	51·2	50·4	55·0	48·2	55·1	50·1
Miano	37·9	36·7	40·1	44·9	40·1	42·6	45·2	45·3	48·9	43·7	44·9	47·1

Hence the difference between the birth-rate of the rich and poor quarters of Naples is also evident, and would be much more so were it not for the changes from one quarter to another, and if the works of the sanitary improvement of the city since 1885 had not caused a large exodus of working-men to the more healthy and elegant quarters, thus producing a greater birth-rate in these last.

The quarter of the city which had the smallest birth-rate in the twelve years elapsing between 1881 and 1892 is the aristocratic quarter of San Ferdinando, the most elegant of all, where the average of births has varied between a *minimum* of 24·3 and a *maximum* of 27·9. The quarter of the city which had the largest birth-rate in the meantime was that of San Lorenzo, which varied between a *minimum* of 39·4 and a maximum of 49·8. At San Lorenzo dwell a great part of the population receiving public relief, and the poorest working-men.

"The demonstration, which connects poverty and the growth of population as cause and effect," says Laings, "is made evident by the fact that in rural districts, where the condition of the peasantry is satisfactory, experience has repeatedly proved that there is no tendency to an excessive increase of population, while in the great cities and in manufacturing districts, where the condition of the great masses of the people is extremely miserable, the rate of increase is very high."[1]

The districts of Italy which have the greatest land cultivation, *Abundant birth-rate in the poor districts of Italy.* and where the mass of wage-earners, who live miserably from day to day, is greatest, are certainly Sicily, Apulia and the Basilicata.[2] And it is precisely here that the population increases most rapidly; while on the contrary, in regions like Tuscany, Emilia, and Liguria, where *métairie* exists, agrarian contracts are relatively equitable, the

---

[1] Laings quoted by Loria : *op. cit.*, vol. ii., p. 402.

[2] *Cf.* Nitti : *Agricultural Contracts in South Italy* in the *Economic Review* of July, 1893. See on the whole question the excellent work of G. Tammeo : *La prostituzione*, Turin, 1891.

number of small proprietors is greater, and the state of labourers less miserable,[1] the birth-rate is less.[2]

The smaller birth-rate of the richer class, in comparison with the poor, should be shown by an accurate study of limited parts and with the use of these principles of accurate demographic study, of which Dumont has given us so luminous an example. It is impossible to draw precise conclusions from general statistics.

Nevertheless, even considering the vagueness of statistical materials at our disposal, we see at once that a great birth-rate always answers to a great depression of the working classes, to smallness of wages, to a bad distribution of wealth, to an absence of social capillarity. The countries where public wealth is most widely divided, such as France, Switzerland and Belgium, are those where the birth-rate is least, while on the other hand, Russia, Servia, Hungary and Germany, that is, where the distribution is worst, are those which have the largest birth-rate.[3]

Confirmation of the law which considers ease as restrictive of fecundity.

This essential truth of the law of population, this principle which makes the abundant and disordered increase of the population to depend not upon the

Fundamental error of the classic theory of population.

---

[1] " The highest quotients of the birth-rate are given by the Neapolitan district, by Sicily and the Roman Province ; the lowest by the northern parts, and particularly by Liguria and Piedmont." *Annuario statistico,* 1889-1890, p. 39. Now if we compare the wealth of each district with the population, and place the private wealth of Italy for 1880-1884 at 100, we shall have, in round numbers, the following result for each inhabitant in Italy, Piedmont and Liguria 16 per cent., Lombardy 14, Latium 13, Tuscany 12, Emilia 10, Venice 9, Naples 7½, the Marches and Umbria 7, Sicily 6½, Sardinia 5. Pantaleoni : *Dell'ammontare probabile della ricchezza privata* in the *Giornale degli economisti* for August, 1890, p. 168. The districts which give the highest quotient of births are the poorest (Naples and Sicily), and those which have the worst distribution of wealth (Latium).

[2] On the fecundity of the various districts of Italy, see the *Movimento dello stato civile* for 1888, Rome, 1850, p. xliv.

[3] Between 1863 and 1883, excluding the still-born, for every hundred inhabitants there were 2·54 births in France, 3·02 in Switzerland, 3·15 in Belgium, while in Russia there were 4·94, in Hungary 4·30, in Servia 4·36, in Germany 3·90.

want of foresight of the poorer classes, but upon the very poverty to which the capitalist organisation condemns them, ruins the entire economic edifice reared by Malthus. For in reality he had no other scope than the condemnation of the aspirations of the reformers, and the being able to tell the mass of working-men that they were the cause of their poverty.

Indeed nothing sounds better to the ears of the comfortable classes than that the workers are themselves the cause of their poverty, and that if they were more continent and virtuous, they would see an end to their difficulties. In this fatalistic reproof, so well adapted to silence scruples, is contained the germ of that economic pessimism, which is so fatal to the development of civilisation and of the moral feelings.

Occasionally, by reason of an industrial crisis, many working-men are dismissed, and the difficulty of finding *Wages and the increase of population.* occupation leads them to have recourse to public assistance, and then population is said to be excessive, and classic economy can suggest no other remedy than abstention from sexual intercourse.

Now the great merit of Marx—a merit allowed him even by his great opposer Lujo Brentano[1]—consists in having shown the falsity of the thesis, according to which wages were considered dependent upon the increase or decrease of the entire population, and not upon the excess existing in single industries.

The latter day Malthusians, now that science has shown the intimate connection between economic and demographic pheno-mena, are obliged to allow that an individual or a class may or may not multiply themselves, without submitting to the conditions of the economic and social surroundings, but by submitting to moral restraint. The cause of the demographic phenomenon is free, according to them. Block ingenuously writes : " The cause is generally free and voluntary."[2]

---

[1] Lujo Brentano : *La question des huit heures en Angleterre* in the *Revue d'économie politique* for November, 1891.

[2] Block : *Les progrès de la science économique depuis, Adam Smith,* Paris, 1890, vol. i., p. 536.

Now the cause is neither free nor voluntary. The masses necessarily submit to the conditions of their econo- Incapacity of the masses to spontaneously restrain their fecundity. mic surroundings, since they in no way possess the opportunity or power of overcoming them. When the mass of the *prolétariat* is over prolific, both in learned Saxony and in uncultured Apulia, in free England and in despotic India, it is clear that it is influenced by one common necessity. Moreover, Malthus, in his famous letter to Senior, has clearly shown his perception of the fact that the masses cannot in any way influence the means of subsistence under the capitalist organisation. The desire of bettering our condition, considered as an influence upon the increase of food, is very weak in comparison with the tendency of the population to multiplication. The most intense desire of improving our condition cannot originate any act which will secure a permanent increase of food in proportion to the tendency to increase of number which the population feels. Indeed this desire, in so much as it influences the working classes, increases food but very slightly. It is not they who accumulate capital in land, and employ it in agricultural improvements, and in the increase of the means of subsistence; *in this respect they are altogether passive.* But, although they cannot help the increase of food, they form the *only* class of the population which can sensibly retard the increase of men by means of moral restraint.[1]

Hence, even according to Malthus, production is limited or increased according to the needs of capital; while the masses remain altogether passive in this respect. But when we have seen that in certain economic phases the increase and decrease of population are merely the effect of given conditions, we are convinced that *moral restraint* has not, and perhaps never had, a great and healthy efficacy, and that the birth-rate is almost exclusively regulated by economic forms.[2]

[1] See Senior: *Two Lectures on Population*, London, 1843, p. 62. Malthus' letter to Senior, dated March 23, 1829.

[2] As Sismondi acutely observes : " The will of man, or, in other words, the legislation under which he lives, and which is the expression of that

Given the constitution of modern society, *the economic situation*
New demographic *does not depend upon the increase of the population,*
laws. *but, on the contrary, not only the number of those*
who live, but even the number of those who are born, depends upon
the economic situation.

Remembering what has been hitherto said, we may draw two
conclusions from this law :

1. *The lower the economic situation and the moral feelings of the*
popular classes, the more restricted are their pleasures to those of
sense, and so much the more is their birth-rate abundant and
disordered.

And on the other hand :

2. *Every improvement of the general condition, every diffusion of*
wealth, every increase of wages, and of the standard of living exer-
cise a useful influence on their birth-rate.

Hence nothing is more certain to fix limits to the birth-rate
The standard of living than high wages and the diffusion of ease.
and the birth-rate.
Countries where the ownership of the soil is
much subdivided, as in France ; countries where the working-man
has succeeded in winning high wages and short days, as in the
United States of America, have a slight birth-rate. Even
England, a country so naturally prolific, now that the economic
causes which heightened the birth-rate have grown less, has a decreasing birth-rate.

It is clearly to be seen that a very high birth-rate always
corresponds with slight wages, long days of work, bad food, and
hence a bad distribution of wealth.

India, the classic country of abundant fertility, is the country
where the economic phenomena referred to are seen much more
intensely than elsewhere.

On the other hand, in the United States of America, notwithstanding the traditional fecundity of the British and Germans who
form the substance of the population, the birth-rate among the

will, have alone arrested the multiplication of the means of subsistence
and with them of human generation.' Sismondi : *Nouveaux principes,*
ii., 272.

native born is very slight, and, putting aside the other reasons of a political and ethical kind, the high standard of living, the large wages, the short days of work exercise their influence in limiting the birth-rate, and make the native-born population but slightly prolific.[1]

All this is not only evident from an economic and statistical standpoint, but also from a psychological point of view. If a man fall into poverty, and be hindered *Psychological causes of the fecundity of the poor.* from every participation in the superior benefits of civilisation, it will be seen that he will find no other pleasures than those of the senses.

Wirchow asked a very poor working-man of Berlin why he had begotten so many children. He replied with a smile : if this be the only pleasure left us !

I have put the same question to very poor peasants in South Italy who were burdened with very large families, and they have answered me with ready Southern intuition, without speaking, but by simply smiling.

This is the explanation why every crisis and disturbance of the economic order, robbing the masses of every advantage which they had gained, almost always end by increasing rather than restraining the birth-rate.

On the other hand, the Malthusian idea that the popular classes have a means of remedying their condition by abstention from sexual intercourse is, to say the *Absurdity of the Malthusian remedy.* least, puerile.

Suppose that a hundred, a thousand, or a hundred thousand men, following the Malthusian precept, became, so to call it, virtuous, their condition would not be altered in the least, because the general conditions would remain unchanged.

But let us suppose for the sake of argument that this abstention were possible in an entire nation. The foundations of capitalist economy would remain the same, and the causes of poverty would remain the same.

In France, for instance, when oliganthropy began to show itself,

[1] Nitti : *I problemi del lavoro.*

the employers turned to foreigners, and the Italians and Germans, belonging to nations which an economic necessity makes prolific, lent themselves to lower the wages of the native working class by their competition.[1]

In Germany the employers opposed the district rates, fearing lest the working-men, availing themselves of the low price of transport, should seek labour elsewhere. M. Leroy-Beaulieu, giving voice to these feelings, and opposing the claims of the French working-men, has even said, that at a not distant day it will be necessary to have recourse to the Chinese.

Hence, in order that the Malthusian precept should act efficiently, it should act throughout the entire world. Individual or national abstention from sexual intercourse is good for nothing. What is necessary is a universal strike in this respect, a kind of May-day of the senses, prolonged for a great time in every part of the world.

The idea of bettering the conditions of the popular classes, by means of this abstention is, says Brentano,[2] a Utopia, in comparison with which any socialist dream seems realisable.

And, on the other hand, when individuals are recommended to practice moral restraint, and it is thought that the good of all consists in the initiative of each individual, there is a want of courage in the examination of the question.

This point about moral restraint is really the great weakness of Insufficiency of moral restraint. the work of Malthus. In fact, after having spoken of the necessity of a preventative restraint, he abandons the individual, leaving him to work, as he puts it, under the influence of the temptations to which he is exposed, that is to his own free will and according to his own conscience.[3] Almost a century has since elapsed, and accepting the moral aberrations into which the neo-Malthusians have fallen, all the followers of Malthus, as Schäffle says, have endeavoured to elude the question.[4]

---

[1] See the *Chronique économique de Gide* in the *Revue d'économie politique*, September and October, 1893.

[2] Brentano : *art. cit.*   [3] Malthus : *Essay*, etc.

[4] Schäffle : *Bau und Leben*, etc., part ii., vii., p. 5.

Objective study clearly shows that if civilisation spontaneously tends to restrict the birth-rate within given limits, without hindering the development of the race, voluntary prevention simply leads to the degeneration of the senses, and the decadence of the race. When pleasure is wished and sought for its own sake, without the responsibility and consequences of having children, matrimony loses its entire purpose, and becomes nothing else but a form of monogamic prostitution.

Moral restraint as a cause of monogamic prostitution.

In the countries which suffer from sterility, the quota of marriages decrease, the proportion of illegitimate births increase, the family ideal decays.[1]

" The carnal instinct," says Buddha, " is sharper than the iron hook with which wild elephants are tamed ; it is more ardent than fire ; it is like an arrow planted in the spirit of man."

The degenerations of this instinct only serve to kill the family ideal, the sentiment of social duty ; to shake the very foundations of civilisation and progress. No society is less disposed to solidarity than that in which individual idealism is powerful ; and nothing predisposes more to individual idealism than practices destined to restrict the family. The French physicians, who had at first adhered to neo-Malthusian practices, now agree in demonstrating its dangers and its evils.[2]

Dangers of moral restraint.

The nations which artificially limit their fecundity arrive at such bestial corruptions as would not only alarm Malthus, who was an honest man and an Anglican pastor, but any tolerant spirit. And if, by chance, some avoid this, on the other hand, a very large number abandon themselves to vice and organic degeneration.

But the argument which ruins the whole Malthusian structure, which made poverty simply dependent upon excess of population, and not upon the economic order, is the fact that the severest poverty has almost always occurred in countries and at times when the means

Permanence of pauperism even in periods of excess of wealth over population.

---

[1] De Foville : *La France économique*, p. 39.

[2] Bergeret : *Les fraudes conjugales.* See also Amelin : *Le libre échange absolu à l'intérieur et à la frontière*, p. 21. And above all see Oettingen : *loc. cit.*

of subsistence sufficed for the population, and far exceeded it. Mill recognises that between 1818 and 1848, the increase of wealth in England far surpassed the increase of population ; [1] and Cairnes, another ardent follower of Malthus, is surprised to perceive that at that very period the means of subsistence exceeded the population. [2]   But even Cairnes is led to confess that in the present capitalist organisation the poor tend to become poorer, while the rich tend to become continually richer. [3]

According to the fundamental theory of the Malthusian system, there should have been no poverty in England between 1818 and 1848.   Now, the poor tax, which in 1801 was hardly four millions sterling, and was yet sufficient, in 1833 reached the enormous sum of £7,500,000, and was insufficient. [4]   But when, after the industrial revolution, and the securing of the permanence of profit, the capitalist class, which had been compelled, in its own defence, to limit the demand for labour and to cause pauperism, had no longer need to recur to such expedients, it limited the funds for alms by the law of 1834, [5] a law which seemed to be the triumph of the new Malthusian theory, but which was merely one of the accustomed expedients of capitalist tactics. [6]

Development of English pauperism in the periods of greatest national wealth.

In very fertile countries, where the production of the means of subsistence has far exceeded the increase of the population, the phenomenon of industrial pauperism, produced with the purpose of crystallising wages to the lowest possible degree, often occurred with great intensity. [7]   We have seen that in the United States of America,

Proportion between the population and the means of subsistence and development of pauperism.

---

[1] Mill : *Principles of Political Economy*, chap. i., p. 185.

[2] Cairnes : *Carattere e metodo logico della economia politica* in the *Biblioeca dell'Economista*, p. 304.

[3] Cairnes : *Alcuni principt fondamentali*, *ibid.*, p. 304.

[4] P. Hubert-Valleroux : *Le charité arant et depuis*, 1789.   Paris, 1890, p. 327,

[5] See an article which Roberts published in the *Fortnightly Review*, reproduced in the *Journal des économistes*, July, 1875.

[6] About the industrial nature of English pauperism, see Loria : *op. cit*,

[7] Loria ; *ibid*,

capital often restricts the demand for labour, and produces, in the greatest period of the development of public wealth, a decrease of wages, the multiplicity of men without work, and pauperism.[1]

In contemporary France food far exceeds the population; yet the persistence of the most squalid poverty, the frequency of crises, the continual agitation of the unemployed, are a standing proof that poverty is not the result of an excess of men over the means of subsistence, but of a vitiated distribution of food.

"For the first time in modern history," says an official publication, "the production of grain exceeds the needs of consumption."[2] But meantime economic mortality spreads; Europe is depressed by a powerful agrarian crisis; capital, menaced into its very existence, becomes unproductive, and the causes of misery increase with pauperism.[3]

An economist, who does not conceal his sympathies with Malthusianism, is compelled by the evidence of facts to declare that "poverty is not simply the result of the excess of population, although it is sometimes, and indeed often, derived from it; many other causes go to produce it, and among them is a vitiated distribution."[4]

Population, pauperism, and the distribution of wealth.

The Malthusian supposition which ascribed poverty to the improvidence of the working classes, and to the excess of population, is therefore erroneous, not only in its practical conclusions but also in its essence, and, as it is impotent to anticipate the causes of poverty, so it is also incapable of explaining them.

But the solution of the problem of population, which has been scarcely ever anything better than utter darkness to the economist, is to be found in the biological theory, which, conceived by Doubleday, afterwards perfected by Darwin, and precisely formulated by Spencer, has revealed new horizons to demographic science. This theory, as we have seen, maintains that the greatest individualism has for necessary con-

The bases of the new law of population. The biological theory

---

[1] Loria : *ibid.*

[2] *Bollettino di legislazione doganale*, 1885, ch. i., p. 282.

[3] *Cf.* Loria : vol. ii., p. 411 and foll.

[4] Messedaglia : *La teoria della popolazione*,

sequence the least genesis; and on the other hand that the least individualism has as a consequence the greatest fecundity. The progress of the human species always tends more and more to the development of individuality. Man, as the being with the strongest individuality, is precisely on this account the least prolific, excepting only the elephant; what is true for the different species is also true of the different races of one species. Individualism is something acquired, generation is something lost; consequently the human races which have developed most are the least prolific. And if the civilised races be more numerous, it is not because they multiply more rapidly, but because they are able to adapt themselves more easily to surroundings, and to eliminate destructive causes.

This law which connects genesis with the greater or lesser degree of individualism has the most absolute confirmation throughout the entire organic world.[1] The rose in its natural state has only five petals, but it multiplies rapidly. When cultivation perfects it and the stamina are changed into petals, the development proceeds at the expense of fecundity, and it can only be reproduced by planting shoots.[2] In the zoological world the widest experience has now unquestionably established that, while the generative power is very high among the inferior species, it is very weak among the superior species. The invisible protozoan after a few hour's life is divided into new individuals, and dies while generating them, transmitting and confounding in them his weak and passing individuality; on the other hand, the more advanced organisms are all reproduced with singular slowness. But experience, which is easy in a comparison made between different species, is rather complicated when a comparison is attempted between variously progressed types of the human species. The reason is that we cannot compare variously progressed races without taking into account many facts which have a considerable influence upon the birth-rate, such as the form of economic organisation, the political *régime*, religion, climate, the

---

[1] *Cf.* Vanni: *op. cit.*, pp. 52-68.

[2] Villey: *Traité élémentaire d'économie politique*, Paris, 1888, book iii.

productiveness of the earth. Nevertheless, even admitted the difficulty of the experiment, we may believe that Spencer's law is substantially true even in social life, and many writers have already clearly shown its essential truthfulness.[1]

Perhaps Spencer has rather exaggerated in attributing the slight fecundity of an advanced civilisation to a

The birth-rate and the psychical factor in an advanced civilisation.

purely biological fact. Moral consciousness has always modified it, and still does so. The primitive savage could have no limit or restraint in his sexual relations; but, as men became civilised, the moral feelings were developed and the sentiment of responsibility widened, the psychical factor also came to be restrictive of the birth-rate.

Guyau,[2] and afterwards Fouilleé,[3] have remarked that in-fecundity, in advanced civilisation, must be far

Guyau and woman.

more dependent upon woman than upon man. The latter, how-ever intense be his intellectual work, is always capable of having a child every year, that is to say a very high fecundity.

" *Même chez les femmes du peuple la gestation et l'accouchement,*" writes Guyau, " *étant le plus dur travail, est aussi celui qui est l'objet de la plus vive répulsion et des protestations de toute sorte. Je n'ai pas vu une femme du peuple qui ne se lamentât d'être enceinte, qui ne préférât même toute autre maladie à cette maladie de neuf mois.—Ah ! nous ne faisons pas, nous recevons, me disait l'une d'elles ; sans cela. . . .—Elle résumait ainsi la situation physio-logique et psychologique de la femme pauvre. Celle qui n'ont pas eu d'enfants, loin de s'en plaindre, s'estiment le plus souvent très heureuses. En tout cas, elles n'en désirent presque jamais plus d'un.*

" *En Picardie et en Normandie, remarque M. Baudrillart, on se moque de la femme qui a beaucoup d'enfants. Ce qui sauve la fécondité de la femme dans les autres provinces—a défaut de la religion—c'est son ignorance. Elle ne connaît pas toujours Malthus. Elle ne trouve qu'un remède au mal qu'elle redoute : fuir son mari. Telle femme d'ouvrier préfère être battue que risquer d'avoir un*

---

[1] *Cf.* above all Vanni : *loc. cit.*

[2] Guyau : *op. cit.*, p. 282.

[3] Fouilleé : *op. cit.*, p. 124-27.

nouvel enfant ; mais, comme elle est plus faible, elle reçoit souvent presque à la fois les coups et l'enfant. La crainte de l'enfant est plus fréquemment qu'on ne croit une cause de dissensions dans les ménages pauvres, comme d'ailleurs dans les ménages riches. Du moment où la femme raisonne au lieu de se laisser guider par la foi, elle ne peut pas manquer de sentir la très grande disproportion qui existe pour elle entre les joies de l'amour et le souffrances de la maternité. Il faudrait qu'une nouvelle idée intervint ici, celle du devoir, et non pas seulement d'une obligation religieuse, dont le mari peut se railler, mais d'une obligation morale."[1]

With the increase of needs, with the advancement of the standard of life, there grows an aversion to a numerous offspring even among the women of the lower classes. In all this there is an instinctive need which it would be vain to combat, and there is an egotistical feeling, which, causing oliganthropy, constitutes one of the great perils of modern nations.

Excessive fecundity has secured the march of civilisation.

Fecundity and civilisation. Civilisation will now fix regular limits to fecundity, and what Malthus and the Malthusians thought an inscrutable and profound mystery will certainly have nothing dangerous or terrible in the future.

Therefore, in the future, the *minimum* of fecundity will corre-

Maximum of individuation, minimum of fecundity. spond with the *maximum* of individuation. But here the difficulty between the followers of the individualist school and of the socialist school becomes greater than ever. The *maximum* of individuation, say the former, is only possible in a society which, allowing perfect freedom of competition, daily causes the prevalence of the stronger beings and the elimination of the weaker. On the other hand, the followers of the second school maintain that a great and general individuation is only possible in a perfectly socialist society, in one where public assistance is perfectly organised, and where the feeling of solidarity is very deep and active. Objective examination leads us to the conclusion that the adherents of the individualist school

[1] Guyau : *op. cit.*, pp. 282, 283. Mill had already recognised that the question of fecundity affects women much more closely than men,

start from false premises, and, consequently, fall into not less false conclusions. For, confusing a purely biological phenomenon with a social phenomenon, they give the character of animal struggles to economic struggles. But the struggle for existence in human society has lost its fatal character; those who conquer in this unequal fight are not the strong; and the vanquished, far from being eliminated, survive and multiply more rapidly than their victors. We have seen, moreover, that the profound differences between various social classes, and the consequent poverty of the lower classes, far from causing a limitation of the birth-rate, are actually a powerful cause of fecundity. A perfect and general individualism will be possible only when the social, not the natural causes, of these profound inequalities shall have been suppressed. *The maximum of individuation will, therefore, be possible only in the maximum of socialisation.*[1]

In support of Spencer's forecasts, according to which the progress of civilisation will necessarily cause a weaker birth-rate, we have statistical proofs of unquestionable value. For hardly did civilisation become widely diffused than fecundity began to everywhere decrease.[2] In some countries the annual birth-rate has decreased in parallel ratio to the marriages; but in many others the average of marriages has remained stationary, or has actually increased, while the birth-rate has increased. Therefore, not fewness of marriages, and hence the diffusion of vice, not the influence of economic crisis, but secret causes which escape the regard of a superficial observer, have influenced the limitation of fecundity.

In France, the number of legitimate births for every marriage has been as follows from the beginning of the century :—[3]

Economic struggles and animal struggles.

Limitation of the birth-rate in advanced countries.

Number of legitimate births for every marriage in France.

. [1] I intend to demonstrate this essential truth of economic science in another work. It has been perceived, moreover, by various authors.

[2] A native of Finland has furnished ample proof in support of this truth. *Cf.* J. V. Tallquist : *Recherches statistiques sur la tendance à une moindre fécondité des mariages.* Helsingfors, 1886.

[3] Levasseur : *op. cit.*

1800-1805	-	-	-	-	-	4·24
1816-1820	-	-	-	-	-	4·08
1836-1840	-	-	-	-	-	3·26
1856-1860	-	-	-	-	-	3·04
1881-1885	-	-	-	-	-	3·03
1886-1889	-	-	-	-	-	2·96

In the period between 1874 and 1890—that is, during a period when the absence of famine and war and the increase of exchanges should have produced a great birth-rate—in almost every civilised country it has rapidly decreased.[1]   (*See* table on p. 173).

With few exceptions, therefore, the fecundity of civilised countries continually tend to decrease.[2]   No apparent cause can explain this satisfactorily to the Malthusian school.   And without Spencer's hypothesis we should be unable to give any explanation of the fact.

My readers will be still more convinced of the reality of the tendency to which I refer, after examining the case of five civilised nations of Europe.   For if we put the birth-rate of their five states as 100 in 1873, we find that it decreased in the following proportion in the years 1878, 1885, and 1890 :—

The birth-rate of five European states between 1873 and 1890.

	Italy.	France.	Germany.	England.	Belgium.
1873	100	100	100	100	100
1878	98	96	97	100	99
1885	101	93	94	87	95
1890	100	87	92	81	92

It is therefore undeniable that there exists this tendency of

[1] Compiled from data furnished by Professor Bodio.

[2] At the Hygienic Congress of Vienna in 1887 Inama Sterneg remarked that the population of Europe has doubled during the last seventy years, but that this increase is an abnormal fact, and that it had proceeded equally with the increase of every branch of human activity.   Now, however, the birth-rate has a tendency to diminish.   See Van der Smissen : *op. cit.*, in the chapter on *Les lois de Malthus,*

BIRTH-RATE FOR A 1000 INHABITANTS.

	1874.	1876.	1878.	1880.	1882.	1884.	1886.	1888.	1890.
Italy...............	34·9	39·0	35·9	33·6	36·9	38·9	36·9	37·6	35·9
France............	26·2	26·2	25·3	24·7	24·9	24·9	24·1	23·2	21·9
Germany.........	40·1	40·8	38·9	37·6	37·3	37·2	37·0	36·6	35·6
England	38·0	36·4	35·6	34·3	33·7	33·3	32·4	30·6	30·2
Scotland.........	35·6	35·6	34·0	34·0	33·3	33·7	32·9	31·3	30·4
Ireland............	26·6	26·7	25·4	24·7	24·1	24·0	23·3	22·9	22·3
Austria	39·7	40·0	38·6	37·7	39·1	38·7	38·0	37·9	36·7
Hungary..........	42·7	45·1	42·2	45·9	43·9	45·2	44·9	43·6	40·6
Belgium	32·6	33·2	31·5	31·1	31·2	30·5	29·6	29·1	28·7
Holland...........	36·1	36·8	35·8	35·4	35·1	34·9	34·6	33·7	32·9
Sweden	30·7	30·7	29·7	29·4	29·3	29·9	29·7	28·7	28·3
Norway...........	30·6	31·6	30·9	30·6	31·1	31·2	31·1	31·0	30·6
Denmark.........	30·9	32·6	31·7	31·8	32·4	33·4	32·6	31·7	30·6
Spain	—	—	36·2	35·6	36·2	36·8	37·2	36·7	38·0
Roumania........	47·8	30·6	26·3	31·9	35·2	37·5	39·6	40·9	—
European Russia.	50·4	49·6	46·4	48·7	50·6	50·4	48·5	—	—
Massachusetts...	28·3	25·5	24·7	24·8	24·9	25·4	25·4	25·9	—
Connecticut......	25·3	23·5	22·3	22·2	19·5	20·5	20·8	21·8	—
Rhode Island....	24·8	23·3	24·0	22·1	24·0	24·0	24·5	24·2	—

civilised countries to limit their birth-rate, and it is undeniable that Spencer's supposition finds its most complete confirmation in statistical inquiry.

But if we admit the Spencerian supposition, we must also

Decadence of individ-
ualism and consequent
development of indi-
viduality. necessarily exclude the Malthusian supposition; for the one naturally destroys the other, and the existence of both is impossible. Malthus believes that man was condemned by necessity to limit his fecundity, and in his disheartening conclusions he can only see a continual struggle between man and nature, and he condemns him inevitably either to the rigour of an inviolable law, or to a severe abstinence and immoral practices; while, on the other hand, the Spencerian theory finds a remedy in civilisation itself, and is devoid pessimism and fatality.

The theorists of economic individualism have naturally accepted the first theory and rejected the second; those of them who adhered to this last, confusing individuality with individualism, have come to the conclusion that a perfect individualism will be possible only with the perfect triumph of individuation.

It is, first of all, necessary to understand the differences which

Differences between in-
dividualism and indi-
viduality. exist between the development of individualism and the development of individuality.

The development of individuality implies an increase of functions, either in number or in density; the development of individualism is simply the prevalence of the egotistical sentiment.

Now while on the one hand the march of civilisation tends to increase human individuality, it tends also to diminish individualism.

Given, in fact, the primitive forms of association, individualism was necessarily very strong; being bound to no one, and checked by no social bond, the primitive man had neither family duties nor duties of association. He was an absolutely individualist being.

But as, under the influences of economic and demographic causes, association advanced and the bonds became closer, individualism decayed.

Every member of the association daily acquires new duties towards the family, the state and collectivity. Law, that is compulsion, makes many of these duties obligatory. The individual, far from being absolutely free, is bound in many ways; he cannot be the absolute arbiter of his own condition, nor the blind fulfiller of his own instincts. Hence individualism declines.

But, on the other hand, as the links of association become closer, individuality increases. Not only is it safe- Individualism and individuality as opposite guarded in life, but, by a succession of secular terms. evolutions, it ends by being so, in his capacity for work, in his moral integrity, even in his liberty. Therefore individuality grows.

We can admit that every development of individuality is nothing else than the decrease of individualism.[1]

Individualism, which is falsely considered as a theory destined to have a large future development, cannot now be regarded as other than a necessary historic phase, through which society has already, in great part, passed. The old legitimist formula *(l'État c'est moi)* has necessarily had a reaction, and a perfectly contrary formula has been arrived at *(les mois sont l'État)*. The atomistic conception of sovereign individuals, which is the foundation of Rousseau's teaching in the *Contrât Social*, has been realised as an indispensable protest; but the historic moment which produced it is now over, and there is no reason why it should continue.

In politics, individualism is a mechanical conception, according to which humanity is nothing else than an ag- Individualism as a political conception. gregate of individuals, social atoms identical in nature, impenetrable and equal to each other. Their agglomerations are purely arbitrary, depending only upon the utility or pleasure of those composing them ; there is not, nor can there be, any other law than the opinion of the whole or the majority of the individuals.[2]

[1] Concerning this difference see Nitti : *Socialismo scientifico e socialismo utopistico.* Florence, 1892.

[2] *Cf.* Ziegler : *op. cit.*, chap. i.   *Cf.* Schmoller : *Ueber einige, Grundfragen des Rechts und der Volkswirtschaft,* Jena, 1875, p. 98 and foll.

In morality individualism places the supreme rule of good and
Individualism as a moral conception. of evil in the personality, in the general conscience
of each ; virtue only consists in following this
individual guide.   Hence, it is not the result but the motive of
the act which makes its morality.   Man is naturally free, and the
law which binds him is a law of his rational nature.

Further, in political economy, the individualist conception
Individualism and its economic basis. takes a purely mechanical character; differing
from every ethical law, this conception really only
sees individuals at war with individuals.   The individual is no
longer considered as a being who maintains moral relations, and
is hence subject to fixed obligations, but as an ideal being (*homo
œconomicus*) who produces, exchanges, and consumes wealth.

Individualism and liberalism once seemed and were synonyms,
Individualism and liberalism. because both were produced by the same need.
But, with the changes of things, the first neces-
sarily leads to the limitation, if not to the destruction of the
second.

Individualism is in reality based upon the supposition that
men are naturally equal and have an equal right to struggle and
to bring about the triumph of their own interests.   But since
this natural equality does not exist, and social institutions and
historical heredity make it quite impossible, it comes about that
the number of those who triumph is continually less, while, on
the other hand, that of the vanquished to whom the enjoyment of
the advantages of liberty continually increases ; thus it happens
that the individualist theory is deficient even in that which
caused its origin, namely, the desire to secure to the largest
possible number of individuals, the largest possible amount of
liberty.

In opposition to this theory, there is another which conceives
Society as an organ- ism. society to be a real organism where every individual is a member and part of the whole, to the
vitality of which he contributes.   Society, producing and consuming, is not, according to this theory, an aggregate of isolated
atoms, but an aggregate, in which the production and distribution

of wealth answer to that which the functions of assimilation and circulation are in a living being.[1] According to the fundamental conception of this theory, the first and greatest need becomes that of the preservation of the social organism. Consequently, individual activities are directed, not simply in an egotistical sense, but for the benefit of collectivity, the interests of which should prevail over those of individuals.

The life of society lends itself to the intervention which reforms and regulates a collective will much more than the life of individuals, and, gradually as the social organism gains cohesion and strength, this function is more and more developed. Far from repressing individual liberty it allows of its development; the intervention of the collective power is extended and justified, by means of the limitation of despotic forms of this intervention, destined to develop the superior forms of self-government to the advantage of individual liberty. Hence the organisation appears not as a repression of the liberty of the majority, but as its defence ; and the state becomes not the antithesis, but the synthesis of individuals.[2]

The intervention which regulates the collective will.

Hence the law, which, starting from a truth which finds the most complete confirmation among the human races, and among the innumerable species of the organic world, associates the *minimum* of fecundity with the *maximum* of individuation, could not be largely developed except in a society of perfect social organisation.

The idea of solidarity is not connected with an unjustified assumption of social justice, but is the consequence of the Darwinian theories.

Unquestionably there exists in human society a solidarity in evil as in good, and no phenomenon can be said to be altogether particular to one class and entirely external to another.

[1] This is the thesis which Schäffle has slightly exaggerated in his now classic work *Bau und Leben des sozialen Korpers* (1875-78), but which is still essentially true. *Cf.* Schmoller : *Zur Litteratur geschichte der Staats und Sozialwissenschaften*, 1888, pp. 211-32.

[2] G. de Greef : *Les lois sociologiques*, Paris, 1893, pp. 150, 151.

Nature itself has compelled us to this ever-increasing solidarity, and nothing but the ignorance of its laws could have led to the excesses of the individualist philosophy.

The microbes of poor quarters also attack richer quarters; just as the vices of the upper classes infect the lower classes, thanks to the law of imitation.

Therefore no real progress is possible in the society of the future without a proportionate development of economic and moral solidarity. [1]

And every development of solidarity, modifying in turn the general conditions and operating a greater diffusion of wealth, will inevitably exercise a useful influence on fecundity.

And it is quite certain that we also tend to definitely abandon
The new demographic phases. the period of blind fecundity, which has so long characterised human history. We are gradually abandoning animal and blind fecundity for a reasonable and methodic development.

No great increase of population will be any longer possible without a parallel development in every branch of human activity. [2]

A great epoch is ending, and another is beginning, and we cannot yet foresee the phases of this last.

The question of population should be studied from a racial
The classic theory contrary to civilisation. standpoint, not less than biologically and econo-
mically. Doubtless Malthus confusedly hoped that the popular classes would adopt restrictive measures, and that hence only the middle and higher classes would remain prolific, and that human progress would receive a new and powerful

---

1 *Cf.* Charles Gide : *L'Idée de solidarité en tant que programme écono-mique* in the *Revue de Sociologie*, Sept., Oct., 1893. See also, for the same, a conference by Gide in the book entitled *Quatres écoles d'économie sociale*, Geneva, 1890, and Durckeim : *La Division du travail social*, Paris, 1893 ; Wagner : *Rede ueber die sociale Frage*, Berlin, 1871; C. Secretan: *Principes de morale ;* etc.

2 Such is also the opinion of Zaborowski : *L'avenir des races humaines* in the *Revue scientifique*, December 17, 1892.

influence from this marvellous process of selection. But facts soon showed that this was a vain Utopia : the only class which has never listened to Malthus and which never listens to him, is the class which he addressed ; the popular classes are still devoted to natural practices, and only the richer classes allow themselves to violate it. Moreover, from this Malthusian tendency of the upper classes, is derived one of the greatest perils for the future of human kind.

Jacoby has demonstrated that every great elevation in wealth, power, and talent, necessarily leads to infecundity. This thesis, which he exaggerated and, consequently, rendered anarchical, was, and is, fundamentally true.[1]

The fecundity of superior types.

And when the superior races and classes of a society have begun to recur to Malthusian practices, the peril, which is already in the nature of things, is necessarily increased.

Galton and Rümelin, two profound thinkers, have acutely pointed out this evil.[2] In the old-standing civilisations, observes Galton, the active and ambitious classes are induced by many reasons to defer the age of matrimony ; and many marriages are dictated by economic motives. Hence there is in old nations a permanent obstacle to the fecundity of the more elevated classes, so that only the weak and improvident are very prolific. Thus the race gradually deteriorates, preserving the appearances of civilisation, until it reverts to barbarism, during the sway of which, however, the race may regain its former strength.

The pessimistic hypothesis of Galton and Rümelin.

And Rümelin, observing that the rich are provident, and the wage-earners improvident and boundlessly prolific, asks in dismay, if this singular fact, which renders the intelligent classes stationary and the uncultured elements more numerous, be not an inversion of the Darwinian selection.

What is true of individuals is also true of races ; the superior races naturally have a low birth-rate, while, on the other hand, the inferior races are very prolific.

Malthusianism contrary to civilisation.

---

[1] Jacoby : *op. cit.*

[2] Galton : *op cit.* ; Rümelin : *op. cit.*

Now, if Malthus could find followers among the inferior races, among the Indians or the Chinese, the harm might not be very great ; on the contrary, he has found them among the superior races, the Latins, the Anglo-Saxons and the Celts. Conceive for a moment that the civilised countries of Europe and America allowed their birth-rate to be less than 20 for every thousand, and that hence the births were only equal to the deaths, or even below them. And if meanwhile the immense populations of China and India continue to multiply abundantly, within a few centuries the best countries will be necessarily inundated by the inferior populations. The future of mankind depends upon the proportion between the inferior and the superior races ; if these last prevail, civilisation is safe ; if the others prevail, it is in peril or it will be destroyed. If science has demonstrated that the superior races are the least prolific, to voluntarily help to intensify this pheno-menon is to unconsciously prepare the decay of civilisation, the brutalising of the world. We have said that if Malthus had found followers among the Chinese and Indians, no great good or evil would be likely to come of it. But the Malthusian proselytes are among the best types, and this is a calamity to the future of the race. A European represents a social capital, at least ten times superior to that of an Oriental ; to impel these to fecundity and the others in a contrary direction is a preference of the worst, and a preparation for the triumph not of the best but of the weakest.[1]

In 1816 it was calculated that Java and Madura had a popula-tion of 4,615,000 ; in 1830, as many as 6,838,000 ; in 1849, 9,584,000, and in 1869, 15,573,000.[2] According to the tables of *Turasschek* in 1889, there were not fewer than 22,818,000 inhabi-tants. It is an instance of the most continuous and rapid increase. Now, if these inferior races which people barbarous Asia and all uncivilised countries develop so rapidly, and if, on the other hand, oliganthropy be artificially brought about in civil-ised countries, it will be seen if civilisation can make resistance for long.

[1] *Cf.* Guyau : *op. cit.*, pp. 269-71.
[2] Levasseur : *op. cit.*, vol. iii., pp. 21, 22.

But these evident truths are strongly opposed by some naturalists. If certain naturalists and biologists object, The biological thesis. statisticians will persistently continue to predict the survival of populations by reason of their quantity and their rate of multiplication, the naturalist will necessarily reject the idea. The survival of a species or of a family does not depend upon quantity but upon quality; thus the most individualised type will prevail by reason of its slow increase.[1]

Here is an evident confusion between a natural phenomenon and a purely social phenomenon, and one which is Insufficiency of the biological thesis. simply dependent upon economic conditions. For, if it be true, on the one hand, that the most civilised societies, by reason of a natural law, abandon a period of abundant and disordered fecundity, and enter upon a period of regular fecundity, it is also true that this happens unconsciously, without a decay of morals, without violent changes, almost imperceptibly. But when the population voluntarily, and through a spirit of egotism, obeys the Malthusian precept and tends to check its fecundity, even individuation must decrease, since, with the failure of moral ties, the change of marriage into monogamic prostitution, the weakening of social solidarity, even the individual ends sooner or later by feeling the effect of the degradation of his surroundings. This argument, therefore, fails in the face of facts, and the last apparent support of Malthusianism fails also.

A last doubt, and one not less grave, is frequently met with in the writings of the new and old theorists of popu- Population in the future. lation. In any case, they say population, even with a light increase, will, in the not distant future, become so great that the production of the means of subsistence of which the earth is capable will not be able to suffice. Then the forecast of Malthus will be realised in all its rigour; human improvidence will find a terrible penalty in the inflexible laws of nature.

But there is a fundamental error in this; for the demographers, who so reason, do not remember the virtual tendency of population to proportion itself to the means of subsistence, and that increas-

[1] Geddes and Thomson : *L'evolution du sexe*, pp. 416, 417.

ing individuation will in the future limit the birth-rate much more than at present.

Treatises on Catholic dogma always have a special chapter *Demographic eschat- ology and the vainness of forecasts.* called *Eschatology* or *the last things*, in which an endeavour is made to give more or less information about the future of life, of which, however, nothing is known.

Economists have lost, and often lose, time in dealing with demographic *eschatology*.

Yet nothing is more stupid than the calculations to which statisticians have abandoned themselves in order to foresee the population of a country, of a continent, or of the earth, within a given number of years or centuries, and to foresee also what will be the production of the substances most necessary to such numerous population.[1] Such hypotheses, being without a scientific basis, are no better than so many arithmetical calculations.

Dr. Bertillon has made very merry over those unwise statisticians who abandon themselves to the more distant prophesyings. These naturally vary at different periods; based upon the medium of increase between 1821 and 1831, they judged a hundred and one years were necessary for the doubling of the population of France; when based upon the rate between 1846 and 1851, they judged a period of a hundred and fourteen years to be necessary.[2] And if their taste for eschatology led them to base their calculation upon recent years, and if they were to suppose that the limitation of the birth-rate were to continue, they could foretell at what date France is destined to disappear.

But these are merely exercises in arithmetic, without scientific value and practical utility.

What will happen in a distant future need not give us trouble. *The problem of population as the problem of the future.* Posterity will have gathered such a mass of facts, observation and study, that it can quite well face the problems, the very existence and nature of which are hidden to us.

---

[1] *Cf.*, among others, Ravenstein in the *Proceedings of the Royal Geographical Society*, January, 1891.

[2] *Cf.* Bertillon in the *Encyclopédie d'hygiène*, tom. i., p. 140.

There is only one thing certain : that no foresight is possible in this matter; and that it depends upon the mental condition of the observer whether he will accept pessimistic rather than optimistic hypotheses. The melancholy philanthropy of The pessimistic conception and the optimistic conception. Malthus looked upon the humanity of the future as the theatre of a tragic struggle between love and hunger. Others make the future depend upon mere scientific discoveries, which, moreover, are quite unrealisable. "*Qu'on se figure,*" says Rénan, "*la révolution sociale qui s'accomplira quand la chimie aura trouvé le moyen, en imitant le travail de la feuille des plantes et en captant l'acide carbonique de l'air, de produire des aliments superieurs à ceux que fournissent les végétaux et les betes des champs . . .*" [1] And an illustrious Italian physiologist adds : " The discovery which would most benefit the world at present would be that of azote, in a form easy of assimilation." One of the most attractive of our scientists, Mantegazza, wrote many years ago : "To feed the poor of Europe with azote, in a form not repugnant to the palate, would be to save them many miseries, and to increase the strength of the nations, and to raise the average life of a country." [2]

Werner Siemens and Eisler have declared it possible to transform inorganic matter into food by means of electricity at no distant period; Liebig, how immense the fertility of the earth could become if certain methods of manuring were in use. Finally, other writers, and all among the most authoritative, have conceived even greater hopes.

When deduction and not induction is used, and forecasts are based not upon concrete facts but upon probable suppositions, excessive pessimism or excessive optimism may be arrived at according to personal disposition and the fundamental principles of the reasoning used. Thus, while economic pessimism, accepting with Malthus a mere probable hypothesis, arrives at disheartening conclusions, economic optimism, also accepting the not less probable hypotheses that the azote of the air might be easily assimilated

---

[1] Rénan : *Dialogues philosophiques.* *Probabilités*, p. 85.
[2] Albertoni : *La fisiologia e la questione sociale*, p. 20.

and become a substance of popular food, arrives at agreeable conclusions.

But let us admit for a moment that the contrasts between the Comparisons between production of men and of the means of subsistence population and the means of subsistence. and the forecasts about the progressions of both have value.

Entering upon the analysis of the problem, it will be well to The problem of popula- note first of all that it now presents itself in a tion a world-wide problem. very different way from formerly. Even at the end of the last century, and in the first half of this century, famines, caused, as we saw, by a bad system of circulation, rather than by insufficient production, were grave and of frequent occurrence.

The markets were then very limited. As we have said, a bad Population and inter- harvest was sufficient to cause a famine ; deaths national exchange. from hunger were very numerous, and reached proportions which now seem almost incredible. And meanwhile, in a neighbouring province or state, there was a crisis of over-production ; and in the year following there frequently occurred an over-abundant harvest in the same district. Economy was then local ; it only became gradually national, with the suppression of internal barriers and the development of communication ; and it is only in times near our own that a world-wide economy has become possible by the abolition of international prohibition tariffs and the development of the means of transport. At present a bad harvest in India, Brazil, or the United States quickly influences the price of European markets ; and there is not a movement of the Bourse of Paris, London, New York, and Hamburg which does not at once attract general notice.

Given a system of world-wide economy, the problem of popula- The problem of popula- tion will also be a universal problem ; it is tion in a system of world-wide economy. impossible to confine it within the narrow limits of a national question.

When markets were very limited, famines were very frequent ; if a district was visited by storms it was sufficient to cause poverty and famine. Now when there is a bad harvest under one degree of longitude, there is another very abundant one ; losses always end by being compensated for by the abundant production of other countries. The production of grain all the world over annually undergoes insignificant changes ; hence prices everywhere tend to become equal, and the losses of one year to become equal with the gains of the year following.

Natural famines cannot, therefore, ever occur ; and if they sometimes occur in some backward country, such as Russia, they have not their former intensity, and they also depend, as has been shown, rather upon social than upon natural causes.[1]

Nations which are in a larger commercial phase find their primary substances in the most different countries, so that the closing of a market may not prove fatal to them. England was supplied thus in 1889 [2] :— The sale of primary articles in the more advanced nations.

Quarters of wheat imported from

Russia	4,264,335
The United States	3,403,250
India	1,843,466
Roumania	572,497
Germany	507,725
Australia	281,212
Canada	23,366

Now almost every latitude and longitude are represented in this list ; there are countries which are at opposite poles ; there are many that differ entirely with regard to climate, production, and population. Hence if the annual production of wheat should be less in any one of them, England could provide herself in a large measure from the markets of the others.

In England, the quota of increase between 1870 and 1880 was as follows :— The quota of increase in England.

---

[1] The great Russian famine is also attributed to the bad distribution of wealth, and to the fact that Russia is but slightly progressed economically. *Cf.* A. A. Jssaïew : *La famine en Russie* in the *Revue d'économie politique,* 1892, p. 739 and foll.

[2] *Cf.* Levasseur : *op. cit.*

Population - - - - -	11 per cent.
Commerce - - - - -	13 ,,
Mercantile Navy - - - -	16 ,,
Mineral production - - -	45 ,,
Railway traffic - - - -	45 ,,

Comparing the commercial data furnished by Dr. Geffcken with those about population supplied by Dr. Longstaff, we find that, in the thirty years elapsing between 1850 and 1880, the increase of international commerce far exceeded that of population.[1]

Increase of population and commerce, 1850-1880 :—

	Increase of Commerce.	Increase of Population.
Great Britain -	258 per cent.	27·4 per cent.
France - -	393 ,,	8·9 ,,
Belgium - -	231 ,,	23·0 ,,
Germany - -	183 ,,	28·4 ,,
Italy - - -	170 ,,	17·9 ,,
Austria-Hungary -	362 ,,	23·0 ,,

Hence the question of population is a universal one, and can henceforward only be considered as such.

Now, when the population of a country increases in a short time, Suppositions about an excessive development of population. and when there is no parallel increase in all the branches of production (we merely formulate a hypothesis, and one which no longer seems possible), two consequences may follow from this phenomenon : either the increase of population causes an increase of production ; or, and this is more probable, a certain portion of the population turns to the uncultivated land or emigrates into distant countries.

As long as there remain uncultivated lands, every newly-born human being will mean an increase of human capital.

[1] Geffcken in the Schönberg *Handbuch*, chap. ii., p. 954; Longstaff : *Studies in Statistics*, p. 183 ; Lyttleton : *loc. cit.*

Fertile, uncultivated land still occupies a very great portion of the earth. Even England, which is the most advanced agricultural country, has an extent of unproductive fields equal to a fifth of its whole surface.[1]

Uncultivated land and population.

When we reflect that Russia, in Europe, has only 16·5 inhabitants for every *kilomètre* q.; that North America has only 4; that South America has hardly 2; and that Australia, with its mild climate and fertile soil, has only 0·35;[2] when we remember that regions, which are perhaps the most fertile in the world, are still inaccessible to European civilisation,[3] and countries, which were once great and flourishing civilised nations, now support only a few poor nomadic tribes, we are justified in concluding that every numerical increase of the human race unquestionably implies a double increase of civilisation and wealth.

According to the despondent philanthropy of Malthus, the numerical increase of men implies bringing poverty and death into the world, and anticipating the period of the complete ruin of nature. The results of scientific inquiry demonstrate, on the contrary, that the theory of pessimistic economy has no foundation in fact.

Inconsistency of the pessimistic thesis.

We can consider the theories about population in two different lights : as theoretical economy and as political economy. Now under the former aspect, the Malthusian principle is nothing better than an unverified supposition, but one which is opposed to all the recent conquests of biology, sociology, and statistics.

The two aspects of the theories about population.

But Malthus' despondent philanthropy was not so much intended to confirm the theoretic truth of a demographic principle, as to give

---

[1] Deconinck : *Le monde économique*, Brussels, 1886, p. 80. The large amount of uncultivated land in England depends almost entirely upon the bad distribution of wealth. In one of his last speeches, at Birmingham, August 27, 1886, John Bright said that half the soil of England belonged to 180 individuals, and the soil of Scotland belonged to ten or twelve persons.

[2] See Schræder's Atlas ; and Van der Smissen : *op. cit.*, p. 16.

[3] See Lavollée's article in the *Reme des deux mondes*, June 15, 1889.

a new direction to political economy. But, since the objective study of social phenomena has shown that poverty is itself a powerful help to disordered fecundity ; when the distribution of wealth appears closely bound up with the demographic phenomenon ; when biology has revealed the close connection between the birthrate and the anatomical and physical progress of mankind ; when the theory of social capillarity has made it clear that the actual constitution of our individualist society is contrary to the development of the species ; when, in a word, new theories on social assistance have triumphed, the Malthusian principle has received a mortal blow not merely in its theoretic essence, but in its practical and positive function.

The nature of Malthus' essay was so profoundly pessimistic, that even Mill, who inclined towards economic optimism, was frequently and directly under its influence. It is sufficient to read his conclusions on the changing vicissitudes of the distinctive features of economic progress (the accumulation of capital, the increase of population, the perfecting of the means of production) to perceive that he shared the cardinal error of Malthusianism, an error which, notwithstanding his premises, led him inevitably into pessimism.[1]

The perils of economic pessimism.

Now nothing is more baneful to all social advancement than this unjustifiable economic pessimism. Indeed, if poverty be regarded as the fated consequence of civilisation, human energy is altogether weakened.

Consequences of economic pessimism.

Unfortunately the majority of economists incline to this pessimistic fatalism, which, since Malthus and Cournot to our own day, has found thousands of adherents, and from which even Mill, as I have said, was not wholly independent.

Several years ago one of the most esteemed German writers, Treitschke, distinctly asserted that " no civilisation was possible without wage-earners," that great inequality " necessarily results from civilisation," that " it is given only to a few to enjoy the superior goods of civilisation," that " the mass must always re-

[1] Mill : *op. cit.* (French edit.), tom. ii., pp. 269, 270.

main such," and that this is "equitable and necessary." He even went further, and from the increase of needs and men, he drew the terrible conclusion, that "the majority of men must live in a mediocre position, and that the average length of labour cannot be decreased."[1]

Is not such fatalistic pessimism, which blindly opposes all the results of science, pernicious to every idea of progress, to every energetic effort, to every development of solidarity ?

If modern science has any merit, it is precisely that of having destroyed the theocratic bases of pessimistic fatalism. The ancient Pagan conception placed the irrevocable golden age before the period of civilisation, and regarded civilisation as a decadence from a former good ; the old Christian idea placed every ideal in a distant world outside of this one. Thus both the Pagan and the Christian theories were imbued with one common practical pessimism, since one placed happiness in a vanished epoch and the other placed it in a sphere external to us.
Ancient fatalism and modern science.

Stuart Mill, who held communism, even in its purest form, possible, but dangerous to civilisation, wished to discover what would be the prevailing demographic form in a communist society, and he concluded that such a system would have impeded the development of population. In a perfectly communist system, according to Mill's forecast, the increase of men would necessarily be exactly proportioned to that of the means of subsistence.[2]
Communism and population: Mill's thesis.

Dumont, on the contrary, says that it is quite clear that the socialist principle of the equality of social functions, if entirely applied, would necessarily imply the destruction of social capillarity and cause a very high birth-
Socialism and population according to Dumont.

---

[1] See the article by him in *Der Sozialismus und seine Gönner* in the *Preussische Jahrbücher*, 1874, vol. xxxiv., pp. 64-110 and 248-301. Moreover, such expressions abound in the works of many economists, especially in those of Leroy-Beaulieu. *Cf.* Julin : *art. cit.*

[2] Mill : *op. cit.*, vol. i., p. 242.

rate. Compelling men to immobility, and suppressing their tendency to ascend, it would produce a very great fecundity.[1]

Each of these opposite views is partly true, or, rather, starting from two principles which each contain some truth; they reach false conclusions by the exaggeration of these principles.

The communist system, which Mill studied and held possible, would not be applicable in the actual state of society and population. On the other hand, a society, like that spoken of by Dumont, which successfully eliminated every power of rising, would be condemned to stagnation and death.

But Mill, imbued with the ideas of Malthus and Ricardo, and perfectly convinced that Dynamism causes poverty and misery to society, prefers the ideal hope of a stationary society.

Mill and economic pessimism.

Now the stable equilibrium is not possible in human societies with a progressive and fatal decadence. The life of society, like the life of individuals and of all organic bodies, is in a perpetual, unstable equilibrium, and this instability is one of the conditions necessary to every increase and progress ; the stable equilibrium would be death.

The stable equilibrium in advanced societies.

The fancy that what mathematicians designate a form-limit, could exist in economy, as in politics, is an absurd idea and unwarranted by any positive observation. In biology a form-limit is not admissible either for the fixity of specific types, or for the duration of life, and it is still less so in human society, which is more plastic and changeable than individual organisms.

The suppression of every kind of struggle, the elimination of every unsatisfied need, would bring about a fatal and irresistible cessation of development in society.

Fallacy of the idea of stages.

And the ideal of absolute communism can only be a passing one.

The ancient communist states of society endured only by limiting fecundity and condemning many newly born to death. Even the aristocratic communism, desired by Plato in his *Republic*, fixes

---

[1] Dumont : *op. cit.*, p. 127.

exactly the number of families and of births, and sets insurmountable barriers to generation.

Therefore, admitting that Mill's supposition be not without some foundation, since it allows the intimate connection between the distribution of wealth and the birth-rate, we cannot allow it any practical value.

Socialism and individualism are merely two great poles in human history ; humanity may approach near to both, but cannot adhere to either.

A completely communist society, even where it were possible, given the high actual number of population, in destroying all individual foresight, could not but injure individuality, and hence cause a very great fecundity.   Finally, it would be the cause of its own destruction.

The same would occur, if it were possible to give reality to the aspirations of pure collectivism and to substitute a purely collective society for that of to-day.

On the other hand, a society strongly organised socially, where the development of individuality could advance equally with that of a conscious and ordered co-operation, would end by restricting the birth-rate within well-defined limits.

Population in a strongly organised state of society.

Every diffusion of wealth, and every increase of solidarity imply, as we have seen, a development of individuality.   Every development of individuality implies a decrease of fecundity.

We may, therefore, conclude that *in every society where individuality will be strongly developed, but where progress of socialisation will not extinguish individual activity ; in every society where wealth will be largely subdivided and where the social cause of inequality will be eliminated by an elevated form of co-operation, the birth-rate will tend to become equal with the means of subsistence, and the regular variations of demographic evolution, will,* not have, *as in the past, an element of fear and terror.*

The new law of population.

This conclusion, which we hold to be scientifically unassailable, and largely proved by the most impartial statis-

Conclusion.

tics, gives a death-blow to Malthusianism and to the principle hitherto maintained by the classic school.

But even when the Malthusian principle will be entirely repudiated; even when the postulates, which seem to be as granite rocks, will end by being destroyed under the dissolving action of truth; even when the theories which we have exposed will have been generally accepted, and the society of our day will accept the principle of co-operation, though guarding against the danger of passing from the dynamic to the static phase; even then the work of Malthus will appear worthy of the greatest respect and of the greatest admiration.

And its fate will be like that of Babylon. Even when the vast city was destroyed and the waters devastated it, and time covered it with oblivion, the vast ruins still filled the astonished beholder with respectful wonder.

Even when Malthus' essay shall have altogether failed, and the current of the new ideas and the new researches shall have buried it, and time which, as Anacreon says, conquers everything, shall have consumed it, it will still appear a wonderful monument of insight and acumen.

THE END.

Printed by Cowan & Co., Limited, Perth.

SOCIAL SCIENCE SERIES.
SCARLET CLOTH, EACH 2s. 6d.

SOCIAL SCIENCE SERIES—(*Continued*).

20. Common Sense about Women. T. W. HIGGINSON
" An admirable collection of papers, advocating in the most liberal spirit the emancipation of women."—*Woman's Herald*.

21. The Unearned Increment. W. H. DAWSON.
" A concise but comprehensive volume."—*Echo*.

22. Our Destiny. LAURENCE GRONLUND.
" A very vigorous little book, dealing with the influence of Socialism on morals and religion."—*Daily Chronicle*.

23. The Working-Class Movement in America.
Dr. EDWARD and E. MARX AVELING.
" Will give a good idea of the condition of the working classes in America, and of the various organisations which they have formed."—*Scots Leader*.

24. Luxury. Prof. EMILE DE LAVELEYE.
" An eloquent plea on moral and economical grounds for simplicity of life."—*Academy*.

25. The Land and the Labourers. Rev. C. W. STUBBS, M.A.
" This admirable book should be circulated in every village in the country."—*Manchester Guardian*.

26. The Evolution of Property. PAUL LAFARGUE.
" Will prove interesting and profitable to all students of economic history."—*Scotsman*.

27. Crime and its Causes. W. DOUGLAS MORRISON.
" Can hardly fail to suggest to all readers several new and pregnant reflections on the subject."—*Anti-Jacobin*.

28. Principles of State Interference. D. G. RITCHIE, M.A.
" An interesting contribution to the controversy on the functions of the State."—*Glasgow Herald*.

29. German Socialism and F. Lassalle. W. H. DAWSON.
" As a biographical history of German Socialistic movements during this century it may be accepted as complete."—*British Weekly*.

30. The Purse and the Conscience. H. M. THOMPSON, B.A. (Cantab.).
" Shows common sense and fairness in his arguments."—*Scotsman*.

31. Origin of Property in Land. FUSTEL DE COULANGES. Edited, with an Introductory Chapter on the English Manor, by Prof. W. J. ASHLEY, M.A.
" His views are clearly stated, and are worth reading."—*Saturday Review*.

32. The English Republic. W. J. LINTON. Edited by KINETON PARKES.
" Characterised by that vigorous intellectuality which has marked his long life of literary and artistic activity."—*Glasgow Herald*.

33. The Co-Operative Movement. BEATRICE POTTER.
" Without doubt the ablest and most philosophical analysis of the Co-Operative Movement which has yet been produced."—*Speaker*.

34. Neighbourhood Guilds. Dr. STANTON COIT.
" A most suggestive little book to anyone interested in the social question."—*Pall Mall Gazette*.

35. Modern Humanists. J. M. ROBERTSON.
" Mr. Robertson's style is excellent—nay, even brilliant—and his purely literary criticisms bear the mark of much acumen."—*Times*.

36. Outlooks from the New Standpoint. E. BELFORT BAX.
" Mr. Bax is a very acute and accomplished student of history and economics."—*Daily Chronicle*.

37. Distributing Co-Operative Societies. Dr. LUIGI PIZZAMIGLIO. Edited by F. J. SNELL.
" Dr. Pizzamiglio has gathered together and grouped a wide array of facts and statistics, and they speak for themselves."—*Speaker*.

38. Collectivism and Socialism. By A. NACQUET. Edited by W. HEAFORD.
" An admirable criticism by a well-known French politician of the New Socialism of Marx and Lassalle "—*Daily Chronicle*.

SOCIAL SCIENCE SERIES—*(Continued)*.

39. The London Programme.   SIDNEY WEBB, LL.B.
  "Brimful of excellent ideas."—*Anti-Jacobin.*

40. The Modern State.   PAUL LEROY BEAULIEU.
  "A most interesting book; well worth a place in the library of every social inquirer."—*N. B. Economist.*

41. The Condition of Labour.   HENRY GEORGE.
  "Written with striking ability, and sure to attract attention."—*Newcastle Chronicle.*

42. The Revolutionary Spirit preceding the French Revolution.
     FELIX ROCQUAIN. With a Preface by Professor HUXLEY.
  "The student of the French Revolution will find in it an excellent introduction to the study of that catastrophe."—*Scotsman.*

43. The Student's Marx.   EDWARD AVELING, D.Sc.
  "One of the most practically useful of any in the Series."—*Glasgow Herald.*

44. A Short History of Parliament.   B. C. SKOTTOWE, M.A. (Oxon.).
  "Deals very carefully and completely with this side of constitutional history."—*Spectator.*

45. Poverty: Its Genesis and Exodus.   J. G. GODARD.
  "He states the problems with great force and clearness."—*N. B. Economist.*

46. The Trade Policy of Imperial Federation.   MAURICE H. HERVEY.
  "An interesting contribution to the discussion."—*Publishers' Circular.*

47. The Dawn of Radicalism.   J. BOWLES DALY, LL.D.
  "Forms an admirable picture of an epoch more pregnant, perhaps, with political instruction than any other in the world's history."—*Daily Telegraph.*

48. The Destitute Alien in Great Britain. ARNOLD WHITE; MONTAGUE CRACKAN-
     THORPE, Q.C.; W. A. M'ARTHUR, M.P.; W. H. WILKINS, &c.
  "Much valuable information concerning a burning question of the day."—*Times.*

49. Illegitimacy and the Influence of Seasons on Conduct.
     ALBERT LEFFINGWELL, M.D.
  "We have not often seen a work based on statistics which is more continuously interesting."—*Westminster Review.*

50. Commercial Crises of the Nineteenth Century.   H. M. HYNDMAN.
  "One of the best and most permanently useful volumes of the Series."—*Literary Opinion.*

51. The State and Pensions in Old Age. J. A. SPENDER and ARTHUR ACLAND, M.P.
  "A careful and cautious examination of the question."—*Times.*

52. The Fallacy of Saving.   JOHN M. ROBERTSON.
  "A plea for the reorganisation of our social and industrial system."—*Speaker.*

53. The Irish Peasant.   ANON.
  "A real contribution to the Irish Problem by a close, patient and dispassionate investigator."—*Daily Chronicle.*

54. The Effects of Machinery on Wages.   Prof. J. S. NICHOLSON, D.Sc.
  "Ably reasoned, clearly stated, impartially written."—*Literary World.*

55. The Social Horizon.   ANON.
  "A really admirable little book, bright, clear, and unconventional."—*Daily Chronicle.*

56. Socialism, Utopian and Scientific.   FREDERICK ENGELS.
  "The body of the book is still fresh and striking."—*Daily Chronicle.*

57. Land Nationalisation.   A. R. WALLACE.
  "The most instructive and convincing of the popular works on the subject."—*National Reformer.*

58. The Ethic of Usury and Interest.   Rev. W. BLISSARD.
  "The work is marked by genuine ability."—*North British Agriculturalist.*

59. The Emancipation of Women.   ADELE CREPAZ
  "By far the most comprehensive, luminous, and penetrating work on this question that I have yet met with."—*Extract from Mr.* GLADSTONE'S *Preface.*

60. The Eight Hours' Question.   JOHN M. ROBERTSON
  "A very cogent and sustained argument on what is at present the unpopular side."—*Times.*

61. Drunkenness.   GEORGE R. WILSON, M.B.
  "Well written, carefully reasoned, free from cant, and full of sound sense."—*National Observer.*

62. The New Reformation.   RAMSDEN BALMFORTH.
  "A striking presentation of the nascent religion, how best to realize the personal and social ideal."—*Westminster Review.*

63. The Agricultural Labourer.   T. E. KEBBEL.
  "A short summary of his position, with appendices on wages, education, allotments, etc., etc."

64. Ferdinand Lassalle as a Social Reformer.   E. BERNSTEIN
  "A worthy addition to the Social Science Series."—*North British Economist.*

SOCIAL SCIENCE SERIES—*(Continued).*

65. England's Foreign Trade in XIXth Century.   A. L. BOWLEY.
"Full of valuable information, carefully compiled, and skilfully marshalled."—
Times.

66. Theory and Policy of Labour Protection.   Dr. SCHÄFFLE.
"Remarkable as an attempt to systematize a conservative programme of reform."
—*Manchester Guardian.*

67. History of Rochdale Pioneers.   G. J. HOLYOAKE.
"The first complete edition, brought down from 1844 to the Rochdale Congress of
1892."—*Co-Operative News.*

68. Rights of Women.   M. OSTRAGORSKI.
"Advocates and opponents will find it an admirable storehouse of precedents,
collected from authentic sources, carefully brought up to date, supported by exact
references, and conveniently arranged."—*Daily Chronicle.*

69. Dwellings of the People.   LOCKE WORTHINGTON.
"An effective and valuable contribution to one of the most pressing problems of
the day."—*Daily Chronicle.*

70. Hours, Wages, and Production.   Dr. BRENTANO.
"Substantially a new work on the relation between wages and hours of labour
and the work done—characterised by all Professor Brentano's clearness of style
and fulness of historical detail."—*Economic Review.*

71. Rise of Modern Democracy.   CH. BORGEAUD.
"A very useful little volume, characterised by exact research and by very clear
political ideas."—*Daily Chronicle.*

72. Land Systems of Australasia.   WM. EPPS.
"A laudable and very useful attempt to place before political thinkers an outline
of the methods which govern the use and alienation of the public land of the
Australasian Colonies."—*Times.*

78. The Tyranny of Socialism.   YVES GUYOT.
Edited with Introduction by J. H. LEVY.
"M. Guyot is smart, lively, trenchant, and interesting."—*Daily Chronicle.*

DOUBLE VOLUMES, Each 3s. 6d.

1. Life of Robert Owen.   LLOYD JONES.
"A worthy record of a life of noble activities."—*Manchester Examiner.*

2. The Impossibility of Social Democracy: a Second Part of "The Quintessence
of Socialism".   Dr. A. SCHÄFFLE.
"Extremely valuable as a criticism of Social Democracy by the ablest living
representative of State Socialism in Germany."—*Inter. Journal of Ethics.*

8. The Condition of the Working Class in England in 1844. FREDERICK ENGELS.
"A translation of a work written in 1845, with a preface written in 1892."

4. The Principles of Social Economy.   YVES GUYOT.
"An interesting and suggestive work. It is a profound treatise on social economy,
and an invaluable collection of facts."—*Spectator.*

5. Social Peace.   Dr. SCHULZE-GAEVERNITZ.
Edited by GRAHAM-WALLES.
"A study by a competent observer of the industrial movement in England, and
the later developments of trade unionism."—*Times.*

SWAN SONNENSCHEIN & CO., LONDON.

NEW YORK: CHARLES SCRIBNER'S SONS.